Life

STUDENT'S BOOK | PRE-INTERMEDIATE

LEARNING

JOHN HUGHES

HELEN STEPHENSON

PAUL DUMMETT

Australia · Brazil · Mexico · Singapore · United Kingdom · United States

Contents

Listening	Reading	Critical thinking	Speaking	Writing
someone talking about a national park near a city a radio interview about long life	a quiz about how well you sleep an article about centenarians an article about how nature is good for you	giving examples	finding out about lifestyle your current life making a town healthier	text type: filling in a form writing skill: information on forms
someone describing an Ironman competition three people talking about competitive sports	an article about crazy competitions an article about female wrestlers in Bolivia	reading between the lines	explaining the rules of a competition talking about your sport preferences your opinions about Olympic sports	text type: an advert or notice writing skill: checking your writing
someone describing a photo of a woman travelling by train in India two people discussing the pros and cons of types of transport a documentary about animal transport	an article about solutions to transport problems an article about the fate of the rickshaw in Kolkata	opinions for and against	talking about and comparing journeys advice on transport a presentation about a pedicab company	text type: notes and messages writing skill: writing in note form
a caver talking about his hobby an impossible decision	an article about adventurers an article about different types of challenges	looking for evidence	asking about your past events you remember telling a story	text type: a short story writing skill: structure your writing
extract from a documentary about a house of recycled materials news about environmental projects	an article about e-rubbish an article about a boat made of plastic bottles, the *Plastiki* an online order	close reading	recycling where you are general knowledge quiz changing attitudes and behaviour	a quiz text type: emails writing skill: formal words
differences between the generations a news item about Mardi Gras	an article about how a couple changed their life an article about how Mardi Gras is celebrated around the world an article about coming-of-age ceremonies	analysing the writer's view	plan the trip of a lifetime your favourite festival planning a celebration describing annual events	text type: a description writing skill: descriptive adjectives

Listening	Reading	Critical thinking	Speaking	Writing
a description of a job in a steel factory an interview with a scientist two people giving instructions	an article about new jobs in an area an article about modern-day cowboys	analysing comparisons in a text	describing past experiences giving directions job satisfaction a job interview	text type: a CV writing skill: missing out words in CVs
a documentary about the importance of technology a science programme about a new invention	an explorer's blog an article about biomimetics	the writer's sources	planning a trip important inventions design an invention for everyday life favourite technology	text type: a paragraph writing skills: connecting words
three people talk about their holidays an interview with a tour guide	a holiday story an article about the two sides of Paris	the author's purpose	a story about a holiday planning the holiday of a lifetime a place you know	text type: an email requesting information writing skill: formal expressions
a description of a producer and his products a programme about a product from the past	an article about some famous logos an article about having less 'stuff'	fact or opinion?	some famous products talk about things you used to do in the past using less stuff planning a new website	text type: a review writing skill: giving your opinion
a historian talking about Scott's hut at the Antarctic a message in a bottle	the history of video gaming an article about stealing history	emotion words	planning a time capsule opinions about games reporting a message a museum in your town	a message in a bottle text type: a biography writing skill: punctuation in direct speech
a description of a photo and the life of a storm chaser a documentary about a photographer	an article about a science blog an article about Jane Goodall	close reading	hopes and dreams questions with *any* interview questions	text type: an article writing skill: planning an article

Life around the world – in 12 videos

Unit 10 Wind turbines

Learn about an innovative product and how it can change lives.

Unit 11   The Golden Record

Voyager 1 carries a message for other life forms in the universe.

USA

UK

Unit 6 Steel drums

Steelband music, or pan, is an important part of the culture in these Caribbean islands.

Trinidad & Tobago

Peru

Unit 1 My local park

How different people spend their free time.

Unit 7 My working life

Some people talk about their working lives.

Unit 9 Living in Venice

Learn what it's like to live in Venice.

Unit 2 Mongolian horse racing

Horse racing at a Mongolian festival.

Unit 8 Ancient languages, modern technology

Find out how technology is being used to record and preserve disappearing languages.

Unit 4 A microadventure

Two friends spend 24 hours in Croatia on a microadventure.

India

Cambodia

Unit 12 Cambodia animal rescue

Rescuing victims of illegal animal poaching in Cambodia.

Unit 5 Recycling Cairo

Find out how recycled objects are used in Cairo.

Australia

Unit 3 Indian Railways

Learn more about the Indian railway system.

UNIT 1
LIFESTYLE

UNIT 2
COMPETITIONS

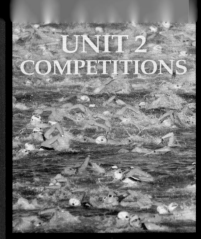

UNIT 3
TRANSPORT

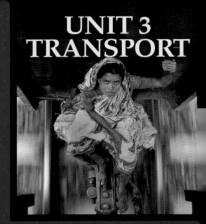

UNIT 4
CHALLENGES

UNIT 5
THE ENVIRONMENT

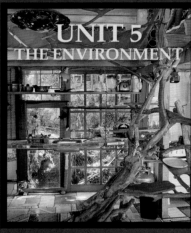

UNIT 6
STAGES IN LIFE

UNIT 7
WORK

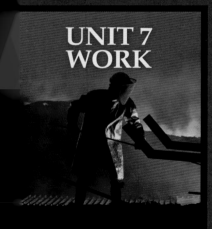

UNIT 8
TECHNOLOGY

UNIT 9
HOLIDAYS

UNIT 10
PRODUCTS

UNIT 11
HISTORY

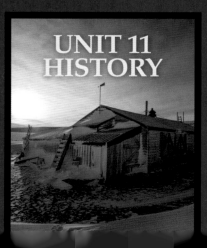

UNIT 12
NATURE

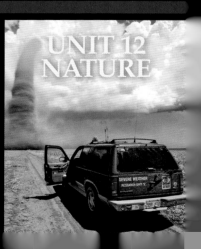

Unit 1 Lifestyle

Bukhansan National Park, Seoul, South Korea

FEATURES

1 Describe the place in the photo. How do you think the person feels?

2 ▶ 1 Listen to a description of the place in the photo. Answer the questions.

1 Where is Bukhansan National Park?
2 How many people visit it every year?
3 Why do they go there?

3 Work in pairs. Look at the activities in the box. Which activities do you often do? When do you do them? Tell your partner.

> cycle through the countryside   do sport and exercise
> chat on social media   cook a meal   go clubbing
> go for long walks   go jogging   play computer games
> play a musical instrument   read books   watch videos

I often go for long walks in the evening.

1a How well do you sleep?

Vocabulary **everyday routines**

1 Work in pairs. Match the two parts of the expressions for everyday routines. Then describe your typical day using some of the expressions.

I often get home late from work …

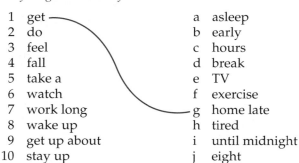

1	get	a	asleep
2	do	b	early
3	feel	c	hours
4	fall	d	break
5	take a	e	TV
6	watch	f	exercise
7	work long	g	home late
8	wake up	h	tired
9	get up about	i	until midnight
10	stay up	j	eight

Reading

2 Read the questionnaire about sleep habits and lifestyle. Answer the questions. Then work in pairs and compare your answers.

▶ 2

3 Turn to page 153 and find out what your answers say about your lifestyle.

Grammar **present simple and adverbs of frequency**

4 Look at these sentences from the questionnaire. Match the sentences (1–2) with their uses (a–b).

1 I work long hours and get home late.
2 The average human needs around eight hours of sleep per night.

a to talk about things that are always true
b to talk about habits and routines

▶ PRESENT SIMPLE	
I/you/we/they sleep	he/she/it sleeps
I/you/we/they don't sleep	he/she/it doesn't sleep
Do I/you/we/they sleep … ?	Does he/she/it sleep … ?

For further information and practice, see page 156.

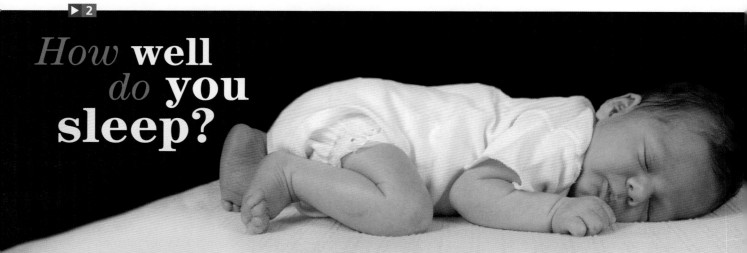

*How **well** do **you** sleep?*

1 Do you often feel tired?
A No, I never feel tired during the day.
B I sometimes feel tired after a long day at work.
C All the time! I'm always ready for bed.

2 How many hours do you usually sleep at night?
A Between seven and eight hours.
B More than nine. I rarely stay up late.
C Fewer than six.

3 Before I go to bed, I often:
A watch TV or read a book.
B do some exercise.
C do some work.

4 At the weekend, I:
A usually sleep the same amount as any other day.
B sometimes sleep for an extra hour or two.
C always sleep until midday! I never get up early.

5 How often do you wake up in the middle of the night?
A I never wake up before morning.
B I rarely wake up more than once, and I usually fall asleep again quite quickly.
C Two or three times a night.

6 Are you often tired during the day?
A No, I'm never tired at work.
B Sometimes, so I take a nap after lunch. After that I'm ready for work again.
C Always! That's because I work long hours and get home late.

take a nap /teɪk ə nap/ have a short sleep during the day

5 Look at the grammar box. Complete the article about sleep with the present simple form of the verbs.

> **The secrets of sleep**
> Why ¹ _do we sleep_ (we / sleep)?
> From birth, we ² _____ (spend) a third of our lives asleep, but scientists still ³ _____ (not / know) exactly why.
> Why ⁴ _____ (we / have) problems sleeping?
> In modern society, many adults ⁵ _____ (not / get) the seven or eight hours sleep they need every night. We ⁶ _____ (work) long hours and we rarely ⁷ _____ (go) to bed at sunset.
> Why ⁸ _____ (we / sleep) differently?
> It ⁹ _____ (depend) on the time of year and also our age. Teenagers usually ¹⁰ _____ (need) more sleep than adults. Lots of elderly people ¹¹ _____ (not / sleep) longer than four or five hours at night, but they often ¹² _____ (take) naps during the day.

6 Pronunciation /s/, /z/ or /ɪz/

a ▶3 Listen to the endings of these verbs. Is the sound /s/, /z/ or /ɪz/?

1	feels /z/	5	goes
2	needs	6	dances
3	watches	7	does
4	sleeps	8	works

b ▶3 Listen again and repeat the verbs. Think about how you say the endings.

7 Discuss the questions.

1 What time do you and your friends normally get up? How late do you stay up?
2 Does anyone in your family ever take a nap in the afternoon?
3 How does this change during the year? Do people sleep longer in the summer or in the winter?

8 Look at the list. Then underline the adverbs of frequency in the questionnaire and write the adverbs in the list.

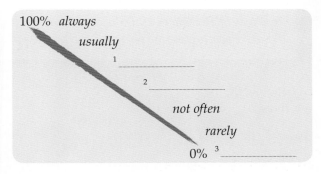

> 100% *always*
>   *usually*
>   1 _____
>   2 _____
>   *not often*
>   *rarely*
>   0% 3 _____

▶ **ADVERBS and EXPRESSIONS OF FREQUENCY**

She's **usually** late for work.
I **often** wake up at seven.
Do you **often** wake up in the night?
She wakes up **two or three times a night**.
Every month I visit my grandparents.

For further information and practice, see page 156.

9 Look at the grammar box. Notice the position of the adverbs and expressions of frequency in the sentences. Then choose the correct options to complete the rules (1–2).

1 An adverb of frequency goes *after / before* the verb *to be,* but it normally goes *after / before* the main verb.
2 An expression of frequency (*e.g. twice a week*) usually goes *at the beginning / in the middle* or at the end of a sentence.

10 Put the adverb or expression in brackets in the correct place in the sentence. Sometimes there is more than one correct answer.

1 My brother⟋plays tennis on Saturday mornings. (always) *[always written above]*
2 We eat out at a restaurant. (about once a month)
3 I take a bus to school. (every day)
4 She is at home in the middle of the day. (rarely)
5 They go on holiday. (twice a year)
6 Are you late for work? (often)

Speaking ⟨ my life ⟩

11 Work in pairs. Find out about your partner's habits. Ask questions with *How often …?* and these ideas. Answer using an adverb or expression of frequency.

A: How often do you eat out?
B: About once a month.

> be late for work/college   take public transport
> eat out in restaurants
> check your phone for messages
> play board games   go on holiday
> check your emails   be stressed at work

12 Work in groups. Prepare a questionnaire about lifestyle for another group. Start each question with *How often …? Are you often …?* or *Do you often …?* and offer three choices of answer (A, B or C).

13 Work with another group and ask your questions from Exercise 12. Tell the class about the other group's answers.

1b The secrets of a long life

Reading

1 Who is the oldest person you know? How old is he or she? How healthy is their lifestyle?

My grandfather is the oldest person I know. He's 83 and still plays golf.

2 Work in pairs. Read the article *The Secrets of a Long Life*. Answer the questions.

1 Where is Okinawa Island?
2 Why is Okinawa famous?
3 What kind of food do the people eat?
4 Which of their activities do you do?
   I don't go fishing but I do gardening.

Wordbuilding **collocations with *do*, *play* and *go***

▶ **WORDBUILDING collocations with *do*, *play* and *go***

We use certain nouns with certain verbs. These are called collocations.
go fishing NOT ~~*do fishing*~~ or ~~*play fishing*~~

For further practice, see Workbook page 11.

3 Look at the wordbuilding box. Read the article again and find the collocations with *do*, *play* and *go*. Complete the table.

Do	Go	Play
	fishing	

4 Add these activities to the table in Exercise 3. Use a dictionary if necessary. Then think of one more activity for each verb.

cards   hiking   homework   nothing
running   shopping   tennis   the piano   yoga
football   karate   surfing

5 Work in pairs. Tell your partner about people you know using the collocations in the table.

*My brother **does** karate. He's a black belt.*

The Secrets of a
Long Life

The island of Okinawa in Japan has some of the oldest people in the world. It's famous for its high number of centenarians – men and women who live beyond one hundred years of age. Some of the reasons for their good health are that they:

• go fishing and eat what they catch.
• do a lot of gardening and grow their own fruit and vegetables.
• go cycling and never drive when they can walk.
• often spend time with friends. They meet at people's houses and play games.
• rarely buy food from a supermarket.
• do regular exercise, go swimming and lead active lives.

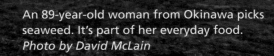

An 89-year-old woman from Okinawa picks seaweed. It's part of her everyday food.
Photo by David McLain

Listening

6 ▶ 5 Listen to a radio interview with photographer David McLain. Tick the topics the speakers talk about.

1 the age of men and women
2 family life
3 sleep
4 food
5 exercise

7 ▶ 5 Listen again. Are the sentences true (T) or false (F)?

1 David McLain is travelling to different countries.
2 He's talking to the radio presenter in the studio.
3 In Sardinia, men don't live the same number of years as women.
4 Sardinian families often eat together.
5 David says life in Sardinia is less stressful than in other places.
6 Younger people are eating more unhealthy food and they aren't doing much exercise.

8 Think about the lifestyle of people in your country. Is it similar to the lifestyle in Sardinia? How traditional is your country? Tell the class.

Grammar present simple and present continuous

9 Look at the sentences from the interview. Which two sentences use the present simple? Why?

1 Well, one man is trying to answer these questions and that man is photographer David McLain.
2 He's speaking to us right now on the phone.
3 Men live to the same age as women.
4 Every Sunday the whole family eats a big meal together.
5 Also, more and more young people are moving to the city these days, and they are doing less exercise because of their lifestyle.

10 The three other sentences in Exercise 9 use the present continuous. How do you form the present continuous?

11 We use the present continuous to talk about something happening now or around now. Match the three present continuous sentences in Exercise 9 with the specific uses (a–c).

a to talk about a changing situation
b to talk about something happening around now, but not necessarily at this exact moment
c to talk about something actually in progress now

▶ PRESENT CONTINUOUS

I'm speaking
you/we/they're speaking
he/she/it's speaking

I'm not travelling
you/we/they aren't travelling
he/she/it isn't travelling

Am I working?
Are you/we/they working?
Is he/she/it working?

For further information and practice, see page 156.

---

12 Complete the sentences with the present simple or present continuous form of these verbs.

check	not / do	not / eat	go	learn	play
read	spend				

1 We __'re learning__ a new language at the moment.
2 My friends and I often _____ time at each other's houses.
3 Can you wait a moment? I _____ my emails.
4 How often _____ you _____ to the gym?
5 I _____ a really interesting book at the moment.
6 Currently, a friend of mine _____ any sweets and he says he feels healthier.
7 I'm nearly eighty, but I _____ any exercise!
8 More old people _____ computer games these days. It isn't just the young people.

Speaking ⌐ my life

13 Write pairs of questions. Use the present simple in one question, and the present continuous in the other.

1 a How / usually spend your free time?
     How do you usually spend your free time?
   b / you / do / much sport these days?
     Are you doing much sport these days?
2 a / often / read novels?
   b / read / any good books at the moment?
3 a Where / normally go on holiday?
   b Where / plan to go this year?
4 a / speak / any other languages?
   b / learn / any new languages?

14 Work in pairs. Ask and answer your questions from Exercise 13.

1c Nature is good for you

Reading

1 Look at the photo. Where is the woman? What can she see?

2 Read the article. Match the topics (a–c) with the paragraphs in the article (1–3).

   a how much time we spend outdoors
   b making nature part of city life
   c studies by doctors

3 Read the article again. Answer the questions.

   1 What do most people think about nature?
   2 What is the main change in how people spend their time?
   3 What is happening at national parks in Canada?
   4 After the maths test, where did some people look at nature?
   5 In Toronto, where did healthier people live?
   6 What are they going to build in Dubai?
   7 Where can children study in Switzerland?
   8 In South Korea, how many people visit the new forests every year?

Word focus *feel*

4 Underline three phrases with *feel* in the first paragraph of the article. Match the phrases to the uses (1–3).

   1 to talk about your emotions or health
   2 to talk about wanting to do something
   3 to talk about an opinion

5 Complete the questions with these words.

better   like   that

   1 What do you usually feel _____ doing after a day at work?
   2 Do you feel _____ nature is good for us? Why? / Why not?
   3 After a difficult day, what makes you feel _____ in the evening?

6 Work in pairs. Take turns to ask and answer the questions from Exercise 5.

   A: What do you usually feel like doing after a long day at work?
   B: Going for a run in my local park and then eating dinner. Sometimes I go out and meet friends.

Critical thinking **giving examples**

7 When writers give an opinion in an article, they often support the idea with examples. Look at these sentences from paragraph 1. Which sentence has the main idea? Which sentences give examples?

   a For example, the number of visitors to Canada's national parks is getting lower every year.
   b Humans are spending more time inside and less time outside.
   c And in countries such as the USA, only 10% of teenagers spend time outside every day.

8 Read paragraphs 2 and 3 of the article. Find the sentence with the main idea and sentences with examples. Underline the words and phrases for giving examples.

   For example, the number of visitors to Canada's national parks is getting lower every year.

9 Complete these sentences in your own words. Use examples from your own life. Then tell your partner.

   1 I relax in my free time in different ways. For example, …
   2 My home town has some places with trees and nature, such as …
   3 There are some beautiful national parks in my country. A good example is …

Speaking   my life

10 Work in groups of four. Imagine your town has some money to make people's lives healthier. Look at the ideas below and think of one more.

   • one hundred new trees in the town
   • a 400-metre running track in the park
   • a new park with a children's play area
   • two cycle paths across the town
   • a bridge across the river with a garden

11 Discuss the ideas in your group and choose the best idea. Give reasons and examples.

   I think cycle paths are a good idea because cycling is good for your health and good for the environment.

12 Present your idea to the class. Then compare your ideas. Try to agree on the best idea.

NATURE
is good for you

▶ 6

How do you feel about nature? After spending hours indoors, do you often feel like going outside for a walk? Or if you work for hours at your office desk, do you feel better when you take a break and visit your local park? Most people think that nature is good for us; it's good for our bodies and good for our brains. However, humans are spending more time inside and less time outside. For example, the number of visitors to Canada's national parks is getting lower every year. And in countries such as the USA, only 10% of teenagers spend time outside every day. Many doctors feel that this is a problem in the twenty-first century, and that it is making our physical health worse.

As a result, some doctors are studying the connection between nature and health: one example of this is the work of Dr Matilda van den Bosch in Sweden. The doctor gave people a maths test. During the test, their heart rate was faster. After the test, one group of people sat in a 3D-virtual-reality room for fifteen minutes with pictures and sounds of nature. Their heart rates were slower than people's in the other group.

The virtual contact with nature helped them feel more relaxed. Another good example of how nature is good for health comes from Canada. In Toronto, researchers studied 31,000 people living in cities. Overall, they found that healthier people lived near parks. 25

Because of studies like these, some countries and cities want nature to be part of people's everyday life. In Dubai, for example, there are plans for a new shopping mall with a large garden so shoppers can relax outside 30 with trees, plants and water. In some countries such as Switzerland, 'forest schools' are popular; schoolchildren study their subjects in the forests and do lots of exercise outside. And South Korea is another good example: it has new forests near its cities and around 35 13 million people visit these forests every year. So after building cities for so long, perhaps it's now time to start rebuilding nature.

heart rate: the speed of the human heart (number of heart beats per minute)

1d At the doctor's

Vocabulary medical problems

1 Look at the pictures. Match the people (1–8) with the medical problems (a–h).

a   I've got a headache.
b   I've got backache.
c   I've got a runny nose.
d   I've got earache.
e   I've got stomach ache.
f   I've got a temperature.
g   I've got a sore throat.
h   I've got a bad cough.

2 What do you do when you have the problems in Exercise 1? Choose the best option (1–3) for each problem. Work in pairs and compare your ideas.

1   I go to bed.
2   I take medicine or pills.
3   I go to the pharmacy or see my doctor.

3 Pronunciation one or two syllables?

a ▶ 7 Listen to these words. Which words have one syllable? Which words have two? Underline the stressed syllable in the two-syllable words.

> ache   headache   ear   earache   stomach
> throat   cough

b ▶ 7 Listen again and repeat.

Real life talking about illness

4 ▶ 8 Listen to two conversations, one at a pharmacy and one at a doctor's. What medical problems does each person have?

5 ▶ 8 Listen again and write the number of the conversation (1–2) next to the medical advice.

a   Take this medicine twice a day. *1*
b   Go to bed.
c   Drink hot water with honey and lemon.
d   Take one pill twice a day.
e   Buy cough sweets.

6 Match the beginnings of the sentences (1–9) with the endings (a–i). Use the expressions for talking about illness to help you.

1   Have you got a
2   You should take
3   It's good for
4   Try drinking
5   Why don't you
6   I've got
7   Do you feel
8   You need
9   If you still feel ill,

a   this medicine.
b   buy some cough sweets?
c   earache.
d   then come back and see me again.
e   a sore throat.
f   hot water with honey and lemon.
g   temperature?
h   sick at all?
i   to take one of these pills.

▶ TALKING ABOUT ILLNESS

Asking and talking about illness
I don't feel very well.
I feel sick/ill. / Do you feel sick/ill?
Have you got a temperature?
How do you feel?

Giving advice
You need to / You should take this medicine.
Why don't you buy some cough sweets?
It's good for stomach ache.
Try drinking hot tea.
If you still feel ill, then come back and see me again.

---

7 Work in pairs.

Student A: You have a medical problem. Choose one of the problems from Exercise 1 and tell Student B what your problem is.

Student B: You are a pharmacist. Ask how Student A feels and give advice.

Then change roles and have a new conversation.

my life   ▶ YOUR HABITS   ▶ YOUR CURRENT LIFE   ▶ MAKING LIVES HEALTHIER   ▶ ILLNESS
▶ FILLING IN A FORM

1e Personal information

Writing filling in a form

1 Work in pairs. Discuss these questions.

- What kinds of forms do you sometimes fill in?
- Think of a form you filled in. What information did you write?

2 Look at these forms. What is each form for?

A

Title		Current occupation	
First name			
Middle initial			
Surname			
Address		Do you smoke?	
Postcode		Yes ☐ No ☐	
Gender		Current medications	
DOB			
No. of dependents			
Country of origin			
First language			
Details of past surgery or operations			

B

PLEASE USE CAPITAL LETTERS

PASSPORT NO.   PLACE OF BIRTH

NATIONALITY   MARITAL STATUS

QUALIFICATIONS (DEGREE, ETC.)

Have you visited this country before? (If yes, give details)

Contact details of person in case of emergency (e.g. spouse, next of kin)

3 Writing skill information on forms

a Match the questions (1–7) with the headings on the forms in Exercise 2 where you write the information.

1 Are you married, single or divorced? *marital status*
2 Do you take any pills or medicine?
3 How many children do you have?
4 What country were you born in?
5 What city/town were you born in?
6 Who can we call in your family if you need help?
7 What is the first letter of your middle name?

b Look at the forms again. Answer these questions. Then check your answers on page 155.

1 How many abbreviations can you find in the forms? What do they mean?
   DOB = Date of birth
2 Under the heading *Title* on forms, we use the abbreviations *Mr, Mrs, Ms* and *Dr*. What do they mean?
3 Which form doesn't want you to write in lower-case letters?

4 Work in pairs. Design a form for new students at a language school.

- List all the information you need about the students.
- Then prepare the form.

5 Exchange your form with another pair. Use these questions to check their form.

- Is their form easy to fill in?
- Do you know what to write in each part?
- Would you change anything on the form?

1f My local park

Park Güell, in Barcelona, is famous for its art and a great place to meet friends.

Before you watch

1 Look at the photo and read the caption. Where is your nearest park? Why do people like going there?

2 Key vocabulary

Read the sentences. The words and phrases in bold are used in the video. Match the words to the definitions (a–f).

1 I like coming to the park **no matter what** the weather is like.
2 Parents push their young children in **prams**.
3 There's a great **view** from the top of the hill.
4 We often come to the park when we're in the **area**.
5 There's a nice **walkway** round the park.
6 In the spring, there are beautiful flowers on the ground and **blossom** on the trees.

a a region or part of a town
b it has four wheels and you move babies or small children in it
c flowers that grow on trees
d it isn't important and it doesn't change my decision
e what you can see around you
f another word for a path or small road only for people

While you watch

3 ▶ 1.1 Watch the video and number a–g in the order you see them.

a A man is cycling.
b A woman is walking with her dog.
c A student is jogging.
d There's a large house near the park.
e Two people are walking down a path.
f A student is doing pull-ups.
g A tractor is cutting the grass.

4 ▶ 1.1 Work in pairs. Look at the table and watch the video again.

Student A: Complete the notes in column 1.

Student B: Complete the notes in column 2.

	Student A When do you come to the park?	Student B Why do you like coming to the park?
	We come to the park very _____. Every _____ after lunchtime, around _____ p.m.	There are a lot of _____ for Jasmine to play with. There are beautiful _____ everywhere.
	I come to the park _____. On sunny days I come here in my lunch _____.	I like this part of the park actually, it's _____ up and there's this beautiful _____.
	When we were a young family and had _____, we used to come here, so it has _____ memories.	It's nicer than the _____ way. It's a _____ park and we like to see the different _____.
	I go through the park _____ and _____ I spend time with my friends.	I like _____ in this park.
	I come to the park _____, I come here about _____ a week.	I like to _____ jogging and I like to do _____ here. The park is quiet and there are lots of _____ and trees.
	I try and come to the park _____.	There are always wild _____ and blossom on the trees. It's lovely to _____.

5 ▶ 1.1 Share your notes with your partner and complete the other column. Then watch the video again and check all your answers.

After you watch

6 Work in pairs. Cover the notes in the table and look at the faces of the different people.

Student A: Choose one person in the video but don't tell Student B. Listen to Student B's questions and give the answers from the video.

Student B: Ask the two questions from the video: When do you come to the park? How often do you come? Listen to Student A's answer. Which person from the video is Student A?

7 Change roles and repeat the activity.

Grammar

1 Choose the correct options to complete the text about a man called Nazroo.

Every day, Nazroo [1] *works / is working* with elephants. In this photo, [2] *he takes / he's taking* his favourite elephant elephant, Rajan, for a swim. [3] *They swim / They're swimming* in the sea around the Andaman Island. Sometimes they [4] *like / are liking* to relax this way after a hard day. Rajan [5] *doesn't seem / isn't seeming* worried about being under the water. I suppose [6] *it feels / it is feeling* good after a long, hot day at work.

2 Write the expression in brackets in the correct place in the sentence. In three sentences, there is more than one correct position.

1 I play computer and video games. (rarely)
2 We're studying Spanish. (at the moment)
3 My family does sport. (every weekend)
4 All my friends are working. (these days)

3 ▶▶ **MB** Rewrite the sentences in Exercise 2 so they are true for you.

I CAN	
ask about preferences	
use adverbs and expressions of frequency	

Vocabulary

4 Match the verbs in A with the words in B. Then complete the sentences with the expressions.

A	fall	take	work	watch	get up

B	long hours	asleep	a break	late	TV

1 I can't _____ _____ because of all the noise outside my bedroom.
2 At work, we always _____ at 11 and have a coffee.
3 We all _____ these days because there is a lot to do.
4 Sometimes I _____ and I miss my bus to school.
5 How much _____ do you _____ in the evenings?

5 Which words can follow the verb in CAPITAL letters? Cross out the incorrect word.

1 DO exercise, housework, relaxing, yoga
2 GO asleep, clubbing, jogging, home
3 PLAY golf, swimming, games, tennis
4 FEEL tired, happy, ache, sick

6 ▶▶ **MB** Work in pairs. Write five sentences using verbs from Exercises 4 and 5, but miss out the verb.

We often _____ yoga when we wake up.

Then work with another pair. Take turns to read your sentences and guess the missing word.

I CAN	
describe daily routines	
talk about freetime activities	

Real life

7 Choose the correct option to complete the conversation between two friends.

A: [1] *How do / Do* you feel?
B: Not very [2] *well / ill*. I've got a [3] *pain / sore* throat.
A: [4] *Do you feel / Have you got* a temperature?
B: I don't know. I feel a bit hot.
A: [5] *Try / You need* drinking some honey and lemon in hot water.
B: Good idea.
A: But you [6] *should / it's a good idea* also see your doctor.

8 ▶▶ **MB** Look at the pictures and answer the questions.

1 What medical problems do the people have?
2 What advice can you give them? e.g. *You should go to bed.*

I CAN	
talk about medical problems and illness	
give advice	

Unit 2 Competitions

Athletes at Cozumel, Mexico, compete for a place in the Ironman championship.

FEATURES

1 Look at the photo. What sport is it? Do you like this kind of sport?

2 ▶ 9 Listen to someone talking about the photo. Answer the questions.

1 How many races are there in the Ironman competition?
2 How many kilometres do the competitors swim and cycle?
3 How many people compete?

3 Look at these words from the same family. Which word is:

1 a verb?
2 an adjective?
3 a noun (thing)?
4 a noun (person)?

competitor   competitive   competition   compete

4 Complete the questions with the words from Exercise 3. Then ask and answer the questions with a partner.

1 In sport, are you normally a _____ or a spectator?
2 Do you ever _____ in sports?
3 What types of _____ do you like?
4 Are you a _____ person? Why? / Why not?

2a Crazy competitions!

Reading

1 Look at the title of the article and the two photos. Why do you think the competitions are 'crazy'?

2 Read the article. Which competition is a race between different teams? Which is a match between two teams?

3 Read the article again and match the sentences (1–6) with the competitions (A–B). One sentence is true for both competitions.

1 Competitors start and end at the same place. *A*
2 The rules are the same as another real sport.
3 The competition is once a year.
4 You use a type of transport.
5 It's for teams.
6 There is a time limit.

4 Which of the two sports would you like to play or watch? Do you have any crazy competitions in your country?

Vocabulary **sport**

5 Look at the highlighted words in the article. Use the words to complete the sentences below.

1 Runners at the Olympic Games get a gold medal when they win a _____ .
2 In football, there are eleven _____ on each side.
3 At the beginning of the championship there are 24 _____ . In the final, there can only be two.
4 A rugby _____ lasts eighty minutes.
5 How many _____ did you score?
6 The ball didn't cross the _____ , so it wasn't a goal.
7 The _____ received a gold medal.

6 Work in pairs. Answer these questions.

1 How many different kinds of race can you think of?
2 How many players are there in your favourite team sports?
3 What are the names of the sports teams in your town or city?
4 In what games do you score goals and in what games do you score points?

▶ 10

CRAZY COMPETITIONS!

There are lots of competitions in the USA and some of them are a bit crazy!

A The Idiotarod

The Idiotarod is an annual race in twenty different US cities. Each team must have five people and a shopping cart. One person usually rides in the cart and four people pull it. Teams can decorate the shopping cart but they can't change the wheels. All the teams have to start and finish at the same place but they don't have to run on the same roads. The members of each team must cross the finish line together and they mustn't finish without the cart!

B The Mud Bowl Championship

Mud Bowl football is similar to normal American football, so players can pick up the ball and run with it. There are also two teams, but the match is shorter. The winner is the team with the most goals at the end of sixty minutes. The really big difference is that the players have to play in a field with half a metre of mud!

Grammar verbs for rules

> ▶ **VERBS FOR RULES**
>
> Each team **must** have five people and a shopping cart.
> They **can't** change the wheels.
> All the teams **have to** start and finish at the same place.
> They **don't have to** run on the same roads.
> They **mustn't** finish without the cart!
> Players **can** pick up the ball and run with it.
>
> For further information and practice, see page 158.

7 Look at the sentences in the grammar box. Complete the explanations (a–d) with the verbs in bold in the grammar box.

   a We use _____ or _____ when the rules say it's obligatory.
   b We use _____ when it's allowed in the rules.
   c We use _____ when something is not obligatory but is allowed by the rules.
   d We use _____ or _____ when it isn't allowed in the rules.

8 Choose the correct option to complete the sentences about different sports.

   1 In golf, you *have to / don't have to* hit the ball into nine or eighteen holes.
   2 Competitors *can / mustn't* argue with the referee.
   3 In football, a goalkeeper is the only player who *can / has to* pick up the ball.
   4 Players *can't / must* throw the ball backwards in rugby.
   5 A referee *can / mustn't* send a player off the pitch when he breaks the rules of the game.
   6 In table tennis, the ball *has to / can't* hit the table.
   7 In tennis, the players *must / don't have to* win every point to win a match.

9 Complete the description of another competition with these verbs. Use each verb once only.

must	have to	don't have to	can't	can

Every year, over three hundred competitors enter the Beard and Moustache competition in Alaska. The rules are simple. You ¹ *must* be over eighteen years old and you ² _____ have a moustache or a beard, or both. Also, you ³ _____ put on false hair! In total, there are eighteen different categories, but competitors ⁴ _____ only enter one category. There are categories for short beards and different moustaches, so you ⁵ _____ have the longest moustache or the biggest beard to win a prize.

Speaking ⟨ my life ⟩

10 Work in pairs. You are going to explain the rules for a sport or competition. Choose one of the following. Make a list of six to seven rules.

   • a popular sport in your country
   • a popular TV quiz show or TV competition
   • an annual national or international competition

   *Baseball is a popular sport in my country. You **have to** play with two teams, a ball and a bat.*

11 Work with another pair. Take turns to explain your rules. Ask questions if you don't understand.

   *Do I **have to** be over 18?*
   *Can I enter the competition on my own or do I **have to** be in a team?*

2b Winning and losing

Wordbuilding suffixes

1 Are any of the sportspeople in the photos famous in your country? Match the people with these words.

> tennis player   runner   footballer   athlete

> ▶ **WORDBUILDING suffixes**
>
> You can add *-er* to some sports to describe the sportsperson: *football* ➔ *footballer*, *golf* ➔ *golfer*
> You can add *player* to some sports:
> *tennis* ➔ *tennis player*, *squash* ➔ *squash player*
> Some sports don't use the suffix *-er* or *-player*:
> *athletics* ➔ *athlete*, *cycle* ➔ *cyclist*
>
> For further practice, see Workbook page 19.

2 Look at the wordbuilding box. What is the word for a person who:

1 boxes? *boxer*
2 motorcycles?
3 plays baseball?
4 swims?
5 plays chess?
6 drives a racing car?
7 does gymnastics?
8 goes surfing?

3 Who are the most famous sportspeople in your country? What type of sportspeople are they? (e.g. *a footballer, an athlete*)

Lionel Messi is very famous in my country. He's a footballer.

Listening

4 Read the quotes with the photos. Do you think winning is always important in sport? Why? / Why not?

5 ▶ **11** Listen to three people talking about competitive sports in schools. Match the speakers (1–3) with the opinions (a–c).

a Speaker _____ thinks non-competitive sport is a good idea.
b Speaker _____ thinks competitive sport is a good idea in schools.
c Speaker _____ thinks sport in schools is a good idea but there can be a problem.

6 Look at these opinions for and against competitive sports in schools. Which are the opinions for (F) and which are the opinions against (A)?

1 Winning and losing teaches students about life. *F*
2 A lot of schools with good results don't have competitive sports. *A*
3 Children get more exercise when they try to win.
4 Winning isn't important as long as you do your best.
5 Children learn to work well in teams when they play in matches.
6 Students learn to work hard with competitive sports.
7 Some parents don't like losing and get angry with their children.
8 All children are different and some aren't good at sport.
9 Competitive sports are fun.

'I don't like losing.' Usain Bolt

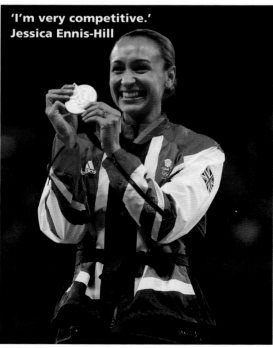

'I'm very competitive.' Jessica Ennis-Hill

'You can't win all the time.' Lionel Messi

7 ▶ **11** Listen again. Which opinion from Exercise 6 does each speaker (1–3) give?

Speaker 1 _____1_____
Speaker 2 _____
Speaker 3 _____

8 Work in groups. Discuss the opinions in Exercise 6. Answer these questions.

1 Which opinions do you agree with?
2 Which do you disagree with?
3 Are there any other reasons for or against competitive sports in schools?

Grammar *-ing* form

> **-ING FORM**

1 *Learning to win and lose is important in a child's education.*
2 *Competitive sports in schools are good for teaching children.*
3 *Some parents hate losing.*

For further information and practice, see page 158.

9 Look at the grammar box. Underline the verbs in the *-ing* form. Then match them with the uses of the *-ing* form (a–c).

a It is the subject of the sentence.
b It comes after a verb, e.g. *like, dislike*.
c It comes after a preposition, e.g. *of*.

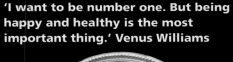

'I want to be number one. But being happy and healthy is the most important thing.' Venus Williams

10 Put the words in order to make quotes by famous sportspeople. Then match the *-ing* forms with the uses (a–c) in Exercise 9.

1 never / thought / losing / of / I
(Muhammed Ali, boxer)
2 love / I just / winning
(Ayrton Senna, racing driver)
3 A champion / afraid / losing / isn't / of
(Billie Jean King, tennis-player)
4 hate / I / losing
(Sachin Tendulkar, cricketer)
5 I'm / more worried about / a good person / being / than being the best football player
(Lionel Messi, footballer)
6 isn't / swimming / winning is / everything,
(Mark Spitz, swimmer)

11 ▶ **12** Choose the correct options to complete this conversation. Then listen and check.

A: What's on TV?
B: ¹ ~~Cycle~~ / *Cycling*. It's the Tour de France. I love ² *watch / watching* it.
A: Oh no! I ³ *think / thinking* it's boring!
B: I really enjoy ⁴ *see / seeing* them on the mountains.
A: ⁵ *Sit / Sitting* in front of the TV all day is not exciting. I'm bored with ⁶ *do / doing* nothing. Are you any good at tennis? We could ⁷ *play / playing* this afternoon.
B: But I want to ⁸ *watch / watching* this.
A: I see. Are you afraid of ⁹ *lose / losing*?

12 Pronunciation /ŋ/

a ▶ **13** Listen to six words. Tick the word you hear.

1 a thin   b think   c thing
2 a win   b wink   c wing
3 a ban   b bank   c bang
4 a sin   b sink   c sing
5 a ran   b rank   c rang
6 a pin   b pink   c ping

b ▶ **12** Listen again to the conversation from Exercise 11. Notice the pronunciation of the *-ing* forms.

c Work in pairs. Practise the conversation.

Speaking ⟨ my life ⟩

13 Work in pairs. Ask questions to find out what sports or leisure activities your partner likes. Then complete the sentences.

*A: What sports do you **love watching**?*
B: Tennis. What about you?

1 I love watching _____ but my partner doesn't.
2 I think _____ is boring but my partner loves it!
3 We both enjoy _____ but we hate _____ .
4 I'm good at _____ but my partner isn't.
5 My partner likes _____ but I prefer _____ .

2c Bolivian wrestlers

Reading

1 Discuss the questions.

1 Do many people watch boxing or wrestling in your country?
2 Why do some people dislike these types of sports?
3 What do you think about these sports?

2 Read the article about wrestling in Bolivia. Which paragraph (1–5) describes:

a the two wrestlers before the fight? *2*
b the popularity of male and female wrestling in Bolivia?
c Yolanda's family life?
d the reason why a fan watches it?
e the fight between the two wrestlers?

3 Find words in the article for these definitions.

1 something people watch for pleasure
  e *ntertainment*
2 the place where two wrestlers fight
  r_____
3 a large group of people   c_____
4 the person who describes the action in a sport
  c_____
5 get very excited, shout and jump up and down
  g_____   c_____
6 people who like a sports person or famous celebrity   f_____
7 the money you earn for work   s_____

Critical thinking **reading between the lines**

4 An article doesn't always tell us about how the people feel, but we can often guess. Match the people from the article (1–3) with the sentences (a–c).

1 Yolanda
2 one of Yolanda's daughters
3 Esperanza

a 'I don't like the days when the wrestling happens.'
b 'I feel wonderful every time I go out there.'
c 'Life is very hard for people like me.'

5 Discuss the questions.

1 How do you feel about the women wrestlers?
2 Would you like to see this sport? Why? / Why not?

Word focus *like*

6 Look at the word *like* in these sentences. Match the sentences (1–4) with the uses (a–d).

1 Most people **like** football.
2 Yolanda and Claudina **are like** famous pop stars.
3 **Would** your daughters **like** to become wrestlers one day?
4 Esperanza **likes** watching the wrestling.

a We use *like* + noun to talk about things we enjoy.
b We use *like* + *-ing* to talk about activities we enjoy doing.
c We use *be* / *look like* to talk about similarities between people / things / actions.
d We use *would like to* + infinitive to talk about future plans or ambitions.

7 Match these questions with *like* (1–4) with the answers (a–d).
1 What do you like doing at the weekend?
2 What kind of music do you like?
3 Are you like anyone in your family?
4 Where would you like to go on holiday next?

a I probably look like my mother.
b Spain. Or Portugal maybe.
c Anything. Rock. Classical. I don't mind.
d Going to the cinema.

8 Work in pairs. Take turns to ask the questions from Exercise 7 and give your own answers.

Speaking ⟨ my life ⟩

9 Work in groups. Can you say ten sports in the Olympic Games?

10 These six sports are not in the Olympic Games. Discuss the questions and give reasons for your answers. Try to agree.

> American football   baseball   chess   karate
> skateboarding   surfing

1 Which of the six sports do you think are the most popular?
2 Which sports don't people like watching?
3 Which two activities would your group like to have at the next Olympics?

BOLIVIAN WRESTLERS

▶ 14

In Bolivia, football is the country's national sport but the country is also famous for another sport – wrestling. Local people like watching the wrestling and it's very popular
5 with tourists. It's an exciting mixture of sport, drama and entertainment. When modern wrestling started in Bolivia in the 1950s, the competitors were all men, but nowadays women are also competing in the ring.

10 The city of El Alto is a good place to watch the wrestling. Hundreds of spectators go to the fights in the evening. This evening, the crowd is sitting round a huge wrestling ring and they shout: 'Bring them on! Bring them on!' Suddenly, the commentator is speaking into a microphone: 'Ladies and
15 Gentlemen. It's time for Yolanda and Claudina!' The crowd is screaming with excitement as two women in colourful clothes enter the ring.

Yolanda and Claudina are like famous pop stars. They smile and wave to their fans. The music stops and the referee starts
20 the fight. Claudina jumps on Yolanda. Then Yolanda throws Claudina on the floor. As Claudina lies on the floor, Yolanda smiles and waves to the crowd. Then, Claudina gets up and pushes Yolanda onto the ground. One minute Yolanda is winning. The next minute, Claudina is winning. The spectators
25 go crazy!

Away from the ring, many wrestlers are women with families. At home Yolanda has a normal and quiet family life. She has two daughters and she makes clothes for a living. Her father was also a wrestler, so it's a family tradition. In answer to the
30 question, 'Would your daughters like to become wrestlers one day?' Yolanda says they wouldn't. She answers: 'My daughters ask me why I do this. It's dangerous and they complain that wrestling doesn't bring any money into the house.' So why does she do it?

35 Yolanda loves wrestling because of her fans, and she has lots of them. One of her fans is called Esperanza Cancina. She pays $1.50 (a large part of her salary) to sit near the ring. Esperanza likes watching the wrestling because she says: 'We laugh and we forget our problems for three or four hours.'

2d Joining a group

Speaking

1 Work as a class or in groups. Interview different people. Find someone who:

1   is a member of a team or club.
2   has to go to regular meetings (e.g. every week).
3   pays to be a member.
4   competes with their team or club.

Real life **talking about interests**

2 Look at the adverts. Which information (1–4) is in each advert. Underline the information.

1   when the club meets
2   the membership fee
3   reasons to join
4   how to contact the club

A

Would you like to get fit and make new friends?

Join our running groups for beginners and for more experienced runners. It's non-competitive and fun.

7 p.m. every Wednesday.

Call Mike for details on 0776 58945.

B

Join us and **WIN** *a new camera!*

The Barton Photography Club welcomes new members. We are a busy club with regular speakers. Join before 1st March and enter our summer photography competition. First prize is a new XP8ii camera! The entry fee is 15 euros (including membership).

Visit **www.bartonphotoclub.com** to join.

C

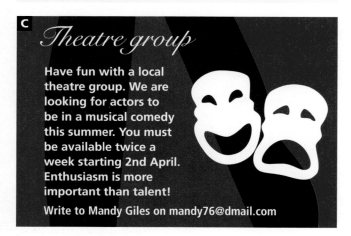

Theatre group

Have fun with a local theatre group. We are looking for actors to be in a musical comedy this summer. You must be available twice a week starting 2nd April. Enthusiasm is more important than talent!

Write to Mandy Giles on mandy76@dmail.com

3 ▶ **15** Two people are looking at the adverts in their local newspaper. Listen to their conversation and number the adverts in Exercise 2 in the order they discuss them.

4 ▶ **15** Listen again and complete the sentences.

1   You're really _____ doing that.
2   Well, _____ joining something else?
3   Are you _____ acting?
4   I _____ standing up in front of people.
5   I'm _____ good at singing.
6   Go _____ . I think you'd enjoy it.
7   I think I'd _____ join this on Wednesday evenings.
8   It _____ like fun. _____ you come too?

5 Match the sentences in Exercise 4 with the three categories in the box.

> ▶ **TALKING ABOUT INTERESTS**
>
> **Talking about interests and abilities**
> Do you like taking photos?
> I'm good at acting.
> I'm (not) interested in photography.
>
> **Talking about plans**
> I'd like/prefer to join a running club.
> I wouldn't like to do it.
>
> **Recommending and encouraging**
> It looks interesting.
> Go on.
> I think you'd enjoy it.
> You should do it with me.

6 Pronunciation **silent letters**

▶ **16** Some letters in English words are not pronounced. Listen to these words from the conversation and cross out the silent letters. Then listen again and repeat.

1   interested
2   should
3   friends
4   write
5   half
6   what

7 Work in pairs. Discuss the questions.

1   Would you like to join one of the clubs in Exercise 2? Why? / Why not?
2   What other types of clubs would you like to join? Why would you like to join them?

my life ▶ RULES FOR A COMPETITION ▶ OPINIONS ABOUT SPORT ▶ OLYMPIC SPORTS ▶ **INTERESTS** ▶ AN ADVERT OR NOTICE

2e Advertising for members

Writing an advert or notice

1 What makes a good advert and a bad advert? Think about adverts you like and don't like in magazines, on TV or online.

2 Read the advice about how to write effective adverts and notices. Then look at the adverts on page 28. Answer these questions.

   1 Which advert follows most of the advice?
   2 How could you improve the other adverts?

> ### *How to* WRITE EFFECTIVE ADVERTS AND NOTICES
>
> - Start with a good headline. You could ask a question or solve a problem.
> - The advert should explain the reasons for buying something or joining a club.
> - If possible, offer something for free or a prize.
> - Include any other important information (dates, times, location, etc.).
> - Photos, pictures or images always help.

3 Work in pairs. You are going to plan a new club. Discuss the questions.

   1 What type of club is it? (e.g. a chess club, a tennis club, a walking group)
   2 Who is the club for?
   3 Are there any rules for members?
   4 Is there a membership fee? How much is it?
   5 How often will it meet?

4 Plan and write an advert for your club.

5 Writing skill checking your writing

a It is important to check your writing for mistakes before people read it. Read these sentences from adverts and find one mistake in each sentence. Circle the mistake and write the correct symbol from the correction code.

   1 Would you like to learn a musical instrument.? *P*
   2 Enter our exciteing competition!
   3 **Are you good at play tennis?**
   4 We meet at Tuesdays and Thursdays.
   5 It's fun way to get fit.
   6 Join this club new!
   7 Get healthy and play yoga.
   8 **Call peter on 077 237 5980.**

Writing correction code		
Sp	=	spelling mistake
MW	=	missing word
P	=	punctuation mistake
Prep	=	preposition mistake
Gr	=	grammar mistake
WO	=	word order mistake
C	=	capital letter mistake
WW	=	wrong word

b Read your advert from Exercise 4 again. Are there any mistakes?

6 Display your adverts around the classroom. Walk around and read about each other's new clubs. Think about these questions.

   - Which clubs would you like to join?
   - Which adverts are effective? Why?

2f Mongolian horse racing

Children compete in a horserace at the Naadam festival, Mongolia.

Before you watch

1 Work in groups. Look at the photo of horse racing in Mongolia. Answer the questions.

1 Do you have horse racing in your country?
2 How popular is it as a sport?

2 Key vocabulary

Read the sentences. The words in bold are used in the video. Match the words and phrases with the definitions (a–h).

1 In the Olympic Games, the winners receive a gold **medal**.
2 I got 100% on the exam so I feel very **proud** of myself.
3 A religious man **blesses** all the people.
4 The grass is very **rich** at this time of year.
5 My horse can run **like the wind**.
6 At the festival, there were **displays** by actors and performers.
7 In the USA, a **rodeo** is very famous for its cowboys and exciting to watch.
8 In this competition, I have one main **rival** who always tries to beat me.

a asks a god (or gods) to protect something
b pleased because you've done something well
c good to eat
d shows or presentations
e a round piece of metal given in competitions
f very quickly
g a competition where people try to stay on wild horses
h person who competes with you

While you watch

3 🎦 **2.1** Watch the video and number these actions in the order you see them.

a Mukhdalai's horse wins the race.
b A horse rider carries a flag *1*
c The riders leave the starting point.
d A religious woman blesses the horses.
e Mukhdalai receives first prize.
f A horse rider picks up poles.
g Two men wrestle.
h Two men ride wild horses in the rodeo.

4 🎦 **2.1** Watch the video again. Choose the correct option (a–b).

1 The 'Naadam' is a type of _____ .
  a festival
  b horse race
2 Mukhdalai and Namjin are _____ who compete against each other.
  a horse riders
  b trainers
3 Mukhdalai and Namjin _____ each other.
  a like
  b don't like
4 There are about _____ horses competing in the race.
  a twenty
  b eighty
5 The starting point is at the _____ of a hill.
  a top
  b bottom
6 _____ is wearing green and white.
  a Mukhdalai's son
  b Namjin's son
7 Mukhdalai's horse is in first place for _____ race.
  a the whole
  b part of the
8 Namjin's horse was in _____ .
  a first place
  b its first race

After you watch

5 Vocabulary in context

a 🎦 **2.2** Watch the clips from the video. Choose the correct meaning of the words and phrases.

b Work in pairs. Ask and answer these questions.

1 What are some annual celebrations in your country?
2 What famous races (e.g. Formula 1 racing) do you watch? Who usually takes the lead and wins? Does the same competitor usually finish a long way ahead of the rest?
3 Do you ever do any races such as running or cycling? Can you keep up with the others? Or do you often slow down and fall back?

6 Work in pairs. Write five questions about the Naadam festival in the video.

What is the Naadam festival famous for?

7 Work with a new partner. Take turns to ask and answer your questions from Exercise 6 about the Naadam.

Grammar

1 Choose the correct options to complete the text about an unusual competition.

The first bed race was in Knaresborough, UK, in 1966. The rules are simple. Each team [1] *can / has to* race with one bed on wheels. There are six people in a team and one passenger. The team [2] *must / doesn't have to* have either six men or six women, or you [3] *can / can't* race with a team of three men and three women. The passenger [4] *has to / doesn't have to* be an adult but he or she [5] *doesn't have to / can't* be younger than twelve years of age. The time limit for the race is thirty minutes and you [6] *mustn't / have to* take longer.

2 **>> MB** Work in pairs. What sports do these people play? Say two rules for each sport.

3 Complete the sentences with the *-ing* form of these verbs.

feel	go	learn	lose	watch	win

1 _____ to speak another language is very useful.
2 Sport is good for _____ healthy.
3 Peter hates _____ any type of game.
4 Trying is more important than _____.
5 We're bored of _____ this match.
6 I love _____ to the cinema after work.

4 **>> MB** Complete the sentences in your own words using *-ing* forms. Then tell your partner.

1 _____ is very good for you.
2 I'm really interested in _____.
3 I don't like _____.

I CAN
use verbs for rules (including modal verbs)
use the *-ing* form

Vocabulary

5 Write the missing vowels in these words connected with sport. Race with your partner to see who can finish first.

1 R_C_
2 G__LS
3 CR_WD
4 M_TCH
5 F_N_SH L_N_
6 B_S_B_LL
7 W_NN_R
8 F_NS
9 T__M
10 B_X_R

6 Answer these questions with four of the words from Exercise 5.

1 What do you have to cross in a race?
2 What is the opposite of *a loser*?
3 What type of competition is Formula One?
4 What are the group of people who like a sports person or team?

7 **>> MB** Work in pairs. Choose four more words from Exercise 5 and write four questions. Then work with another pair and ask and answer your questions.

I CAN
talk about sport and sports people

Real life

8 Complete the conversation. Write one word in each gap.

A: Are you interested [1] _____ painting? There's a new evening course at my college.
B: I'm afraid I'm not very good [2] _____ art.
A: I'm not either, but I'd like [3] _____ learn. Go [4] _____. You should do it with me.
B: Sorry. What about doing something else?
A: [5] _____ you like taking photos? There's also a course for that.
B: Actually, that looks interesting.

9 **>> MB** Complete these sentences in your own words. Then tell your partner.

1 I'm good at …
2 I wouldn't like to …
3 I'm also interested in …
4 I think I'd enjoy learning …

I CAN
talk about my interests

Taking the train in Dhaka, Bangladesh

FEATURES

1 Look at the photo. Where is the woman? Why do you think she is travelling like this?

2 ▶ 17 Listen to someone talking about the photo. Why isn't the woman inside the train?

3 Work in pairs. Which ways of travelling would you prefer for the activities (1–10)? Give your reasons.

by bicycle	by bus	in my car	on a ferry	on foot
by lorry	on a motorbike	by plane	on a ship
in a taxi	by train

1 visit relatives
   *I'd prefer to **visit** my **relatives by bicycle** or **on foot** because they only live five minutes from my house.*
2 move house and furniture
3 get to the airport
4 go on holiday
5 cross an ocean
6 get to the railway station
7 go out in the evening to a party or restaurant
8 take children to school
9 commute to your place of work or study
10 go shopping

3a Transport solutions

Reading

1 Work in pairs. Answer the questions.

1 How do you go to your place of work or study?
2 Do you use public transport?
3 Are there often traffic problems?

2 Read the article about four solutions to transport problems. Match the paragraphs (A–D) with the photos (1–4).

3 Look at the photos and read the article again. Which types of transport (A–D) do you think the sentences describe? Some sentences describe more than one type.

1 It moves over people's heads.
   B, D
2 It's a faster way to commute.
3 It needs human energy.
4 It uses energy from the wind or the sun.
5 It makes travel cheaper.
6 It isn't for long distances.

Vocabulary **transport nouns**

> ▶ **WORDBUILDING compound nouns**
>
> We can join two nouns to make a new noun: *bus + stop = bus stop*,
> *air + port = airport*
> A compound noun can be two words *(bus stop)* or one word *(airport)*.
>
> For further practice, see Workbook page 27.

4 Find these compound nouns in the article. Match the nouns with the definitions (1–7).

> carbon emissions   city centres   container ships   fuel costs
> rush hour   speed limit   traffic jam

1 the maximum speed you can legally drive   *speed limit*
2 a long line of vehicles moving slowly on the road
3 the time in the day when lots of people travel to/from work
4 the money you spend on petrol or diesel in transport
5 the amount of CO_2 that a type of transport produces
6 the middle of cities
7 transport for moving products around the world

5 Work in pairs. Discuss the questions.

1 Which of the four transport solutions in the article do you think are a good idea?
2 Which traffic problems will they solve in your area?

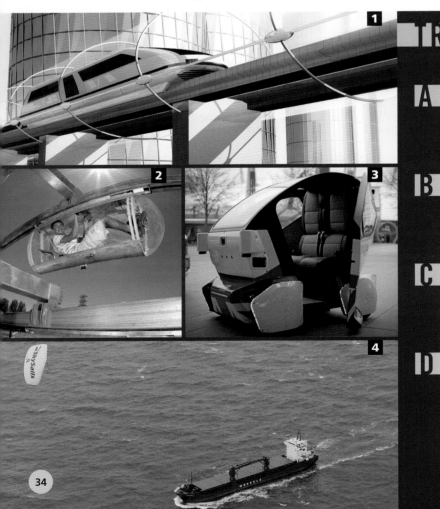

TRANSPORT SOLUTIONS

▶ 18

A BMW, Volvo, General Motors and Google are all currently working on driverless cars. Some driverless cars use solar energy, so they are good for the environment. They are also safer because the computer controls the speed and they can't go faster than the **speed limit**.

B This monorail in New Zealand is a new solution for commuters in **traffic jams** during the **rush hour**. The passenger sits in a pod and can cycle over people's heads. Google has already invested over $1 million in the idea.

C At sea, large **container ships** travel thousands of kilometres and use a lot of fuel. Now, a German company is testing huge kites on these ships. The wind pushes the kite and this moves the ship. It reduces the **fuel costs** and lowers **carbon emissions**.

D In the future, the Hyperloop could be a common type of public transport. It's a long tube with no air inside, and passengers sit inside pods which travel at 1,200 kilometres per hour. There are already plans for the first Hyperloop between the **city centres** of San Francisco and Los Angeles. The distance is around 600 kilometres and it would only take 30 minutes.

Grammar comparatives and superlatives

6 ▶ **19** Listen to a short conversation between two colleagues at work. Which types of transport do they talk about? What advantages and disadvantages do they mention?

7 ▶ **19** Listen again. Choose the correct option in these sentences.

1 Eight thirty is the *bad / worst* time for traffic.
2 My bicycle is *faster / fastest* than your car in the rush hour!
3 I travel *far / further* than you.
4 They're *better / best* for the environment.
5 They're better but they're also *more / most* expensive.
6 A new electric car is the *more / most* expensive type of car.
7 The *faster / fastest* bus takes over an hour.

▶ **COMPARATIVES and SUPERLATIVES**

Regular adjectives	Comparative	Superlative
fast	faster	fastest
big	bigger	biggest
expensive	more expensive	most expensive

Irregular adjectives		
far	further	furthest
good	better	best
bad	worse	worst

For further information and practice, see page 160.

8 Look at the grammar box. Answer these questions.

1 What letters do we add to short adjectives (*fast, cheap*, etc.) to form comparative and superlative adjectives?
2 We use *more* before longer adjectives to make the comparative. What do we use to make the superlative?
3 What is the comparative and superlative form of these irregular adjectives: *far, good, bad*?
4 Which word often comes after a comparative adjective? Which word normally comes before a superlative adjective?

9 Pronunciation *than*

a ▶ **20** Listen to the pronunciation of *than* in these sentences. Notice how we say /ðən/ not /ðæn/.

1 Cars are faster than bicycles.
2 Bicycles are better for the environment than cars.

b ▶ **20** Listen again and repeat the sentences.

c Practise saying these sentences.

1 I travel further than you.
2 A train is more expensive than a bus.

10 Complete this report about a transport survey. Write the correct comparative or superlative form of the adjectives.

Report on local transport

For commuting and daytime travel in our town, the ¹_____ (popular) form of transport is the bus because it's ²_____ (cheap) than going by car or taxi. However, some people in the survey want ³_____ (good) cycle paths because the bus is ⁴_____ (slow) than a bicycle in the rush hour. Everyone said that parking in the town centre is the ⁵_____ (big) problem, so people don't often use their cars. As a result, taxis are ⁶_____ (popular) than private cars in the evenings, even though taxis are the ⁷_____ (expensive) type of transport.

Speaking ⟨ my life ⟩

11 Work in pairs. Make comparative and superlative sentences with these transport words and adjectives. How many sentences can you make in three minutes?

trains	cars	taxis
buses	planes	
ships	bicycles	
motorbikes		

fast	cheap	bad
slow	popular	
expensive	safe	
quick	good	

*Trains are **quicker than** cars but planes are **the fastest** type of transport.*

12 Find out about your partner's journey to work or college. Ask these questions.

1 How far do you travel to work or college?
2 How long does it take?
3 How much does it cost every week?

13 Make sentences comparing your journeys.

*My home is **further** from college **than** yours. / Your home is **nearer than** mine.*

14 Work with another pair. Compare your information. Find out:

1 who lives the nearest to / furthest away from work / college
*Mario lives **the nearest to** work and Ahmed lives **the furthest away**.*
2 who has the shortest / longest commute
3 who has the cheapest / most expensive journey each week
4 which type of transport is the least / most popular in the group

3b Transport around the world

Listening

1 Work in pairs. Look at the photos of the camel and the huskies. Where in the world do you think they are? What are the advantages of using animals for transport in these parts of the world?

2 ▶ 21 Listen to a documentary about animal transport. Why does the presenter say camels and huskies are better than cars?

3 ▶ 21 Listen to the documentary again. What do these numbers describe? Make notes.

Camels

50 degrees

40 kilometres

3 to 5 days

160 words

Huskies

-50 degrees

6 and 8 huskies

1,600 kilometres

Grammar *as ... as*

> ▶ **AS ... AS**
>
> 1 *In some parts of the world, animal transport is **as** popular **as** these modern types of transport.*
> 2 *In winter, northern Alaska can be **as** cold **as** the North Pole.*
> 3 *For long distances, modern vehicles are **not as** good **as** camels.*
> 4 *A camel is**n't as** comfortable **as** a car.*
>
> For further information and practice, see page 160.

4 Look at the grammar box and answer these questions.

  a Which two sentences say two things are the same or equal?
  b Which two sentences say two things are different, and one thing is less than the other?

5 Read the first sentence. Then complete the second sentence. Use *as ... as* or *not as ... as* and the adjective in brackets.

  1 An underground train across London costs £6 and a taxi costs £15.
     An underground train across London is*n't as expensive as* a taxi. (expensive)
  2 A ferry from England to France takes 90 minutes. A train through the tunnel takes 35 minutes.
     A train from England to France is _____ a ferry. (slow)
  3 In the New York rush hour, cycling to work and going by bus takes the same amount of time.
     In the New York rush hour, cycling to work is _____ going by bus. (fast)
  4 In Germany and in Finland, 9% of journeys are by bicycle.
     Cycling in Germany is _____ in Finland. (popular)
  5 London Heathrow airport has 75 million passengers per year. Atlanta airport has over 100 million passengers per year.
     London Heathrow airport is _____ . (busy)

6 Pronunciation sentence stress

▶ 22 Listen to these sentences. Underline the stressed words in each sentence.

1 Cycling is as popular as jogging.
2 Trains aren't as expensive as taxis.
3 Los Angeles airport is as busy as London Heathrow.
4 A car isn't as fast as a bicycle in a traffic jam.

7 Work in pairs. Ask questions to find out how similar or different you are. Then write sentences.

Is your partner … as tall as you? / as old as you? / as interested in sport / music / films as you?

Is your partner's … family as large as yours? / day at work or college as long as yours? / English book as new as yours?

Carlos is as tall as me. / Carlos isn't as short as me.

Vocabulary transport adjectives

8 Read part of a news article about taxis in London. What does it compare?

BATTLE OF THE TAXIS

When you travel in London, the city's famous black taxis or black 'cabs' are a **convenient** type of transport. On any main road there are **frequent** cabs, and even with four or five people they're **comfortable** to ride in. But now the **traditional** black cab has competition from private hire taxis such as Uber, Karhoo or Addison Lee. Using your mobile phone, you can book a private hire taxi for a certain time and they are very **punctual**. Sometimes these private taxis are also a bit cheaper and a little faster. However, in bad traffic, black-cab drivers say their cabs are much faster. They have to learn all the roads around London, so they don't use sat nav, and they know the best routes around the city. They think that private taxis are a lot less **reliable** in rush-hour traffic.

9 Find these words in the article. Then match them with the definitions (1–6).

| convenient | frequent | comfortable |
| traditional | punctual | reliable |

1 It's always on time.
2 It comes often or regularly.
3 It's always been the same.
4 It's nice to sit in.
5 It's near or easy to use.
6 It does what you need it to.

Grammar comparative modifiers

▶ COMPARATIVE MODIFIERS

Sometimes these private taxis are **a bit** cheaper and **a little** faster.
Black cab drivers are **much** faster because they know the best routes.
They think that Uber taxis are **a lot** less reliable.

For further information and practice, see page 160.

10 Look at the grammar box. Complete these rules with the correct modifiers.

1 To talk about a small difference, we use _____ or _____ before a comparative adjective.
2 To talk about a big difference, we use _____ or _____ before a comparative adjective.

11 Work in pairs. Look at the information about transport for visitors to London. Write sentences using these ideas and comparative modifiers.

1 A London bus is / expensive than …
  A London bus is a lot less expensive than a black cab.
2 London buses are / frequent than …
3 The river boat is / comfortable than …
4 A black cab is / convenient than …

	River boat	**Black cab**	**London bus**
Prices	£14.70 per day for travel anywhere on the river	£6 per mile (minimum price £2.40)	£5 per day for travel anywhere in the city centre
Frequency	One boat every 20 to 30 minutes; 15 different stops	All the time at taxi ranks and on busy streets	About every five minutes on busy routes
Other information	Guaranteed seat; food and drink sold on board	Seats for five people plus luggage	Buses to every part of London; space for standing and sitting

12 Make three more sentences with comparative modifiers using the information about London transport in Exercise 11.

Speaking ⟨ my life ⟩

13 What advice would you give a visitor who arrives in your country for the first time? What are the best ways to get around? Tell your partner.

From the airport to the city centre, there are buses. They're a lot more frequent than the trains.

3c The end of the road

Reading

1 You are going to read an article about a city in India. Write one thing you know about India. Then tell the class.

2 Read the article. Which paragraph talks about:

a why people like rickshaws in Kolkata?
b modern transport in Kolkata?
c the end of the old rickshaws in Kolkata?

3 Read the article again and answer the questions.

1 What is the population of Kolkata?
2 Why is Kolkata noisy?
3 Where is it safer for pedestrians to walk? Why?
4 In paragraph 2, why do these people take rickshaws?
   • children
   • commuters
   • housewives
   • tourists
5 Some politicians want a new type of rickshaw. Why is it different?
6 How many people pull the old rickshaws in Kolkata?
7 Why don't the drivers want the new rickshaws?

Vocabulary **transport verbs**

4 Find the verbs (1–8) in paragraphs 1 and 2 of the article, and match them with the words (a–h).

1	catch	a	the underground
2	get on	b	a taxi
3	go	c	your bus
4	pick up	d	a train
5	miss	e	children
6	take	f	with your shopping
7	go by	g	rickshaw
8	drop you off	h	on foot

5 Replace the verbs in bold with a verb or verb phrase from Exercise 4.

1 I'd **travel by** taxi to the airport. It's much quicker. _take a / go by_
2 I can **collect** the children from school on my way home from work. ....
3 I need to go now if I want to **get** the next train. ....
4 You'd better leave now or you will **not get** your flight. ....
5 Let's park the car here and **walk** to the city centre. ....
6 Tell the driver to **leave you** outside the restaurant. ....

Critical thinking **opinions for and against**

6 There are five different groups of people in the article: shoppers, tourists, politicians, parents and rickshaw drivers. Which groups:

1 are for hand-pulled rickshaws in Kolkata?
2 are against the rickshaws?

Underline the reasons in the article for each group's opinions.

7 Do you think the writer gives a balanced view of the opinions on both sides? Why? / Why not?

Speaking ⟨ my life ⟩

8 Look at this advert for pedicabs. Do you have them in your country? Why are they popular?

✓ Pedicabs are greener than taxis
✓ They take two passengers
✓ Friendly drivers cycle you anywhere
✓ No engine, so it's quieter
✓ Great for sightseeing

9 Work in groups. You want to start a pedicab company in your town or city. Discuss the questions and make notes.

1 Who are your main customers? (commuters, tourists, etc.)
2 Why are pedicabs better than other types of transport (buses, taxis, etc.)?
3 How much do you charge? Are you cheaper or more expensive than other transport?
4 What is the name of your business? How can you advertise your business? (on the internet, on TV, etc.)

10 Give a presentation about your pedicab company to the class. Listen to other groups and compare your ideas. Which group has the best ideas?

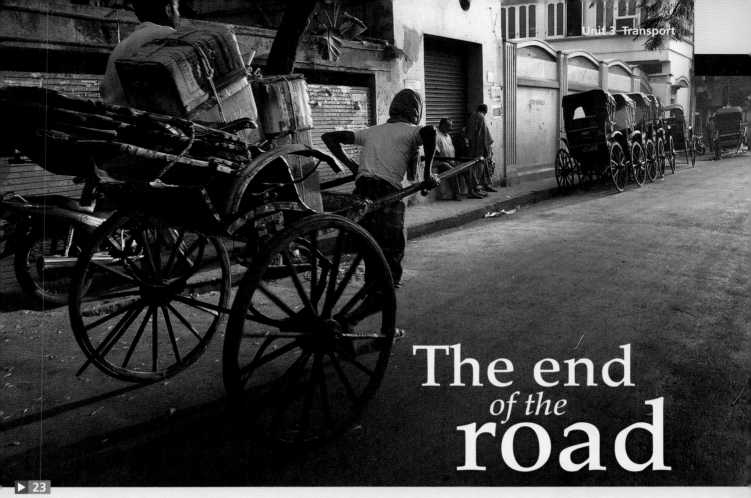

The end *of the* road

▶ 23

Kolkata is the capital of West Bengal in India. It has a population of around 15 million people and the rush hour starts early in the morning. All day there are traffic jams with cars, public buses, taxis, motorbikes and pedicabs, and drivers honk their horns from morning to night. You can also catch the train or get on the underground, but those are busy too. For pedestrians, Kolkata can be dangerous – crossing the road is especially difficult. Fortunately, the old parts of the city have smaller streets which are better if you go on foot. Cars can't drive down them so they are much quieter and a lot safer.

In these old streets, you'll see men pulling rickshaws. They are a traditional type of transport in the city and local people still like using them. Early in the day, the drivers pick up children and take them to school. And if you miss your bus to work, a hand-pulled rickshaw is much cheaper than taking a taxi. Then, later on in the day, housewives often prefer to go by rickshaw to the local markets. The driver drops the women off with their shopping outside their house; no other type of public transport can do that! So rickshaws are popular with many local people. When the traffic is very bad, you can go anywhere by rickshaw. Kolkata is one of the last cities in the world with hand-pulled rickshaws, so the drivers also make money from tourists. Visitors to the city often want to get a photograph sitting on a rickshaw because it's a famous symbol of Kolkata. 25 30 35

However, not everyone thinks the famous rickshaws are a good idea. Some local politicians don't like this old type of transport because they think it's wrong for one human to pull other humans. Instead, they want more rickshaw drivers to use pedicabs or modern electric rickshaws, which are clean and fast. The problem is that Kolkata has around 2,000 rickshaw drivers who pull their passengers by hand. They are often men from villages in the countryside and they don't have any other job. The new electric rickshaws are very expensive, so these drivers can't afford them. For these men, it's probably the end of the road for the traditional rickshaw and their way of life. 40 45

electric rickshaw (n) /ɪˈlektrɪk ˈrɪkˌʃɔː/ a modern type of rickshaw with an electric engine
honk your horn (exp) /hɒŋk jɔː hɔː(r)n/ make a loud noise in a car to tell people you are there
pedicab (n) /ˈpedɪkæb/ a type of taxi with no engine. The driver cycles.

3d Getting around town

Vocabulary taking transport

1 Look at these pairs of words. Match the words with the correct definition (a or b).

1 stop / rank
  a where you can get a taxi
  b where you can get a bus

2 fare / price
  a the money you pay for a journey by bus, train or taxi
  b the amount of money something costs

3 change / receipt
  a the money you get back when you pay more than the price
  b the piece of paper you receive to show you paid for something

4 gate / platform
  a where you get on a train
  b where you get on a plane

5 book / check in
  a when you buy a ticket in advance
  b when you confirm your flight or leave your bags

Real life going on a journey

2 ▶ 24 Listen to five conversations. Javier and Shelley are going to the airport, but they take different transport. Answer the questions.

1 At the taxi rank: where does Javier want to go?
2 In the taxi: how much is the fare? Does Javier want a receipt?
3 At the bus stop: where does Shelley want to go? What type of ticket does she buy?
4 At the train station: how much is the ticket? Which platform does the train leave from?
5 At the airport: what does Shelley give the woman? How many bags does she check in?

3 ▶ 24 Look at the expressions for going on a journey. Then listen to the conversations again. Tick the sentences you hear.

> ▶ **GOING ON A JOURNEY**
>
> **In a taxi**
> I'd like to go to the station please.
> You can stop here.
> How much is that?
> Do you have change?
> Do you want a receipt?
>
> **On a bus**
> Do you stop at the airport?
> A single or return ticket?
> Please stop at the next one.
> That's two pounds.
>
> **At the train station**
> A return ticket to the airport, please.
> First or second class?
> Single or return?
> Which platform is it?
>
> **At the airport**
> Can I see your passport?
> How many bags are you checking in?
> I only have this carry on.
> Window or aisle?
> Can I have a seat next to my friend?

4 Pronunciation intonation

a ▶ 25 In everyday English, people don't always use full questions. For example, they can say *Single or return?* instead of *Do you want a single or return ticket?* Listen to these questions. Mark the intonation ⤴ or ⤵.

1 Single or return?
2 Window or aisle?
3 Credit card or cash?
4 Bus or train?
5 North or south?
6 First or second class?

b ▶ 25 Listen again and repeat the sentences.

5 Work in pairs. Look at the four situations (a–d) with people going to an airport. Act out conversations using the expressions for going on a journey to help you.

Student A: You are the passenger.

Student B: Take the other role in the conversations (e.g. the taxi driver).

Then change roles and repeat.

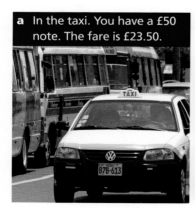
a In the taxi. You have a £50 note. The fare is £23.50.

b On the bus.

c At the train station.

d At the airport. You have two bags.

my life ▶ EVERYDAY JOURNEYS ▶ TRAVEL ADVICE ▶ ALTERNATIVE TRANSPORT ▶ GOING ON A JOURNEY ▶ NOTES AND MESSAGES

3e Quick communication

Writing notes and messages

1 How do you normally send notes and messages to friends and colleagues? By text or email? What other ways do you use?

2 Read the notes and messages (1–8). Match them with the reasons for writing (a–e).

a thanking
b apologizing
c giving travel information
d suggesting a time and place
e giving a message from someone else

3 Writing skills writing in note form

a People often miss out words in notes and messages. Look again at the notes and messages in Exercise 1. Find places where the writers have missed out these kinds of words.

- articles (e.g. *a, the*)
- pronouns (e.g. *I, me*)
- auxiliary verbs (e.g. *do, are*)
- polite forms (e.g. *Would you like to …? Can we …?*)

(Can we) Meet outside (the) airport at 2? (Is that) OK?

b Rewrite these phone messages as shorter text messages.

1 'I'm sorry but I'm stuck in a traffic jam. I'll see you in half an hour.'
   Sorry. Stuck in traffic. See you in 30 mins.
2 'Thank you for booking the train tickets. I'll pay you when we meet at the station.'
3 'Take the underground to Oxford Street and the Moon café is opposite the station.'
4 'Peter wants to come with us in the taxi. Can you call him and tell him where to meet us?'
5 'My flight is an hour late. Meet me in the arrivals area at five o'clock.'

4 Work in pairs. Write a short note or message for each situation.

1 You have to work late. Write a text to your friend. Say you will arrive at the bus station an hour later.
2 You are meeting tonight in the city centre. Suggest your friend takes a taxi from the taxi rank outside the train station.
3 You cannot travel with your friend on the underground to the airport. Explain you will travel by bus and meet him/her at the check-in desk.

5 Write a short message to your partner. Then exchange messages. Can you understand the other person's message? Write a reply if necessary!

1
Meet outside airport at 2?
OK?

2
Sorry. Bus late. Will be 15 minutes late.

3
Javier called. Call him back.
0770 657 655.

4
Train leaves platform 6.

5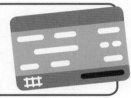
Thanks for getting tickets.
Here's the money.

6
Plane at gate 6.

7
Am in taxi. See you outside in 5?

8
Afraid I was late so missed meeting. My apologies.

Indian Railways

At the Victoria Terminus in Mumbai, India, it always seems to be rush hour.

Before you watch

1 Work in groups. Look at the photo and the caption. Why do you think trains are a popular type of transport in India?

2 Key vocabulary

a Read the sentences. The words in bold are used in the video. Guess the meaning of the words.

1 Don't walk on the railway **track**! A train might come.
2 Some of the trains in India have **impressive** names like *The Himalayan Queen*.
3 I live in a **rural** village about thirty miles from the nearest town.
4 This toy train is a **miniature** of the real thing.
5 My company has a large **workforce**. We employ over five hundred people.

b Match the words in bold in Exercise 2a with these definitions.

a important-sounding
b the metal line that a train runs on
c the group of people who work for a company
d in the countryside
e a small copy

While you watch

3 **3.1** Watch the video about Indian Railways with the sound OFF. Number these actions in the order you see them (1–6).

a A man is checking the railway track.
b A train is travelling in the Indian countryside.
c Hundreds of people are walking on a platform during the rush hour.
d People are playing a game.
e A man with a white beard is dancing with two swords.
f Someone is serving food.

4 **3.1** Watch the video with the sound ON. Underline the correct words.

1 Every day approximately *two hundred thousand / two million* passengers pass through Mumbai train station.
2 There are over *two billion / one billion* people in India.
3 The British built the railways in India in the *eighteenth / nineteenth* century.
4 The first steam train in India was in eighteen *thirty-three / fifty-three*.
5 There are over *thirty-eight thousand / three thousand eight hundred* miles of railway track in India.
6 The Grand Trunk Express has travelled through India since *nineteen thirty-nine / nineteen twenty-nine*.
7 India's railways carry *four billion / four million* passengers every year.
8 Indian Railways employ *one hundred thousand / one and a half million* staff.

After you watch

5 **3.2** **Vocabulary in context**

a Watch the clips from the video. Choose the correct meaning of the words and phrases.

b Work in pairs. Ask and answer these questions.

1 Does your country have an enormous public transport system? Is the transport system in your country in good condition? Why / Why not?
2 What everyday situations do you find most stressful (e.g. taking exams, driving in busy traffic)? Why?
3 In your region, which company is one of the largest employers? What do they make or provide?

6 **3.3** You are going to prepare a narration for a new version of the Indian Railways video. It's called *A one-minute journey on the Indian Railways*. As you watch, take notes about what you see in each part.

• Rush hour in Mumbai (0–15)
• On the train (16–38)
• The workforce (39–50)
• At the station (51–60)

7 Now write a script for the new video. Describe what you can see in the video and any important facts and figures about the Indian railway. Try to use some of these words and phrases.

> checking the track
> cities and rural villages
> dancing
> enormous
> good condition
> passengers
> platform
> playing games
> rush hour
> station
> stressful
> workforce

8 Work with a partner. Your teacher will play the video twice. As you watch, take turns to read your script and narrate the video.

Grammar

1 Complete the article with the correct form of the adjectives.

Santiago is the ¹_____ (large) city in Chile. It has a population of five million people and it's the ²_____ (busy) city in the country. It has some of the ³_____ (beautiful) buildings in the world, but in the past, it was the ⁵_____ (polluted) city in Chile. Its streets weren't as ⁶_____ (clean) as they are today.

Nowadays, public transport around the city is much ⁷_____ (good) and the city centre isn't as ⁸_____ (noisy). Cycling is also a lot ⁹_____ (popular) these days because there are new cycle paths and people can use electric bikes.

2 ▶▶ **MB** Work in pairs. Make four sentences to compare your town or city to Santiago. Talk about:

- size and population
- buildings and streets
- traffic and public transport
- walking and cycling

I CAN	
use comparative and superlative adjectives	☐
use as … as	☐

Vocabulary

3 Match words from A with words from B to make compound nouns. Then complete the sentences with the compound nouns.

A: traffic	rush	city	bus	speed

B: hour	stop	limit	jam	centre

1 There's a _____ _____ on the motorway. Nothing's moving.
2 _____ starts at about seven in the morning.
3 Wait at the _____ _____ and the number 39 comes every twenty minutes.
4 Slow down! The _____ is only 30 kilometres an hour on these roads.
5 The _____ is closed to cars on Sundays.

4 Which words can follow the words in CAPITAL letters? Cross out the incorrect word.

1 GO BY: car, foot, plane, bicycle
2 GO ON: a taxi, a ship, foot, a ferry
3 CATCH: a train, a plane, a taxi, a bus
4 DROP OFF: your shopping, your children, the underground

5 ▶▶ **MB** Work in pairs. Look at the photos (a–e) and answer the questions (1–7). Give reasons.

1 Which types of transport are slow but reliable?
2 Which are comfortable and convenient?
3 Which are the cheapest?
4 Which goes the furthest in a short time?
5 Which lands at a gate?
6 Which stops at a rank?
7 Which are good for sightseeing in a city?

I CAN	
talk about transport	☐

Real life

6 Complete the conversation at a train station with these words.

platform	ticket	single	return	receipt

A: I'd like a _____ to Glasgow.
B: _____ or return?
A: _____, please.
B: That's twenty-one pounds fifty. Do you want a _____?
A: Yes, please. Which _____ is it?
B: Three.

7 ▶▶ **MB** Work in pairs. Write a similar conversation between two people at an airport. Use these phrases.

see your passport	checking in	a carry on
window or aisle		

I CAN	
buy tickets and use different types of transport	☐

Unit 4 Challenges

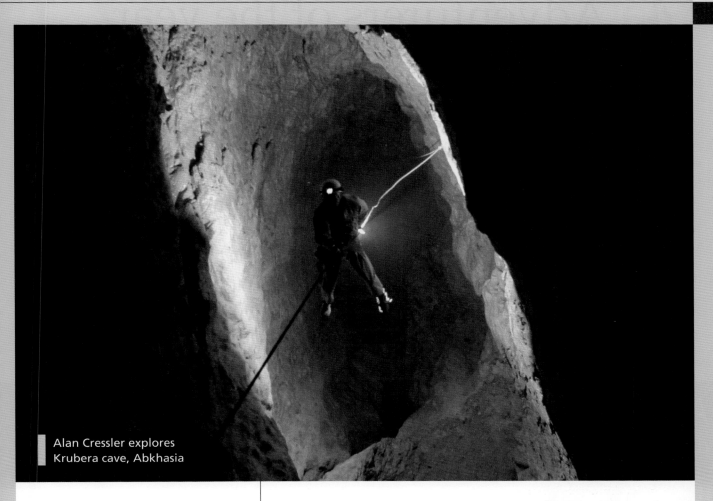

Alan Cressler explores
Krubera cave, Abkhasia

FEATURES

1 Look at the photo. Where is the man? Do you think this activity looks exciting or dangerous? Would you like to do this?

2 ▶ 26 Listen to another caver talking about his hobby. Answer the questions.

1 Why do colleagues at work think he is 'a bit crazy'?
2 Why do cavers work in teams?
3 How do you get to Rumbling Falls Cave?

3 Look at these sentences from Vic's description. Match the words in bold with the definitions (a–c).

1 Sometimes you have to **take a risk** when you go caving.
2 Every cave gives you a new **challenge**.
3 Rumbling Falls cave was probably my biggest **achievement** as a caver.

a do something which can be dangerous
b success in something after a lot of hard work and effort (e.g. passing an examination)
c something very difficult to do

4 Work in groups. Discuss the questions.

1 Are you a person who takes risks or are you usually very careful?
2 What is a big achievement in your life so far?
3 What will be a big challenge for you in the future?
4 Is there any kind of risky activity you would like to try in the future?

4a Adventurers of the year

Reading

1 Read the article. Are these sentences about Pasang, Marjan, or both of them? Write 1–6 in the diagram.

1 She was born in Nepal.
2 Her father helped her.
3 She started when she was a teenager.
4 She trained for her job.
5 She competed in other countries.
6 She changed other people's lives.

Pasang   Marjan

1

Both

2 Read the article again. Work in pairs and discuss the questions.

1 What do you think was Pasang's biggest challenge?
2 Why is she famous?
3 What was Marjan's ambition?
4 What were her team's achievements?

Grammar past simple

> **PAST SIMPLE**

We use the past simple to talk about finished actions, events or situations in the past.
*Pasang Lhamu Sherpa Akita **lived** with her younger sister in Lukla.*
*Marjan Sadequi **grew up** in the capital city of Kabul.*
*People **didn't have** homes or food.*
*It **wasn't** easy to practise around the roads of Kabul.*

For further information and practice, see page 162.

▶ 27

ADVENTURERS of the YEAR

EVERY YEAR, READERS OF *NATIONAL GEOGRAPHIC* MAGAZINE VOTE FOR THEIR ADVENTURERS OF THE YEAR. HERE ARE TWO OF THEM.

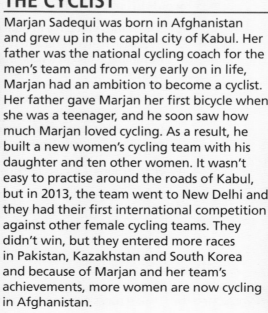

THE MOUNTAINEER

As a child, Pasang Lhamu Sherpa Akita lived with her younger sister in Lukla, a town in northeastern Nepal. Her parents died when she was young. As a teenager she trained as a mountaineer. She worked as a mountain guide and she climbed Mount Everest when she was only 22. In 2015, there was a terrible earthquake in Nepal and many people didn't have homes or food, so Pasang helped them. Nowadays she also works to improve education in Nepal and is famous for her voluntary work as well as her mountaineering.

THE CYCLIST

Marjan Sadequi was born in Afghanistan and grew up in the capital city of Kabul. Her father was the national cycling coach for the men's team and from very early on in life, Marjan had an ambition to become a cyclist. Her father gave Marjan her first bicycle when she was a teenager, and he soon saw how much Marjan loved cycling. As a result, he built a new women's cycling team with his daughter and ten other women. It wasn't easy to practise around the roads of Kabul, but in 2013, the team went to New Delhi and they had their first international competition against other female cycling teams. They didn't win, but they entered more races in Pakistan, Kazakhstan and South Korea and because of Marjan and her team's achievements, more women are now cycling in Afghanistan.

3 Look at the grammar box on page 46. Underline the past simple forms in the article. Which are regular? Which are irregular?

4 Answer these questions.

1 What do we add to regular verbs to form the past simple? What do we add if the verb ends in *-e*? What if the verb ends in *-y*?

2 What is the infinitive form of the irregular verbs you underlined?
grew up – grow up

3 How do we form the negative of most past simple verbs? How do we form the negative of *be*?

5 Pronunciation /d/, /t/ or /ɪd/

a ▶ **28** Listen to the *-ed* ending of these regular verbs. Is the sound /d/, /t/ or /ɪd/? Notice how /ɪd/ comes after the letters *t* or *d* and adds an extra syllable.

1	lived	/d/	5	waited
2	finished	/t/	6	looked
3	wanted	/ɪd/	7	decided
4	studied		8	climbed

b ▶ **28** Listen again and repeat.

6 Complete the text about another adventurer with the past simple form of the verbs.

THE PHOTOGRAPHER

Reza ¹ _____ *was* _____ (be) born in Tabriz, Iran, in 1952. He ² _____ (study) architecture at the university in Tehran but he ³ _____ (not / become) an architect. When he was a teenager, Reza ⁴ _____ (love) photography, and after university, he ⁵ _____ (get) a job with a local newspaper as a photographer. But he ⁶ _____ (not / want) to take photos of local news, so in 1978 he ⁷ _____ (go) abroad and he ⁸ _____ (take) photos of wars. Nowadays he works for *National Geographic* magazine.

7 Read the text about Reza again. Answer the questions.

1 When was Reza born?
2 Where did he study architecture?
3 What did he love when he was a teenager?
4 What did he do after university?
5 Did he want to take photos of local news?
6 When did he go abroad?

▶ **PAST SIMPLE QUESTIONS**

When **was** Reza born?
Where **did** he **study** architecture?
Did he **want** to take photos of local news?

For further information and practice, see page 162.

---

8 Look at the grammar box. Choose the correct option (a–b) to complete these rules.

1 With most regular and irregular verbs, we make questions with:
   a the past simple form of the verb.
   b *did* + infinitive.

2 With *be*, we make questions with:
   a *was* and *were*.
   b *did* + infinitive.

9 Read these questions and answers from interviews with Pasang and Marjan. Complete the questions.

1 I: Where _*did you live*_ as a child?
   P: In Lukla, in northeastern Nepal.
2 I: When _____ Mount Everest?
   P: When I was 22 years old.
3 I: Who _____ after the earthquake?
   P: People with no homes and no food.

4 I: _____ you born?
   M: In Afghanistan
5 I: _____ your first international competition?
   M: In 2013.
6 I: _____ the race in New Delhi?
   M: No, we didn't.

Speaking ⌐ my life

10 Write six questions to ask your partner about the past. Use some of these ideas.

where / be / born?   where / grow up?
when / learn / to ride a bike?
when / start / studying English?
where / go / holiday / last year?
go / abroad / last year?   go / university?
what / be / first job?

11 Work in pairs. Take turns to ask and answer your questions. Make notes about your partner.

12 Work with a new partner. Describe your first partner's life.

4b An impossible decision

Vocabulary **personal qualities**

1 Work in groups. Read this English expression and discuss the questions.

'Two heads are better than one.'

1 What do you think the expression means?
2 Do you have a similar expression in your language?
3 What are the advantages and disadvantages of working in teams with other people?
4 What do you think makes a good team member?

2 Read the sentences (1–7) about what makes a good team member. Match these adjectives with the sentences.

experienced	friendly	hard-working
intelligent	kind	patient	positive

A good team member:
1 likes meeting people and gets on with everyone. *friendly*
2 is a good listener and thinks about other people.
3 gives people the time they need and waits for them.
4 is always happy and looks for the good things in life.
5 works extra hours when it's necessary.
6 knows a lot about his or her area of work.
7 is good at learning and understanding.

3 Work in pairs. Which qualities in Exercise 2 do these people have? Why?

a close friend	a language learner
a manager	a parent	a president	a teacher

A good teacher is patient because the students need time to learn.

Listening

4 What difficult decisions do people have to make in life? What decisions do you have to make at work or for your studies? Tell your partner.

I left my old company last year. It was difficult because I had lots of good colleagues there. But I wanted a new job.

5 ▶ 29 Listen to the first part of a true story about two climbers called Joe Simpson and Simon Yates. Number these pictures in the correct order (1–6).

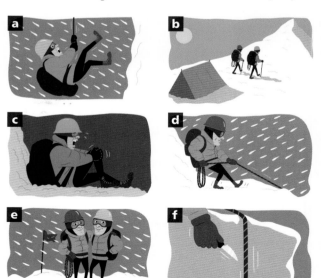

6 Work in pairs. What was Yates' impossible decision at the end? What do you think he did?

7 ▶ 30 Now listen to the whole story and answer the questions.

1 What two personal qualities from Exercise 2 did Simpson and Yates have?
2 Why didn't they stay at the top of the mountain for very long?
3 What decision did Yates make in the end?
4 The next day, what did Yates think about Simpson?
5 What did Yates hear in the night?
6 How did the story of Yates and Simpson become famous?

Grammar past continuous and past simple

> **PAST CONTINUOUS and PAST SIMPLE**
>
> *While they **were going** down the mountain, Simpson **fell**. He **wasn't moving**, but he **was** still **breathing**.*
> Note: We often use *when* and *while* to talk about one action happening at the same time as another.
>
> For further information and practice, see page 162.

8 Look at the sentences in the grammar box. Answer these questions.

1 Which verb(s) talk about completed actions?
2 Which verb(s) talk about actions in progress at a moment in the past?
3 We often use the two verb forms together. Which verb form is used for the longer, continuing activity? Which form is used for the shorter, finished action?
4 What is the auxiliary verb in the past continuous? What is the form of the main verb?

9 ▶ 30 Read the sentences from the story about Simpson and Yates. Choose the correct option. Then listen and check.

1 The sun *shone / was shining* when Simpson and Yates left their tents on the first day.
2 When they reached the top of the mountain, it *snowed / was snowing*.
3 While they were going down the mountain, Simpson *broke / was breaking* his knee.
4 For an hour, Yates held the rope, but it *pulled / was pulling* him off the mountain.
5 Yates was sleeping in his tent but he suddenly *woke up / was waking up*.
6 Finally, he *found / was finding* Simpson on the ground.

10 Complete the sentences with one verb in the past continuous form and one verb in the past simple form.

1 I ___*was working*___ (work) on my own when a group of people ___*came*___ (come) into my office.
2 We _____ (met) them when they _____ (live) above our apartment.
3 They _____ (not get on) very well, so the team _____ (agree) to have a meeting.
4 The weather _____ (be) cold this morning but it _____ (not rain) so I cycled to work.
5 I saw you across the street but I _____ (not stop) because I _____ (run) to my job interview!
6 What _____ he _____ (do) when you _____ (phone) him?
7 Which cities _____ they _____ (visit) while they _____ (travel) through Brazil?
8 Why _____ you _____ (answer) that call while we _____ (watch) the film?

11 Pronunciation *was/were*

a ▶ 31 Listen to sentences 1 to 4 from Exercise 10. Notice the pronunciation of *was, were, wasn't* and *weren't*. Which are stressed and which are unstressed?

b ▶ 31 Listen again and repeat the sentences.

Speaking ⌐ my life

12 Which of these events happened to you in the past? Write some sentences about them and say when the events happened.

> broke a bone
> achieved something with a team of other people
> first fell in love
> got my first job
> had an accident
> had an argument with a close friend
> received really good news
> was late for an important meeting

I broke a bone in my arm on my sixth birthday.

13 Work in pairs. Take turns to tell your partner about the things that happened to you. Ask and answer questions about what you were doing when it happened.

A: I broke a bone in my arm on my sixth birthday.
*B: What **were you doing** when it happened?*
*A: I **was riding** my first bicycle when I **fell off**.*

4c Challenge yourself

Reading

1 Work in pairs. Do you like doing crosswords, quizzes or puzzles? How much time do you spend playing video and computer games every week? Tell your partner.

2 Answer this riddle and solve the matchstick puzzle, then take the numbers memory challenge on page 51. Turn to page 155 to find the answers.

A riddle: *What is yours, but other people use it more than you?*

A puzzle: Move two matchsticks and make four equal squares.

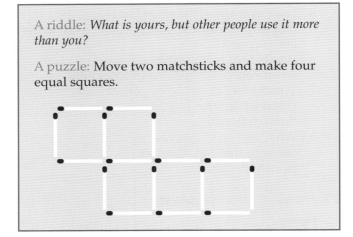

3 Why do you think people like taking these types of challenge?

4 Read the second part of the article. Are these sentences true (T) or false (F)?

1 Professor Rubik taught students about architecture.
2 He made the cube to teach his students about puzzles.
3 Professor Rubik solved the problem of the cube straight away.
4 A robot can solve a Rubik's cube faster than a human.
5 Some scientists think puzzles and games are only good for older people's brains.
6 A study showed some adults over sixty are better at video games than other adults over sixty.

Critical thinking looking for evidence

5 *Evidence* is factual information to support an idea. Which three types of evidence does the writer use in the article? Which does he not use?

• facts from history
• data (e.g. numbers and amounts)
• quotes from people
• results from a scientific study

6 Read these ideas from the article and answer the questions (1–2).

a The Rubik's cube became one of the most popular toys in history.
b Our brain naturally loves solving problems.
c Some scientists think puzzles and games can improve memory in the elderly.

1 Which two ideas have lots of evidence in the article to support them? Underline this evidence.
2 Which idea doesn't have much evidence in the article? (It's the writer's opinion.)

Wordbuilding verbs and nouns

> ▶ **WORDBUILDING verbs and nouns**
>
> Some words have a verb form and a noun form.
> Sometimes the verb and noun form are the same:
> *challenge* (v) *challenge* (n)
> Sometimes the forms are different:
> *achieve* (v) *achievement* (n)
>
> For further practice, see Workbook page 35.

7 Look at the wordbuilding box. Complete this table with words from the article.

Verb	Noun
challenge	a challenge
achieve	an achievement
1 _____	a solution
2 _____	an answer
3 _____	player
memorize	4 _____
5 _____	a study
test	6 _____
7 _____	a score

Writing and speaking 〔my life〕

8 Complete these questions about learning English with a verb or noun from the table. Then ask your partner the questions.

1 What do you think is the biggest _challenge_ when learning English?
2 Do you like _____ problems in English on your own or working with other learners? Why?
3 What do you think is the best way to _____ new words in English?
4 When you study for a _____ or exam, how do you do it?

9 Work in pairs. Write a list of tips for someone who is a beginner in English. Give them advice about the best ways to learn.

CHALLENGE YOURSELF

THE NUMBERS MEMORY CHALLENGE

Cover the groups of numbers in this list. Then look at the first group, cover it again, and try to say the numbers. Then look at the second group of numbers, cover them and try to say them.

Continue down the list. When do you stop remembering all the numbers in a group?

▶ 32

```
4 9 2 6
5 7 8 4 3
9 5 3 4 5 6
7 4 3 0 6 7 3
8 9 3 1 4 2 8 9
6 3 9 8 1 8 5 3 1
9 2 7 8 3 6 9 7 0 8
```

In 1974, Professor Erno Rubik was looking for an interesting way to teach his architecture students about 3D geometry. To do this, he made a cube with nine other cubes on each of its sides. The smaller cubes were different colours and you could turn them in different directions. The challenge was to make each side all one colour. The problem was that there were 43 quintillion (43,000,000,000,000,000,000) ways to move the cubes. As a result, it took Professor Rubik over a month to solve his own problem.

In the end, the Rubik's cube became one of the most popular toys in history. Over 400 million Rubik's cubes have been sold around the world and one in seven people have played with one. In 2008, a Dutch teenager called Mats Valk solved the Rubik's cube in 5.55 seconds. It's still the world record for a human; a robot beat him with a time of 1.019 seconds.

So why do humans love challenging themselves with puzzles like the Rubik's cube? It's the same reason we like crosswords and puzzles in newspapers, or why we play video games on our phones and tablets. Our brain naturally loves solving problems.

Some scientists also think puzzles and games can improve memory in the elderly. In one study at Illinois University, the researchers studied how video games help older people's mental health. In their study, twenty adults over the age of sixty played a video game for a long period, while another twenty adults over sixty did not. Afterwards, they gave all forty adults a test of memory and mental skill. Overall, the video game players scored higher on the test, which means a challenging video game could be good for our brains.

3D (dj) /ˌθriːˈdiː/ three dimensional
geometry (n) /dʒiːˈɒmətri/ mathematical subject about shapes and sizes

4d True stories

Real life **telling a story**

1 Do you ever go camping at weekends or on holiday? Why? / Why not?

2 ▶ **33** Listen to two friends talking about a camping trip. Answer the questions.

   1 Was the start of the weekend good or bad?
   2 When did Mark and the others leave the house?
   3 What happened to the car?
   4 Who helped them?
   5 What was the problem when they found the campsite?
   6 Where did they go instead?

3 ▶ **33** Listen again. Complete the conversation.

   A: Hi Mark. How was your camping trip?
   B: It was great in the end, but we had a terrible time at the beginning.
   A: Why?
   B: ¹_____, we left the house late, and then after only half an hour the car broke down.
   A: Oh no! ² _____?
   B: ³_____ there was a garage nearby and the mechanic fixed the problem. But ⁴_____ we arrived at the forest, it was getting dark. ⁵_____ we drove around for about an hour, we ⁶_____ found the campsite, but it was completely dark by then. And it was raining!
   A: Really? So ⁷_____?
   B: We found a nice, warm hotel down the road!
   A: That was lucky!
   B: Yes, it was a great hotel and ⁸_____ we stayed there for the whole weekend.
   A: ⁹_____!

4 Look at the expressions for telling a story. Match the expressions (1–9) in Exercise 3 with the headings (a–d).

> ▶ **TELLING A STORY**
>
> **a Sequencing the story**
>   At the beginning … Then … Next … While …
>
> **b Introducing good and bad news**
>   Luckily … But … Unfortunately …
>
> **c Reacting to good and bad news**
>   Why? Really?
>   That was a good idea!
>   Oh no!
>
> **d Asking about the next part of the story**
>   What did you do?
>   What happened?

5 Pronunciation **intonation for responding**

▶ **34** Listen to the expressions for reacting to good and bad news. Notice how the listener uses intonation to show interest. Listen again and repeat.

Why?
Really?
That was a good idea!
Oh no!

6 Work in pairs. Practise the conversation from Exercise 3. Take turns to be person A. Be careful with your intonation when you are responding.

7 Work in pairs. Practise telling a story and responding.

Student A: Use these ideas to tell a story to your partner.

   • You had a terrible journey to work.
   • You were cycling and it started raining.
   • A car hit your bike.
   • You weren't hurt.
   • The driver was very nice. He owns a bicycle shop.
   • He gave you a new bike! It's much better than your old one!

Student B: Listen to your partner and respond with comments and questions.

8 Now change roles.

Student B: Use these ideas to tell a story to your partner.

   • You went hiking with a friend in the mountains.
   • It started snowing.
   • You went back towards the town, but it was getting dark.
   • You passed a large house with the lights on.
   • The people in the house invited you in. They made you dinner and you stayed the night.
   • The next day the sun was shining. You reached the top of the mountain.

Student A: Listen to your partner and respond with comments and questions.

9 Think of a bad journey you had. Did it have a happy ending? Make a list of the events. Then tell your partner the story.

4e A story of survival

Writing **a short story**

1 What is an interesting story in the news at the moment? Is it good news or bad news?

2 Stories in the news answer some or all of these questions. Read the short story and answer the questions.

1 Where did it happen?
2 What was the weather like? Who was there? What were they doing?
3 What went wrong?
4 What surprising event happened? Who was there? What were they doing?
5 Did the story have a happy or sad ending?

Boys survive
50 DAYS *lost at sea*

T he islands of Atafu are in the middle of the Pacific Ocean and the people there go fishing every day. One day, the sun was shining and the sea was calm, so three teenage boys went fishing in a small boat. In the evening, they didn't arrive home, so the islanders went out and looked for them. After many days there was no sign of them and everyone thought the boys were dead.

Fifty days later, some fishermen were sailing in the middle of the Pacific Ocean when they saw a small boat in the distance. The three boys were in the boat, over 1,500 kilometres from their home. They were living on fish from the sea and rainwater. In the end, they returned to their families alive and well.

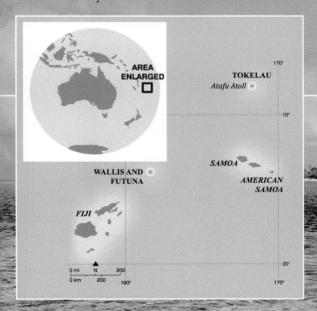

3 Writing skill **structure your writing**

The story has a five-part structure. Number the parts (a–e) in the correct order (1–5).

a The day the story starts, the background events (such as the weather) and what happened at first.
b An important moment when something goes wrong, and what happens next.
c There is a happy (or sad) ending.
d The place and the typical lives of the people. *1*
e A surprising (and often positive) change in the story after a long time.

4 Time expressions help the structure of a story. Look at this example and underline the other time expressions in the story.

> The islands of Atafu are in the middle of the Pacific Ocean and the people there go fishing <u>every day</u>. <u>One day</u>, the sun was shining and the sea was calm, so three teenage boys went fishing in a small boat.

5 You are going to write a short story. Use a story from your own life or a story in the news. Plan the story using the five-part structure and make notes to answer the questions in Exercise 2.

6 Write your short story in about 80–100 words. Use some time expressions to help the structure.

7 Work in pairs. Take turns to read your stories. Does your partner use the five-part structure and time expressions?

4f A microadventure

Alastair and Temujin during their adventure in Croatia.

Before you watch

1 Make a list of things you did in the last 24 hours. Write as many things as you can in two minutes. Then work in pairs. Take turns to read your lists. Who wrote the longest list?

I got up, I brushed my teeth, I ate breakfast, …

2 You are going to watch a video about two friends. They are spending 24 hours in Croatia on a 'microadventure'. Complete these sentences from the video in the past simple, using the irregular verb in brackets.

a We _____ a photo of the city lights below. (take)
b We _____ the city. (leave)
c We _____ next to this rock. (wake up)
d We _____ some bread, some grapes, some meat. (buy)
e We _____ swimming in the Mediterranean Sea. (go)
f We ___*ate*___ an ice cream. (eat)
g Al _____ on a wall. (sit)
h We _____ some water and watched the sunset. (have)
i We _____ a sandwich. (make)
j We _____ a river. (find)

While you watch

3 🎥 **4.1** Watch the video. Number the sentences in Exercise 2 in the order they happen (1–10).

We ate an ice cream. *1*

4 🎥 **4.1** Choose the correct option to complete the sentences. Sometimes, more than one option is possible. Then watch the video again to check.

1 Alastair Humphreys is:
  a a filmmaker.   c a writer. ✓
  b an adventurer. ✓
2 They hired:
  a a car.   c bicycles.
  b motorbikes.
3 They drove:
  a through a tunnel.   c round a bend.
  b over a bridge.
4 They saw:
  a a fish.   c a butterfly.
  b a dragonfly.
5 They stopped:
  a at a river.   c at a restaurant.
  b at a castle.
6 On the mountain, they could hear:
  a people.   c music.
  b animals.
7 In the morning, Alastair:
  a ate a banana.   c phoned his mother.
  b brushed his teeth.
8 Afterwards, they had:
  a a shower.   c breakfast.
  b a coffee.

After you watch

5 **Vocabulary in context**

🎥 **4.2** Watch the clips from the video. Choose the correct meaning of the words and phrases.

6 Work in pairs. Watch the video again with the sound OFF. Try to describe what happened in the microadventure as you see each action on the screen.

7 Work in pairs. You are going to plan a 24-hour microadventure. Discuss these ideas and make your plans.

• Where will you go?
• What will do?
• What will you see?

At 9 o'clock we'll take the train to … and visit …

8 Work with another pair and describe your plans for your microadventure.

A dragonfly

Grammar

1 Complete the text with the past simple form of the verbs.

In 2013 Aleksander Doba [1] _____ (cross) the Atlantic Ocean in a kayak. He [2] _____ (start) his journey in Lisbon, Portugal and he [3] _____ (arrive) in Florida six months later. He [4] _____ (travel) 12,427 kilometres and it [5] _____ (be) a difficult journey. His kayak [6] _____ (break) near the Bahamas, so he [7] _____ (stop) to fix it. He also [8] _____ (have) other challenges – his satellite phone [9] _____ (not work) for 47 days so he [10] _____ (not have) any communication. Aleksander [11] _____ (be born) in Poland in 1946 and he [12] _____ (not begin) kayaking until the age of 34.

2 Complete the questions about Aleksander Doba.

1 How did _____ ? In a kayak.
2 How long did _____ ? Six months.
3 How far _____ ? 12,427 kilometres.
4 Did he _____ ? Yes, his phone didn't work for 47 days.

3 >> MB Work in pairs. Answer the questions about the story in Exercise 1.

1 What were the personal qualities of Aleksander Doba?
2 Why do you think people like Aleksander take risks and give themselves challenges?

4 Choose the correct options.

The sun [1] *shone / was shining* as the plane turned onto the runway. As it [2] *took off / was taking off*, the passengers inside the plane sat quietly. They [3] *took / were taking* their first parachute jump. Everyone [4] *was / was being* nervous and no one [5] *talked / was talking*. When the plane [6] *reached / was reaching* the correct height, their teacher shouted, 'Right everyone. It's time to jump!' She [7] *opened / was opening* the door on the side of the plane and, in the next moment, everyone [8] *jumping / was jumping* out of the plane towards the ground.

I CAN
use the past simple and past continuous

Vocabulary

5 Complete the sentences with these words.

challenging   experienced   intelligent   kind
patient   positive

1 Don't get angry when things don't happen as fast as you want. Learn to be _____ .
2 He's a very _____ climber. He started mountaineering when he was a child.
3 It's very _____ of you to help me with my homework.
4 Even when things go wrong, it's important to stay _____ .
5 My friend is the most _____ person in our class. She always gets 100% on tests.
6 Finishing the marathon was very _____ , but I did it in the end.

I CAN
talk about personal qualities and challenges

Real life

6 >> MB Work in pairs. Look at the pictures (1–5).

Student A: Tell the story to your partner using some of these words.

at the beginning   but   luckily   next   while

Student B: Listen to the story and react to good and bad news with some of these phrases.

Oh no!   Really?   What happened?   Why?

I CAN
tell a story
react to good and bad news

Unit 5 The environment

Uruguayan artist Jaime built this home in Florianapolis, Brazil, from recycled materials.

FEATURES

1 Look at the photo and the caption. What do you think of the home in the photo? Would you like to stay there? Which of these materials did Jaime use?

cardboard   glass   leather   metal   paper   plastic   wood

2 ▶ 35 Listen to part of a documentary about Jaime and the house in the photo. Answer the questions.

1 What everyday objects does the speaker talk about?
2 What did Jaime do with these objects?
3 What does he want people to think about?

3 Look at the highlighted expressions for talking about objects. Make similar sentences about the everyday objects in the box.

A dictionary is made of paper. You use it for looking up words.

a dictionary   a mobile phone   a pen   scissors   a tin can

4 Work in pairs. Think of other everyday objects. Don't tell your partner the object, but describe what it's made of and what you use it for. Your partner has to guess the object.

5a Recycling

Vocabulary recycling

1 What kind of rubbish do you throw away or recycle every week? What percentage of each type (a–e) is in your rubbish?

About 25% of my rubbish is glass.

a electronics   d metal
b glass   e plastic
c paper and cardboard

2 Match these objects to the type of rubbish (a–e) in Exercise 1. Some items match two categories.

1 computer *a*   6 tin can
2 bottle *b, e*   7 TV
3 jar   8 cereal box
4 aluminium foil   9 magazine
5 milk carton   10 bag

 36

Reading

3 Look at the photos with the article. What do you think *e-rubbish* is? Why is the boy holding part of an old computer?

4 Read the article and check your ideas from Exercise 3.

5 Read the article again and answer these questions.

1 Where did Peter Essick follow the e-rubbish to?
2 What did he find in the markets of Ghana?
3 Why do people melt parts of the broken computers?
4 Why is recycling the metal dangerous?
5 What is it bad for?
6 What types of electronic products are environmentally friendly?

E-RUBBISH

Do you ever throw away any electronic rubbish (or *e-rubbish*)? Perhaps you have some old technology that doesn't work, like an out-of-date phone, or a slow computer. But when you throw away these objects, do you know where they go? The journalist Peter Essick has followed this e-rubbish to different countries around the world.

Essick found a lot of e-rubbish in Ghana, with thousands of old computers in the local markets. Here, the sellers resell a few computers to people for their homes and offices, but you can't sell many computers in the market because a lot of them don't work. So they melt some parts of the computers to recycle the metal. These parts don't have much metal, but sometimes there is a little gold inside.

Unfortunately, recycling the metal can be dangerous for the workers because it produces a lot of chemicals which are bad for workers' health. As a result, Peter Essick thinks we shouldn't send any e-rubbish to other countries. It's bad for the environment and it's bad for people's health. He believes we need to produce more environmentally-friendly electronics in the future; in other words, electronic products which you can recycle safely and in the country where they were made.

Grammar quantifiers

6 Which of these nouns are countable? Which are uncountable? Write C or U.

> rubbish *U*   computer *C*   plastic   bag   box
> magazine   paper   metal

> ▶ **QUANTIFIERS**
>
> We use *quantifiers* with countable and uncountable nouns to talk about quantity.
> *Do you ever throw away **any** electronic rubbish?*
> *Perhaps you have **some** old technology that doesn't work.*
> *Essick found **a lot of** e-rubbish in Ghana.*
> *The sellers resell **a few** computers.*
> *You ca**n't** sell **many** computers in the market.*
> *These parts do**n't** have **much** metal.*
> *There is **a little** gold inside.*
> *We should**n't** send **any** e-rubbish to other countries.*
>
> For further information and practice, see page 164.

> **melt** (v) /melt/ to heat an object until it turns to liquid
> **toxic** (adj) /ˈtɒksɪk/ poisonous, dangerous for your health

7 Look at the sentences in the grammar box. Then complete these sentences with the correct quantifiers.

1 We use ___*some*___ and ___*a lot of*___ in affirmative sentences with countable or uncountable nouns.
2 We use _____ in questions with countable or uncountable nouns.
3 We talk about small quantities with _____ in affirmative sentences with countable nouns.
4 We talk about small quantities with _____ in affirmative sentences with uncountable nouns.
5 We use *any* and _____ in negative sentences with countable nouns.
6 We use _____ and _____ in negative sentences with uncountable nouns.

8 Choose the correct quantifier. In one sentence both quantifiers are correct.

1 How *much* / *many* rubbish do you recycle?
2 I recycle *a few* / *a little* things, like glass and plastic bottles.
3 I don't recycle *many* / *much* glass.
4 I recycle *a few* / *a little* paper each week.
5 Do you have *much* / *any* recycling bins?
6 There are *some* / *any* old TVs for sale at the market.
7 A lot of people on my street don't recycle *many* / *much* plastic.
8 You shouldn't throw away *many* / *any* paper! Always recycle it.
9 Nowadays, *a lot of* / *some* cities and towns have special places to take recycling.

Speaking ⏵ my life

9 Read these sentences about recycling. If necessary, change the words in bold so the sentences are true for you.

1 I throw away **a lot of** paper every week.
2 In my area, **a few** places have recycling bins.
3 My school / place of work **doesn't have any** recycling bins for paper.
4 **Some** people in my country think recycling is important.

10 Work in pairs. Ask and answer questions about your sentences in Exercise 9. Start your questions like this:

1 How much paper …?
2 Do any places …?
3 Does your school / place of work …?
4 How many people …?

A: How much paper do you throw away?
*B: I don't throw away **any paper**. We recycle it in the special green bins.*

5b Managing the environment

Vocabulary **results and figures**

1 Discuss the questions.

1 How often do you read news about the environment? Is it always bad news?
2 Do you have any good news about the environment in your country?

2 Read a newspaper report about Portugal. Is it good news or bad news?

> Portugal powered the whole country using only solar, wind and hydroelectric energy for **about a hundred** hours last week. **Exactly a year** ago, the country produced **under a quarter** of its electricity from wind power and **nearly half** of its total energy came from renewable energy. So it's a huge achievement for the country to live off renewable energy for **over four days**.

3 Look at the phrases in bold in the newspaper report. Find the phrases that have a similar meaning to the exact information a–e.

a 48%
b 107
c from May 7 to May 11
d 22%
e 12 months

You can see the Sahara desert on this satellite photo of Africa.

4 Work in pairs. Answer these questions about your life using *over, under, nearly* and *about*.

1 How much of your day do you spend looking at a screen (e.g. computer, TV)?
   I spend about a third of my day looking at a screen.
2 How many hours a week do you spend shopping?
3 How many people live in your town or city?
4 How much money a month do you spend on buying clothes?
5 How many months a year do you spend at school or at work?

Listening

5 ▶ 37 Listen to a news report about two environmental projects and answer the questions.

1 What four deserts does the report mention?
2 Where are the two environmental projects?
3 What type of wall are the countries building?

6 ▶ 37 Listen again and answer the questions.

1 What percentage of the Earth's land is desert?
2 When did the Chinese start planting the great green wall?
3 Why did they plant it?
4 How many trees are in the wall now?
5 How long will it be by 2050?
6 How many countries are working together on the wall in Africa?
7 What will the new forest stop the desert doing?
8 How big will the forest across the Sahara be?

Grammar articles

▶ **ARTICLES *a/an*, *the*, or no article**

1 *In 1978 the Chinese started planting **a wall** of trees. Now **the wall** has 66 billion trees.*
2 *It's **the largest** hot desert in **the world**.*
3 ***The Gobi Desert** is getting larger.*
4 *Countries in **Africa** plan to build a wall.*
5 ***People** know about the Great Wall of China.*

For further information and practice, see page 164.

7 Look at the grammar box. Read the sentences and look at the words in bold. Complete these rules with *a/an*, *the*, or no article.

a We normally use _____ when we talk about something which isn't specific or it's the first time we mention something. When we talk about something specific or talk about it again, we use _____ .

b We also use _____ when something is unique (there is only one), with superlatives or with the names of some places (e.g. oceans, deserts, mountain ranges).

c We use _____ when we talk about people or things in general, and with the names of most places (e.g. continents, countries, cities, lakes).

8 Read about two more ways to manage the environment. Choose the correct option. Choose – if no article is needed.

Ice towers
In the spring and summer there is often a water shortage in [1] *the* / – Himalayan mountains. So during the winter, [2] *a* / – people make ice towers. They put one end of [3] *a* / – long pipe into a river high in the mountains and then they take the other end of [4] *a* / *the* pipe down to a village. The water comes out of the pipe and freezes in a fountain to make [5] – / *an* ice tower in the village. Then it melts in the spring so [6] *a* / – farmers can use it on their land.

Fog collectors
[7] *The* / – Atacama desert in [8] *the* / – Chile is one of the driest parts of [9] *a* / *the* world. There is very little rain, but there is fog, and fog contains [10] – / *the* water. To get this water, some scientists are trying to collect the water in [11] *the* / *a* big net. [12] *The* / *A* net catches drops of water, and it can collect between five and thirty litres of water per day.

9 Pronunciation /ðə/ or /ðiː/

a ▶ 38 Listen to the difference in the pronunciation of *the* before a consonant sound and a vowel sound.

/ðə/	/ðiː/
the wall	the Earth

b ▶ 39 Listen and circle /ðə/ or /ðiː/. Then listen again and repeat.

1	the river	/ðə/	/ðiː/
2	the ice	/ðə/	/ðiː/
3	the world	/ðə/	/ðiː/
4	the desert	/ðə/	/ðiː/
5	the oldest	/ðə/	/ðiː/
6	the largest	/ðə/	/ðiː/
7	the Atacama desert	/ðə/	/ðiː/

10 Look at the questions from a general knowledge quiz. Complete the questions with *a/an* or *the* where necessary. Then try to answer the questions.

Around the world quiz
1 There is _____ river between _____ Brazil, Colombia, Peru and Ecuador. What is its name?
2 _____ White House is in _____ USA. Who lives there?
3 There's _____ natural satellite which goes round _____ Earth every day. What is it?
4 In 1997, Larry Page and Sergey set up _____ global search engine. What is its name?
5 _____ Arctic Ocean is _____ smallest ocean in the world. Which is _____ largest?

11 Check the quiz answers on page 155.

Writing and speaking ⟨ my life ⟩

12 You are going to write five more quiz questions. Work in two pairs in a group of four.

Pair A: Turn to page 153 and follow the instructions.

Pair B: Turn to page 154 and follow the instructions.

13 Work in your group. Ask and answer your five questions. Find out which pair has the best knowledge of the world.

5c A boat made of bottles

Reading

1 Look at these words from the article on page 63. What do you think the article is about?

> boat   plastic bottles   recycle   sail   San Francisco
> Sydney   the Pacific Ocean

2 Read the article and check your ideas from Exercise 1.

3 Complete the fact file with numbers about the Plastiki.

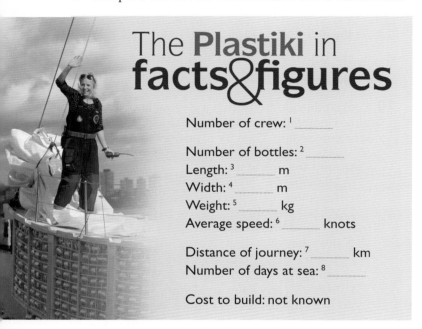

The **Plastiki** in facts&figures

Number of crew: ¹ _____

Number of bottles: ² _____
Length: ³ _____ m
Width: ⁴ _____ m
Weight: ⁵ _____ kg
Average speed: ⁶ _____ knots

Distance of journey: ⁷ _____ km
Number of days at sea: ⁸ _____

Cost to build: not known

Critical thinking **close reading**

4 Read the sentences (1–8). Choose the correct option (A–C) for each sentence.

A = The sentence is true. The information is in the text.
B = The sentence is false. The information is in the text.
C = We don't know if it's true or false. The information isn't in the text.

1 The *Plastiki* is made of the same material as other boats.
2 Nowadays, humans recycle most of their plastic bottles.
3 Plastic in the sea is killing animals.
4 The boat doesn't use renewable energy.
5 The crew only ate vegetables for the whole journey.
6 The size of the 'Great Garbage Patch' is growing.
7 The journey took longer than de Rothchild planned.
8 De Rothschild wants to sail the Plastiki again one day.

Word focus *take*

5 Find five expressions in the article with the word *take*. Match the expressions with the uses (1–4).

> **take** /teɪk/
> _____
> 1   transport: *take a taxi*
> 2   daily routines: *take a walk*
> 3   lengths of time: *take a few days*
> 4   idioms: *take time (to do something)*

6 Complete the sentences with the correct form of *take* and these words.

> a break   many days   care   a plane   time

1 Most people ___*take a plane*___ from San Francisco to Sydney so they don't know about the pollution in the ocean.
2 The journey across the Great Garbage Patch _____ .
3 The work was tiring and the crew sometimes needed to _____ and relax.
4 The Pacific Ocean can be dangerous, so everyone on the ship had to _____ .
5 For this kind of project, it's important to _____ to plan things carefully.

Speaking my life

7 Work in groups and discuss these questions.

1 Do you think environmental projects like the Plastiki make a difference to people's attitudes to rubbish? Will de Rothschild's journey make people change their behaviour? Why? / Why not?
2 In your country, does anyone (e.g. the government, the police, charities) try to change people's behaviour in these areas?
   • recycling more rubbish
   • stopping smoking cigarettes
   • driving over the speed limit
   • eating too much food
   • anything else?
   The government tries to stop people smoking cigarettes.
3 How do they try to do this? What are some good ways to change people's attitudes and behaviour? (e.g. TV advertising, making people pay a fine)

A BOAT *made of* BOTTLES

▶ 40

A boat with a difference

The *Plastiki* looks similar to many other boats in Sydney harbour. It's eighteen metres long, six metres wide and it weighs about twelve thousand kilogrammes. It carries a crew of six people and has an average speed of five knots. However, once you get near to the *Plastiki* you realize there's a big difference. It's made of twelve thousand five hundred re-used plastic bottles.

How did the *Plastiki* begin?

David de Rothschild is an environmentalist who has crossed Antarctica and explored the Ecuadorian Amazon. One day he was reading some information about all the plastic in the seas and oceans. He couldn't believe what he was reading. For example, humans throw away four out of every five plastic bottles they use, and plastic rubbish causes about eighty per cent of the pollution in the sea. In addition, scientists think that around one million seabirds die every year from plastic pollution. De Rothschild decided he wanted to help the fight against pollution in the sea. To help more people understand the problem, he started building a boat made of plastic bottles.

Designing the *Plastiki*

As well as building the boat with recycled plastic, it was important for him to make the boat environmentally friendly and user-friendly. The boat uses renewable energy such as wind power and solar energy. The crew can make meals with vegetables from the small garden at the back of the boat. They can take a break from work and get some exercise by using the special exercise bicycle. The energy from the bike provides power for the boat's computers. And if anyone needs to take a shower, the boat's shower uses saltwater from the sea.

The journey

De Rothschild sailed the *Plastiki* across the Pacific Ocean from San Francisco to Sydney. That's fifteen thousand three hundred and seventy-two kilometres. On the way, de Rothschild took the special boat through the 'Great Garbage Patch'. It is a huge area in the Pacific with 3.5 billion kilogrammes of rubbish. You can see every kind of human rubbish here: shoes, toys, bags, toothbrushes, but the worst problem is the plastic. It kills birds and sea life.

How well did the *Plastiki* survive the journey?

The journey wasn't always easy and de Rothschild and his crew had to take care during storms. There were giant ocean waves and winds of over one hundred kilometres per hour. The whole journey took one hundred and twenty nine days. Originally, de Rothschild thought the boat could only travel once, but it lasted so well that he is planning to sail it again one day.

knot (n) /nɒt/ measurement of speed at sea (1 knot = 1.8 km/hr)
garbage (n) /ˈgaːbɪdʒ/ (US Eng) rubbish (UK Eng)
patch (n) /paetʃ/ area

5d Online shopping

Reading

1 Do you normally go shopping or do you prefer shopping online? Why?

2 Read the website and email order. What did the customer order? What is the problem?

WWW.TECOART.COM

| HOME | MY ACCOUNT | SHOPPING CART | CHECKOUT |

We have lots of different clocks and they are all made from recycled computers!

Computer Hard Drive Clock with Circuit Board. £39.00

Apple iPod® Hard Drive Clock on a Circuit Board. £35.00

Order number: 80531A   Ms Jane Powell
Order Date: 20 March   90 North Lane

Thank you for your order. Unfortunately, the model you ordered is currently not available. We expect delivery in seven days. We apologize for the delay. For further information about this order, speak to a customer service assistant on 555-01754.

Item Number	Description	Quantity	Price
HCV1N	Hard drive clock	1	£35

Real life **phoning about an order**

3 ▶ 41 Jane Powell telephones customer services about her order. Listen to the conversation. Answer the questions.

1 What information does the customer service assistant ask for and check?
2 Why does Jane want the clock quickly?
3 How much does the other clock cost?
4 What does Jane decide to do?
5 What will the customer service assistant email her?

4 ▶ 41 Look at the expressions for phoning about an order. Then listen to the conversation again. Tick the sentences the customer service assistant uses.

> ▶ **PHONING ABOUT AN ORDER**
>
> **Telephone expressions**
> Good morning. Can I help you?
> I'm calling about an order for a clock.
> Can I put you on hold for a moment?
> Is there anything else I can help you with?
>
> **Talking about an order**
> Do you have the order number?
> Would you like to order a different product?
> Would you like to cancel the order?
> Would you like a refund?
> Would you like confirmation by email?
>
> **Checking and clarifying**
> Is that A as in alpha?
> Let me check.
> So that's F for Freddie?
> That's right.

5 Pronunciation **sounding friendly**

a ▶ 42 Listen to the sentences from a telephone conversation. Does the speaker sound friendly (F) or unfriendly (U)?

1 Good morning. Can I help you?
2 Can I put you on hold?
3 Is that A as in alpha?
4 I'm calling about an order.
5 Is there anything else I can help you with?
6 Do you have an order number?

b ▶ 43 Listen to the sentences again. This time they are all friendly. Listen and repeat with a similar friendly intonation.

6 Work in pairs. Practise two phone conversations similar to the one in Exercise 3.

Student A: Turn to page 153 and follow the instructions.

Student B: Turn to page 154 and follow the instructions.

A: Good morning. Can I help you?
B: Hello, I'm calling about some clothes I ordered.

5e Emails about an order

Writing emails

1 Read the correspondence between a customer and a customer service assistant. Put the emails in order (1–5).

A
> Dear M Cottrell
>
> I would like to inform you that the e-book reader you ordered is now in stock. I would be delighted to deliver this item immediately. Please reply to confirm you still require this item.
>
> Charlotte Lazarro

B
> Dear Sir or Madam
>
> I recently ordered an 'e-book reader'. However, I received an email which said this was not currently available. Please refund my money back to the credit card.
>
> Yours sincerely
>
> Mr M Cottrell

C
> Thanks, but I bought the same product at a shop yesterday. Therefore, please cancel the order and, as requested, send me my refund.
>
> M Cottrell

D
> As requested here is the order number: 80531A

E
> Dear M Cottrell
>
> Thank you for your email. I apologize for the difficulties with your order. In order to provide you with the necessary assistance, could you please send the order number?
>
> Best regards
>
> Charlotte Lazarro
>
> Customer Service Assistant

2 Read the emails in Exercise 1 again. Underline any phrases and expressions that ask for something or give instructions.

3 Writing skill formal words

a The language in the emails in Exercise 1 is fairly formal. Match the formal language in the emails to these less formal verbs and phrases (1–9).

1 get   *receive*
2 be happy
3 ask for
4 give
5 give back (money)
6 help
7 say sorry
8 tell
9 want

b Work in pairs. Make these sentences more formal.

1 I want my money back.
2 I'm writing to tell you that I didn't get the delivery.
3 Do you want any help?
4 Please give us your credit card details.
5 Sorry, but I can't give you your money back.

4 Imagine you ordered a printer online two weeks ago. You paid for delivery within 24 hours but it hasn't arrived. Write an email to the supplier and request a refund.

5 Work in pairs. Read your partner's email. How formal is the language?

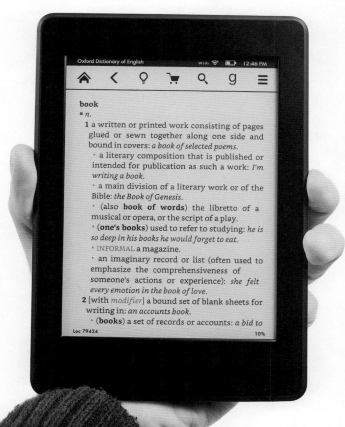

5f Recycling Cairo

Using Egypt's greatest natural resource on the rooftops of Cairo

Before you watch

1 Key vocabulary

Match these words with the pictures (1–6).
Two words have the same meaning and match
one picture.

water tank	satellite dish	goat	trash
solar panel	rooftop	garbage	

2 Work in pairs. You are going to watch a video
about using recycled objects in Cairo. What do
you think is the connection between the words
in Exercise 1?

While you watch

3 ▢◀ **5.1** Watch the video. Were your predictions
in Exercise 2 correct?

4 ▢◀ **5.1** Watch the video again and answer the
questions.

   1 How does the narrator describe the streets of
Cairo?

   2 How does he describe the rooftops of Cairo?

   3 When did Cairo start to 'go green'?

   4 What is Thomas Culhane helping to do?

   5 What is Egypt's great natural resource?

   6 When Culhane measures the temperature of
the water, how hot is it?

   7 The new solar heaters provide hot water, so
what do they reduce?

After you watch

5 Vocabulary in context

▢◀ **5.2** Watch the clips from the video. Choose
the correct meaning of the words and phrases.

6 Write a short summary of the video (about 100
words). Use these phrases.

> People in Cairo use the rooftops for …
> Thomas Culhane is helping some local
> people to …
> They make the solar water heaters out of …
> The new heaters provide …
> Culhane thinks the solar heaters
> demonstrate that …

7 ▢◀ **5.3** Work in pairs. You are going to be the
narrator on the video. Watch a shorter version of
the video with no sound. As the video plays, take
turns to read your summary to your partner.

8 In the video, Thomas Culhane says: 'One man's
garbage is another's goldmine.' Choose the correct
meaning (a–c) for this expression.

   a Everyone thinks the rubbish is worth a lot of
money.

   b Some people think the rubbish is useless but
other people think it's very useful.

   c You can sell the rubbish for a lot of money.

9 List some things that people often use and throw
away, which other people could recycle or reuse.

> **figure out** (v) to work something, to solve a problem
> **found materials** materials we use every day and all around us
> **informal communities** poorer areas of a city
> **garbage/trash** US English for *rubbish* (British English)

Grammar

1 Choose the correct options to complete the article about recycling.

Recycling
around the
World

A new report looks at recycling in different countries and what they can learn from each other.

Switzerland

[1] *A / The* Swiss have different types of recycling bins and so local people only throw away [2] *a little / a few* household items. For example, they recycle about 80% of their plastic bottles which is a lot higher than other countries in [3] *– / the* Europe.

USA

Overall [4] *– / the* USA doesn't recycle as [5] *many / much* rubbish as a country like Switzerland but it's introduced [6] *a lot of / any* new projects in recent years. This year it recycled 48% of its paper, 40% of its plastic bottles and 65% of its cans.

Senegal

Senegal recycles [7] *a few / a little* of its waste industrially, but people don't throw away [8] *any / much* items that they can use for something else. For example, you can buy shoes made from old plastic bags and drinking cups made from tin cans.

2 >> MB Work in pairs. Look at the photos. Answer the questions for each photo.

1 What is the name of this?
2 What was the purpose of it?

I CAN
use quantifiers and articles

Vocabulary

3 What material are these objects made of? Match the objects to the materials 1–6.

| book | bottle | calculator | can | envelope |
| jar | magazine | mobile phone | radio | |

1 cardboard   4 metal
2 electronics   5 paper
3 glass   6 plastic

4 >> MB Work in pairs. Think of two more objects for each material in Exercise 3.

5 Look at the percentages in the article in Exercise 1. Match the percentages to these phrases.

1 over three quarters
2 nearly a half
3 over a third
4 about two thirds

6 >> MB Write the percentage of time you spend doing these things each week. Then work in pairs. Explain how you spend your time.

- at work or at school
- sleeping
- going out and meeting friends
- cleaning your room or the house
- shopping

I spend over a third of my day at school.

I CAN
talk about materials
talk about results and figures

Real life

7 Work in pairs. Practise making a telephone call about an order. Take the roles of someone who works for the company (A), and a customer (B). Use these ideas.

A: Hello. Can / help ?
B: calling / an order / a clock. It hasn't arrived.
A: Do / you / order number?
B: It / AG-100234L
A: Sorry, can / repeat /?
B: Yes, it's /
A: Let / check. Is / A / Alpha?
B: That's correct.
A: Sorry, we don't / this product anymore. Would / change / order?
B: No. I'd like / refund.
A: That's fine. Would / like confirmation / email?
B: Yes, please.
A: Is / anything else / can help you with?
B: No / goodbye

8 Practise the conversation again, but this time Student B closes their book. Then change roles.

I CAN
phone about an order

Women chat on the station platform in Winterthur, Switzerland.

FEATURES

1 Work in pairs. The photo shows three generations of people. Which words in the box describe their stage in life?

> child   teenager   young adult   adult
> middle-aged   elderly

2 ▶ 44 Listen to someone talking about the photo. Why does the speaker like the photo?

3 Look at these different life events. Answer the questions.

> get a pension   get your driving licence
> go to college or university   get married
> learn to ride a bicycle   leave home
> start a family   start your career
> retire from work   buy your first home

1 At what age do people in your country do these things?
2 Do you think there is a correct time in your life to do each one?

6a Changing your life

Vocabulary **describing age**

1 In some countries it is rude to ask the question
'How old are you?' Is it rude to ask this question
in your country? What does it depend on?

2 We use the phrases in B to talk about general age,
e.g. *He's in his mid-twenties*. Match the ages in A
with the phrases in B. Which words on page 69
also describe these ages?

> **A** 25   14   83   39   53

> **B** early teens   mid-twenties   fifties
>   late thirties   early eighties

3 Work in pairs. Think of five people you both
know (e.g. the leader of your country, a famous
celebrity). What age do you think they are?

Reading

4 Read the article on page 71 about Rich and
Amanda. What was their stage in life when they
left their jobs? Why did they decide to leave?

5 Read the article again and answer the questions.

1 Did they do anything fun at the weekends?
2 What did they realize they wanted to do?
3 Why did they buy a campervan?
4 Where did they plan to travel to by container
   ship?
5 What did colleagues find difficult to
   understand?
6 What did friends think they were crazy to do?
7 What did Rich and Amanda start to do after
   they left home?

Grammar *to* + infinitive

> ▶ **TO + INFINITIVE**
>
> 1 We **intend to leave** our jobs.
> 2 Let's **buy a campervan to travel** in.
> 3 It's **difficult to understand** your decision.
>
> For further information and practice, see page 166.

6 Look at the grammar box. Match the sentences
(1–3) with the different forms (a–c).

a a verb + *to* + infinitive
b an adjective *to* + infinitive
c *to* + infinitive explains the purpose of an action

7 Read about three people's future plans. Choose the
correct options to complete the three texts. What is
each person's stage in life?

'One day I plan ¹ *go / to go* to university, but this
year I'm working in a supermarket ² *earn / to earn*
some money. Then I'd ³ *like / to like* to travel round
the world for six months.'

'I'm so happy ⁴ *retire / to retire*! Some people tell me
I should ⁵ *relax / to relax* at this stage in my life, but I
don't want ⁶ *sit / to sit* at home doing nothing.'

'These days it's really difficult ⁷ *buy / to buy* a house.
Me and my husband can't ⁸ *afford / to afford* one, so
we're living with his parents and saving money ⁹ *buy /
to buy* a place of our own. It's hard ¹⁰ *don't feel / not
to feel* unhappy about it.'

CHANGING your life

▶ 45

Rich and Amanda Ligato were professional people with successful careers. Every week, they worked hard. They always intended to do something fun and exciting at the weekend but, in the end, there was never time. One day they asked themselves, 'Is this all there is?'

They realized that they wanted to stop working and to go travelling. Or, as Rich said, 'to buy our freedom'. But first they needed to save some money. Every month they lived on Rich's salary and saved Amanda's. Then they bought a campervan to travel from the bottom of South America to Brazil, and from there they hoped to get to Africa on a container ship.

Colleagues at work found it difficult to understand their decision. Even their closest friends thought they were crazy to go on this kind of journey, but finally, the day came. They left their home and started to live their dream.

8 Look at the correct options in Exercise 7. Which options use *to* + infinitive? Match them to the uses (a–c) in Exercise 6.

9 Match the beginnings of the sentences (1–6) with the endings (a–f).

1 One day I intend to
2 I want to take a year off
3 I'd be
4 In the future, I'd like to learn
5 When I get older, I
6 These days, it's difficult

a hope to spend more time with my family.
b happy to live in another country.
c buy my own house.
d not to take work home.
e to play a musical instrument.
f to travel overseas.

10 **Pronunciation** /tə/

▶ 46 Listen to the sentences from Exercise 9. Is *to* pronounced /tuː/ or /tə/? Listen again and repeat.

11 Write your own sentences using the sentence beginnings (1–6) in Exercise 9. Then work in pairs. Read out your sentences and compare your ideas.

1 One day I intend to start my own business.

Speaking ⟨ my life ⟩

12 Work in groups. You plan to take six months off from your job or your studies and have the trip of a lifetime! Discuss the following questions and make notes about your plans. You can use the world map on pages 6–7 to help your planning.

- Which countries and continents do you plan to visit?
- Why do you want to visit these places?
- What type of transport do you intend to use?
- What do you hope to do in each place that you visit?
- What do you think will be easy to do on the trip? What do you think will be difficult to do?

13 Present your 'trip of a lifetime' to the rest of the class.

*We **plan to visit** parts of Asia. First of all, **we want to visit** Vietnam **to see** its beautiful and ancient places …*

6b World party

WORLD PARTY ▶ 47

People in different countries celebrate Mardi Gras with live music, costumes, fireworks, parades and lots of good food. The most famous celebrations are in New Orleans, Venice, Rio de Janeiro and Port-of-Spain.

New Orleans, USA
Small parties for Mardi Gras began in the 1700s. By the 1800s they were huge events with masks, costumes and jazz bands. Visitors also have to try 'king cake' with its gold, purple and green decorations.

Venice, Italy
Mardi Gras is called *Carnevale* in this beautiful city. The first celebrations were in the 11th century and it is still a big celebration today. Visitors to the city can enjoy the costumes, candles and fireworks at night from a gondola in Venice's canals.

Rio de Janeiro, Brazil
The world-famous parades started in the mid-1800s, with decorated floats and thousands of people dancing to samba. People eat a famous meat and bean stew called *feijoada*.

Port-of-Spain, Trinidad
The French arrived here in the 18th century and brought Mardi Gras with them. Nowadays, everyone enjoys the parties and concerts with the famous steel drums playing from morning to midnight.

Reading and vocabulary celebrations

1 Which events do you celebrate in your country? When do you have parties?

When a child is born, everyone in the family comes to a big party.

2 Look at the first paragraph of the article. Why is the article called *World party*?

3 Read the article. Match the sentences (1–6) with the four places in the article.

1 There were no Mardi Gras celebrations here before the mid-1800s.
2 It has the oldest celebration.
3 One type of food is decorated with different colours.
4 One type of musical instrument is especially important.
5 One type of music is especially important.
6 People can travel to the party on a type of boat.

4 Find words in the article for these pictures.

1 .... 2 .... 3 ....

4 .... 5 .... 6 .... 7 ....

5 Work in groups. Describe your favourite festival or celebration in your country. Answer these questions.

- When and why did it begin?
- Is there any special food?
- Do people wear special costumes or masks?
- Do people walk round the streets or ride on floats? Do you have fireworks in the evenings?
- Is music important? What kind of music is there?

Listening

6 ▶ 48 Listen to a report about one of the celebrations in the article. Which celebration is it about?

7 ▶ 48 Listen again. Answer the questions with *Yes, No* or *Don't know* (if the news report doesn't say).

1 Are a lot of people going to come?
2 Is the woman riding on the float on her own?
3 Is she wearing her mask when the interview starts?
4 Does she think she'll have a good time?

Grammar **future forms**

> ▶ **FUTURE FORMS**

1 *Are you **going to be** in the parade this afternoon?*
2 *Everyone **is meeting** at the float at six fifteen.*
3 Interviewer: *Do you have a mask?*
   Lorette: *Sure. Here it is. **I'll put** it on.*

For further information and practice, see page 166.

8 Look at the grammar box. Answer these questions.

a Which sentences (1–3) use these future forms: the present continuous, *will* + infinitive, *be going to* + infinitive.
b Which sentence is about a general plan or future intention? (It was decided before the conversation.)
c Which sentence is about a decision at the time of speaking?
d Which sentence is about an arrangement for a fixed time, made before the conversation?

9 Choose the correct option in these sentences.

1 A: Did Geoff email the times of the parade?
   B: I don't know. *I'll check / I'm checking* my inbox right away.
2 *You'll / You're going to* visit New Orleans! When did you decide that?
3 A: Hey, this costume would look great on you.
   B: Maybe. *I'm trying / I'll try* it on.
4 One day when I'm older, *I'm visiting / I'm going to visit* Venice.
5 A: What time *will we meet / are we meeting* everyone for the parade?
   B: At two in the main square.
6 A: What *are we going to give / will we give* Mark for a present?
   B: We planned to give him a new shirt and tie.
7 A: What time *will you leave / are you leaving*?
   B: Straight after the firework display. I need to go to bed early tonight.

10 **Pronunciation contracted forms**

▶ 49 Listen to sentences 1–4 in Exercise 9. Notice how the contracted forms are pronounced. Listen again and repeat.

11 Complete the sentences with a future form of the verb.

1 At the end of this year I .... (leave) my job and write a book.
2 What time .... we .... (meet) everyone today?
3 A: My car won't start and I've got a meeting at nine!
   B: Don't worry. I .... (take) you in my car.
4 Next year I .... (do) more exercise, but I'm not sure what kind of exercise.
5 The lesson .... (start) half an hour later tonight, at eight o'clock.
6 We also need to get more food and drink for the party, so I .... (buy) that.

Speaking ‿ my life

12 Work in groups. Imagine your town is going to be five hundred years old. Have a town meeting to plan and prepare the celebration. Discuss this list. Decide what you would like to do and who is in charge of organizing each thing.

- type of celebration
- type of food
- type of music
- type of place
- date and time
- anything else

*A: So we're **going to** have a party with fireworks! I'll buy the fireworks. What about the food?*
B: I'll buy the food!

13 Present your final plans to the whole class. Explain what you are going to do.

‿ my life   ▶ THE TRIP OF A LIFETIME ▶ **PLANNING A CELEBRATION** ▶ EVENTS IN THE YEAR ▶ AN INVITATION   ▶ A DESCRIPTION

6c Coming of age

Reading

1 Discuss these questions.

1 At what age can people legally do these things in your country?

> drive a car   get married   buy cigarettes
> leave school   buy fireworks
> open a bank account

2 At what age do you think teenagers become adults?
3 Do you have special celebrations in your country for young people as they become adults?

2 Look at the photos and the title of the web page on page 75. What do you think the expression 'coming of age' means? Read the introduction and check your ideas.

3 Read the three posts about different coming-of-age ceremonies. Are these sentences true (T) or false (F)?

1 The celebration of *Quinceañera* is common in many different countries.
2 The writer thinks the Spanish introduced coming-of-age celebrations to South America.
3 The Hamar bridegroom's family must pay money to the wife's family.
4 In Hamar culture, when the husband dies, the wife gives her cows to the younger brothers.
5 In Japan, you have more legal rights when you are twenty.
6 The attitudes of some young people to *Seijin-no-Hi* in Japan are changing.

4 These pairs of words are on the web page. Match the words with the definitions (a–b).

1 country / culture
  a the way a group of people do things
    culture
  b an area of land with its own government
    country
2 celebration / ceremony
  a a social event such as a party
  b a traditional and formal event on a special day
3 bride / groom
  a the man at a wedding
  b the woman at a wedding
4 legal rights / social traditions
  a what the law allows you to do
  b activities based on the past

Critical thinking **analysing the writer's view**

5 The three posts on the web page are by different writers. Match the posts with these three ways of looking at the topic (a–c). Underline the words that help you decide.

a Historical view: The writer includes information about the past.
b Social view: The writer includes information about society and how it is changing.
c Economic view: The writer includes information about money.

6 Work in pairs and compare your ideas.

Word focus *get*

7 Look at the web page again and find four examples of the word *get*. Match them with these meanings.

> become   receive   start

8 Read the description of a wedding. Match the uses of *get* (1–7) with the meanings (a–g).

> Once the couple ¹**get** engaged, people start to
> ²**get ready** for the big day! On the morning of
> the wedding, everyone ³**gets up** early. Family and
> friends sometimes have to travel long distances
> but it's always a great chance for everyone to ⁴**get
> together** again. After the main ceremony, the couple
> ⁵**get** a lot of presents. Nowadays, many couples go
> abroad on their honeymoon so they leave to ⁶**get**
> their plane. When they ⁷**get back**, they move into
> their new home.

a become   e receive
b catch   f return
c meet and socialize g start the day
d prepare

Speaking ⟨ my life ⟩

9 Work in pairs. Choose one of these events and make notes about what happens in your country on this day. Then work in pairs. Describe the day to your partner. Try to use the word *get* three times in your description.

> a birthday   a religious day or period
> New Year's day   your country's national day
> Valentine's day   another special occasion

COMING of AGE

For some people, the age when you become an adult is the age you learn to drive or leave your parents' home. It can also be when you get married, buy a house and have children. Or perhaps it's when you leave school and get a job. Different cultures have their own ideas and their own celebrations to symbolize coming of age. 5

Quinceañera

In Latin-American cultures, *Quinceañera* is a well-known celebration for girls around their fifteenth birthday. Many people believe the celebration started when the Spanish first came to parts of the Caribbean, Central America and South America. Of course, ancient tribes like the Inca, Maya and the Aztecs probably had their own coming-of-age ceremonies already, but the Spanish changed these to include European features such as the *Quinceañera* waltz, which was introduced in the 19th century by Emperor Maximilian and his wife Carlota. This waltz between the teenage girl and her father symbolizes her coming of age.

Cattle jumping

The whole economy of the Hamar tribe in southern Ethiopia is based on traditional farming. The importance of farming is seen in the coming-of-age ceremony in Hamar culture. As part of the celebration, young men must jump over a line of fifteen cows. They have to do this before they can marry. After that, the man's family chooses a wife and they have to pay the bride's family about thirty goats and twenty cows. Sometimes the man will have to pay the family back over his whole life. Because of the costs involved, Hamar men are usually in their mid-thirties and the women aged about seventeen when they marry. As a result, the husband often dies many years before his wife, and traditionally, she then gets financial control over the husband's younger brothers' money (if the parents are also dead) and all their cattle.

Seijin-no-Hi

The second Monday of January is a public holiday in Japan. It's a day when all twenty-year-olds are supposed to celebrate their coming of age. It's called *Seijin-no-Hi* and the young men and women wear formal clothes and attend ceremonies. Twenty is an important age in Japanese society because you get several adult legal rights, such as voting in elections. However, in recent years, the number of young people celebrating *Seijin-no-Hi* has decreased. This is partly because of Japan's low birth rate, but maybe it's also because it's too expensive and modern twenty year-olds are less interested in these kinds of social traditions.

economy (n) /ɪˈkɒnəmi/ the system of money and business in a society
feature (n) /ˈfiːtʃə(r)/ a quality or important part of something
symbolize (v) /ˈsɪmbəlaɪz/ represent
tribe (n) /traɪb/ a group of people who live far away from towns and cities and share the same language and culture
waltz (n) /wɔːls/ a traditional and formal dance

6d An invitation

Speaking

1 Which of these events are very formal? Which are less formal?

> an end-of-course party   an engagement party
> a barbecue with family and friends
> a leaving party for a work colleague
> your grandfather's ninetieth birthday party
> going out for dinner with a work client

Real life inviting, accepting and declining

2 ▶ **51** Listen to two conversations. Answer the questions.

Conversation 1
1   What event does Ian invite Abdullah to?
2   Why does Abdullah decline the invitation at first?
3   How does Ian convince Abdullah to come?
4   Does Abdullah need to get anything?

Conversation 2
5   When is Sally leaving?
6   Where does Joanna invite Sally?
7   Does Sally accept the invitation?
8   Do you think this conversation is more or less formal than conversation 1? Why?

3 ▶ **51** Look at the expressions for inviting, accepting and declining. Listen to the conversations again. Tick the expressions the speakers use.

INVITING, ACCEPTING and DECLINING	
Less formal	**More formal**
Inviting	
Do you want to …? How about -*ing*? Why don't you …?	Would you like to come …? I'd like to invite you to / take you to …
Accepting	
It sounds great/nice. Thanks, that would be great. OK.	I'd like that very much. That would be wonderful. I'd love to.
Declining	
Thanks, but … Sorry, I can't. I'm …	I'd like/love to, but I'm afraid I … It's very nice of you to ask, but I …

4 Pronunciation emphasizing words

a ▶ **52** Listen to these sentences. Underline the word with the main stress.

1   I'd love to.
2   That would be wonderful.
3   It's very nice of you to ask.
4   I'd like to, but I'm afraid I'm busy.

b ▶ **52** Listen again and repeat the sentences with the same sentence stress.

5 Work in pairs. Take turns to invite each other to different formal and informal events from Exercise 1. Think about how formal you need to be. Practise accepting and declining.

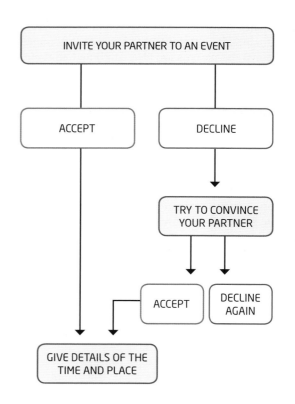

INVITE YOUR PARTNER TO AN EVENT

ACCEPT   DECLINE

TRY TO CONVINCE YOUR PARTNER

ACCEPT   DECLINE AGAIN

GIVE DETAILS OF THE TIME AND PLACE

my life   ▶ THE TRIP OF A LIFETIME   ▶ PLANNING A CELEBRATION   ▶ EVENTS IN THE YEAR   ▶ AN INVITATION
▶ A DESCRIPTION

6e A wedding in Madagascar

Writing a description

1 Read this post from a travel blog. Which of the things in the box does the writer describe?

> food and meals   clothes   festivals and ceremonies
> nature and geographical features   people
> towns, cities and buildings   transport

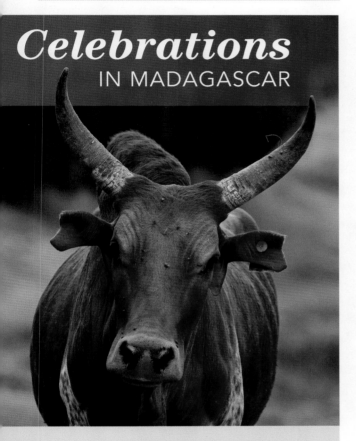

Celebrations
IN MADAGASCAR

I was staying in Madagascar with a family and they invited me to their daughter's wedding. On the big day, I arrived outside an enormous tent. There was a zebu (a type of cow) at the entrance and it looked miserable. Inside the tent, there were beautiful decorations and over 300 excited relatives and guests were waiting for the bride and groom to arrive. The women wore colourful dresses. The older men wore smart suits but the younger men were less formally dressed. I even saw jeans and T-shirts. Finally, the ceremony began with some very long and sometimes dull speeches. But the crowd listened politely and sometimes they laughed and applauded. Finally, it was dinner and I suddenly realized what the zebu was for. We ate from massive plates of meat. I felt sad for the zebu but the meat was the best part of the ceremony! It was delicious!

2 Writing skill descriptive adjectives

a When you write about places or special events, it's important to use interesting and very descriptive adjectives. Match the highlighted adjectives in the travel blog with these less descriptive adjectives (1–4).

1 big ___enormous___ , _____
2 unhappy _____
3 nice ___beautiful___ , _____ , _____ ,
    _____
4 boring _____

> ▶ **WORDBUILDING synonyms**
>
> Some words have the same meaning, or a similar meaning. These are called synonyms.
> *old = ancient, big = huge, boring = dull*
> Using synonyms can improve a description and make it more interesting to read.
>
> For further practice, see Workbook page 51.

b Work in pairs. Improve these sentences with more descriptive adjectives. You can use words from Exercise 2 or your own ideas.

        beautiful   *ancient*
1 Venice is a ~~nice~~ city with lots of ~~old~~ buildings.
2 In the USA, you can buy big burgers.
3 The parade was a bit boring after a while.
4 The crowd was happy because the nice fireworks started.
5 All the costumes were nice.
6 I was very sad to leave Paris.
7 I tried sushi for the first time and it was really good.
8 The view of the mountains was nice.

c Work in pairs. Look at the topics in Exercise 1. Think of two or three interesting adjectives for each one. Use a dictionary to help you. Then work with another pair and compare your adjectives.

food and meals – delicious, tasty, disgusting

3 Choose one of these topics and write a short description (one paragraph) for the travel blog.

- a day you remember from a holiday
- your favourite place in the world
- a special occasion in your life
- a festival or celebration

4 Work in pairs. Read your partner's description. Does he/she use interesting adjectives?

6f Steel drums

Steel drumming competition in Port of Spain during Trinidad's Carnival celebrations.

Before you watch

1 Look at the photo on page 78 and discuss the questions.

1 What kind of musical instrument is the woman playing?
2 How important is music in your country?
3 Does your country have a traditional type of music and musical instrument?

2 Key vocabulary

Read the sentences. The words in bold are used in the video. Match the words with the definitions (a–e).

1 Before you can play a guitar, you have to **tune** it.
2 Young children are **influenced** by their parents.
3 Oil companies store and transport the oil in **drums.**
4 In some countries, smoking is **banned** in public places.
5 The didgeridoo is a long wooden musical instrument and it**'s native to** the aboriginal people in Australia.

a comes from
b affected or changed
c round metal containers
d stopped (by law)
e change the sound of the instrument so it sounds nice

While you watch

3 ▶ 6.1 Watch the video. Number these things in the order you see them.

a Beverley and Dove learn to play the drums.
b A steel band with children and adults playing together.
c A person runs into the sea.
d Honey Boy with a drum.
e People sell food in the market.

4 ▶ 6.1 Watch the video again and answer the questions.

1 What are the islands of the Caribbean region famous for?
2 When did people invent this musical instrument?
3 Why did Trinidad have many oil drums?
4 Where did the music come from?
5 Do most people here play by reading music?
6 What is the name of the person who tunes the drums?
7 Who do you find in a 'panyard'?

After you watch

5 Vocabulary in context

a ▶ 6.2 Watch the clips from the video. Choose the correct meaning of the words and phrases.

b Complete the information about the Australian didgeridoo with these words.

play	performers	backgrounds	goes back
escape			

The didgeridoo is an important symbol and a musical instrument which [1] _____ about 1,500 years. The instrument is made from a long piece of wood with a hole down the middle. Aborigines of different tribes and [2] _____ play the didgeridoo; they don't read from music but [3] _____ by ear. As you travel around Australia, you can't [4] _____ its famous sound and you'll often see [5] _____ playing the instrument at special Aboriginal celebrations because it's an important symbol of their culture.

6 Work in pairs and discuss these questions.

1 Musical instruments can be important national and cultural symbols. What are some other important symbols of your country or culture? (e.g. your country's flag)
2 Plan a short two-minute video about your country's symbols. Which ones will you show in the video? What will you say about them? (e.g. their history, how they are made, how people use them)
3 Present your idea for the video to the class.

Grammar

1 >> **MB** Work in pairs. Look at these sentences about the future. Can you explain the difference in meaning between the different verb forms?

1 I'm going to study English at university.
2 I think I'll study for my English test next.
3 I'm meeting my friend to study English together.
4 I plan to study English at university.

2 Choose the correct option to complete the sentences.

1 We *hope to / 're going to* visit my family this weekend, but we aren't sure yet.
2 A: I need someone to carry these books for me.
   B: I *'m helping / 'll help* you!
3 It isn't easy *win / to win* the lottery.
4 A: When *are you going to / will you* bring the cake?
   B: In a few minutes.
5 Rachel *will have / is having* a party tonight. She arranged it months ago.

3 >> **MB** Work in pairs. Tell each other about:

• your plans for this weekend.
• your future career intentions.

I CAN	
use *to* + infinitive	☐
use different future forms	☐

Vocabulary

4 Match the verbs in A with the words in B to make phrases

A get	go	buy	learn	start

B your first job	to school	your own clothes
to drive	a family	

5 >> **MB** Work in pairs. Look at the phrases in Exercise 4 and answer these questions.

1 What order do these things normally happen in life?
2 Which things have you done?
3 What age were you when you did them? (e.g. thirteen or early teens)
4 How did you feel at the time?
5 When do you plan to do the other ones?

6 Complete the text about the Notting Hill Carnival with these words.

costumes	decorations	drums	floats
parades			

Every year at the end of August, the London neighbourhood of Notting Hill is full of colourful ¹_____ for the biggest carnival in Europe. Over 40,000 volunteers help by putting up ²_____ along the streets of West London and welcoming over one million visitors to the party. Many of them make and wear their own ³_____. The Caribbean community of London started the event in 1966. You'll see many decorated ⁴_____ and hear loud music and traditional steel ⁵_____.

I CAN	
talk about age and the stages in life	☐
talk about parties and celebrations	☐

Real life

7 Look at the sentences (1–4). Replace the words in bold with these phrases.

I'd like you to	I'd like to	that sounds
would you like		

1 **Do you want** to go for a coffee?
2 **Why don't you** come with me to the cinema?
3 **It's nice of you to ask**, but I'm out this evening.
4 Thanks. **That'd be** great.

8 Work in pairs. Invite each other to do something this week. Accept or decline the invitation.

I CAN	
invite people and accept or decline invitations	☐

Woman working in a steel
factory in Pennsylvania, USA

FEATURES

1 Work in pairs. Look at the photo of a woman working in a steel factory. Describe her job using some of these words.

| interesting | dangerous | physical | hard | boring | skilled |
| challenging | tiring | | | | |

2 ▶ 53 Listen to someone talking about the job in the photo. Choose the correct option.

1 She had a *full-time / part-time* job in a restaurant when she left school.
2 She did some *office / manual* work for a construction company.
3 At first, her job in the steel mill was *low-paid / well-paid*.
4 It's *easy / hard* work with *normal / long* hours.
5 She works *in a team / on her own*.

3 We often make words for jobs with two words, e.g. *steel + worker = steel worker*. Make five jobs with words from A and B.

| **A** | hotel | sales | police | fashion | shop |

| **B** | assistant | designer | representative | officer | receptionist |

4 Work in pairs. Describe each job in Exercise 3 with words from Exercise 1. Which of the jobs would you enjoy doing? Which wouldn't you enjoy? Give reasons.

7a Changes in Pennsylvania

Vocabulary jobs

1 In the UK, some jobs are difficult to fill because there aren't enough people qualified to do them. Work in pairs. Look at these jobs. Which five jobs do you think are difficult to fill? Check your answers on page 155.

> accountant   chef   computer programmer
> electrician   engineer   journalist
> marketing manager   nurse   shop assistant
> teacher   waiter

> ▶ **WORDBUILDING suffixes in job words**
>
> We often make words for jobs by adding suffixes to verbs and nouns.
> verb + suffix: *teach – teacher*
> noun + suffix: *journal – journalist*
> Some job titles do not use a suffix: *chef, nurse,* etc.
>
> For further practice, see Workbook page 59.

2 Look at the wordbuilding box. Underline the suffixes in the jobs in Exercise 1.

▶ 54

3 Make jobs from these words using the suffixes from Exercise 1.

> farm   economics   science   drive   politics
> build   train

Reading

4 Read the article about people living and working in Pennsylvania. Match the jobs (1–3) with the people in the article.

1 businessman
2 trainee driver
3 farmer

5 Read the article again and answer the questions.

1 When did the first energy company discover natural gas in Pennsylvania?
2 What does Donald get from the energy company?
3 What job does Lee want to get?
4 What training is she doing?
5 What kind of company does Paul run?
6 Why is Paul's business 'looking good'?

WHEN JOBS CAME TO PENNSYLVANIA

In 2004, an energy company discovered gas under the ground in the State of Pennsylvania in the USA. Now there are lots of energy companies in Pennsylvania and many people's lives have changed.

Donald Roessler lives on a farm. He has lived there for most of his life, but he hasn't made much money from it. Two years ago, however, an energy company wanted the gas under his farm. Now they pay Donald a regular monthly income for the energy.

Lee hasn't had a job since she lost her old job at a bottle factory. But recently, a lot of the energy companies have employed new drivers, so now she's learning to drive trucks.

Paul Battista has run his company selling construction equipment for about thirty-five years. He's had some bad times, but since they discovered natural gas, Paul's profits have increased and business is looking good.

Grammar present perfect and past simple

> ▶ **PRESENT PERFECT and PAST SIMPLE**
>
> 1 *In 2004, an energy company **discovered** gas under the ground.*
> 2 *Many people's lives **have changed**.*
> 3 *Donald Roessler **has lived** on his farm for most of his life, but he **hasn't made** much money from it.*
>
> For further information and practice, see page 168.

6 Look at the sentences in the grammar box. Underline the verb in the past simple and circle the verbs in the present perfect. Then choose the correct option in these sentences (a–c).

  a   If we say when something happened, we use the *past simple / present perfect*.

  b   If we don't know or don't say when something happened, we use the *past simple / present perfect*.

  c   For something that started in the past and continues now, we use the *past simple / present perfect*.

7 Underline other verbs in the article in the present perfect (*have / has* + past participle). Write the past participles in the correct category.

  • Regular past participles:
     changed, lived
  • Irregular past participles:
     made

8 Read about an engineer in Pennsylvania. Choose the correct options.

> ¹ *I've gone / I went to* university when I was nineteen and ² *I qualified / I've qualified* as an engineer about four years later. Now I live here in Pennsylvania with my wife and children, but we ³ *haven't lived / didn't live* here very long. ⁴ *I've worked / I worked* in six other places and last year ⁵ *I've spent / I spent* three months working overseas. But now I think we'll stay in Pennsylvania. ⁶ *It's been / It was* good for us living here. At first some of the local people ⁷ *haven't been / weren't* friendly because they were worried about the local environment, but the natural gas industry ⁸ *has created / created* new jobs and ⁹ *has improved / improved* the local economy, so things are better now.

9 You are going to listen to an interview with a scientist for a natural gas company. Write questions to ask about his life. Use the present perfect or the past simple.

  1   how long / work / for your company?
     How long have you worked for your company?
  2   when / you / go to college?
  3   you / always / live / in Pennsylvania?
  4   when / you / move back here?
  5   you / ever / work / overseas?
  6   it / be / easy living here?

10 ▶ **55** Listen to the interview. Check your questions from Exercise 9 and write the scientist's answers.

Grammar present perfect with *for* and *since*

> ▶ **PRESENT PERFECT with *FOR* and *SINCE***
>
> Journalist: *How long have you worked for your company?*
> Scientist: ***For** five years. **Since** I left college.*
>
> For further information and practice, see page 168.

11 Look at the grammar box. Read the scientist's answer to the question and complete this sentence with *for* and *since*.

   We use ¹ _____ and a point in time (e.g. 2015, yesterday) and we use ² _____ and a period of time (e.g. ten minutes, six months).

12 Complete the phrases with *for* or *since*.

  1   _____ 2008
  2   _____ two weeks
  3   _____ six days
  4   _____ one o'clock
  5   _____ I started work
  6   _____ 1st January
  7   _____ 24 hours
  8   _____ I was ten

Speaking ⌐ my life

13 Work in pairs. Practise asking and answering questions about these topics using the present perfect and past simple.

> current job / studies   where you live   travel
> languages   people you know
> interests / hobbies

   A: ***Have** you ever **studied** Chinese?*
   B: *No, I **haven't**, but I study Arabic.*
   A: *Really? How long **have** you **studied** it?*
   B: ***For** about **three years**.*
   A: *Why **did** you **want** to learn Arabic?*

7b X-ray photographer

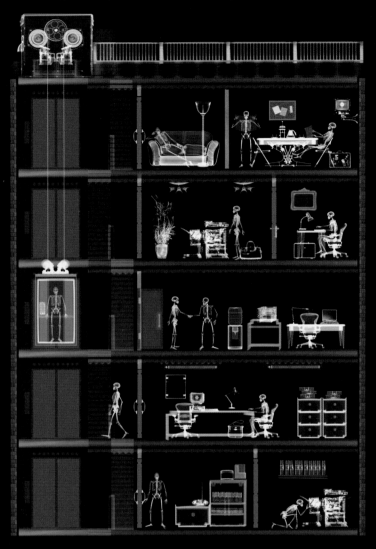

Nick Veasey is a photographer who works with X-rays. Nick likes taking photos showing the inside of people, buildings, flowers and everyday objects. This photo of an office building was made by taking a series of X-ray photographs and putting them together in one picture.

Vocabulary parts of a building

1 Look at the photo and read about the photographer. Answer the questions.

  1 What type of photography is it?
  2 How did Nick make this photo?
  3 Do you like this kind of photography?

2 Complete the sentences (1–8) with these parts of an office building.

> basement   canteen   corridor   emergency exit
> entrance   ground floor   lift   office
> reception   stairs

  1 I work in an _____office_____ on the second floor.
  2 You can park your car outside the _____ to the building.
  3 Speak to the person at _____ when you arrive.

  4 I work on the _____ . Walk down the _____ and my office is on the left.
  5 When the _____ isn't working, we have to walk up the _____ .
  6 In case of a fire, leave the building by this _____ .
  7 I normally have my lunch in the _____ or I go out to the café down the road.
  8 You can get more paper from the _____ below the ground floor.

3 Work in pairs. Think about the building you are in now. Which parts from Exercise 2 are in your building?

4 Look at the photo of the office building again. With your partner, describe different parts of the building and say what the people are doing there.

On the ground floor, someone is fixing the photocopier.

Listening

5 ▶ **56** Listen to two telephone conversations with people who work in the building in the photo. Answer the questions.

Conversation 1
1   Where is Geoff calling from?
2   Where is Kristina sitting on the photo?
3   Where is the price list?

Conversation 2
4   Why is the man visiting the building?
5   Where is Richard's office on the photo?

6 ▶ **56** Listen again and write in the missing prepositions.

1   I'm _____ home but I'm about to leave for a meeting.
2   Is it _____ your desk?
3   I think it's _____ my computer.
4   Maybe I left it _____ one of the drawers _____ you.
5   Try the top drawer _____ the left.
6   I'm standing _____ the entrance.
7   You need to come _____ the entrance to the building.
8   Go _____ the third floor.
9   Go _____ the door on your right and the photocopying room is there.
10 My office is _____ it.

Grammar prepositions of place and movement

▶ **PREPOSITIONS OF PLACE AND MOVEMENT**

Prepositions of place
*It's **opposite** the door.*
*It's **on** the third floor.*
*It's **at** the top of the building.*

Prepositions of movement
*Go **down to** the basement.*
*Come **up** the stairs.*
*Walk **out of** the building.*
Note: prepositions of movement follow verbs of movement (e.g. *go, come, walk*)

For further information and practice, see page 168.

7 Look at the grammar box. Then look at the sentences in Exercise 6. Which sentences have prepositions of place? Which have prepositions of movement?

8 Choose the correct option.

1   There's coffee *on / in* the table. Help yourself.
2   You need to go *up / down* these stairs to get to the basement.
3   I need some fresh air. Let's go *inside / outside* for a walk.

4   Wait there and I'll come and meet you *at / on* reception.
5   When you go *past / through* a post box, can you post this letter for me?
6   The canteen is *opposite / between* the main building.
7   Go *along / on* the corridor and my office is *at / on* the left.
8   Park your car on the left and walk *across / out of* the road to the building opposite.

9 Complete the messages with these prepositions.

at   down   in   into   next to   on
through   up

> Let's meet [1]_____ the coffee area at 11. It's the room [2]_____ the top of the building. See you there.

> Can you fix my printer for me? My office is [3]_____ the third floor. The printer is [4]_____ my desk.

> The lift is out of order today so please go [5]_____ the reception area to the fire exit and walk [6]_____ the emergency stairs.

> We got [7]_____ the lift on the fifth floor and now it won't go [8]_____ to reception. Please help!

10 Pronunciation **intrusive** /w/

▶ **57** Sometimes when a word ends in a vowel and the next verb starts in a vowel, we add the /w/ sound. Listen and repeat these examples with *go* + preposition.

1   go /w/ in
2   go /w/ on
3   go /w/ out
4   go /w/ into
5   go /w/ up
6   go /w/ across

Speaking ⟨ my life ⟩

11 Work in pairs. Take turns to give directions from where you are now to these parts of the building. Listen to your partner and name the part of the building.

the lifts or stairs   your favourite café
the toilets   another classroom/office
the reception area

7c Twenty-first century cowboys

Reading

1 Look at the photo. What is a cowboy? Which country is most famous for cowboys?

2 Read the article on page 87. Which sentence (1–3) best summarizes the article?

1 How modern cowboys really live and work.
2 The truth about Hollywood cowboys.
3 Why people don't want to be cowboys anymore.

3 Read the article again. Choose the correct option (a–c) to complete these sentences.

1 The writer explains that real life as a cowboy is:
   a like a Hollywood actor.
   b adventurous and romantic.
   c hard work and not well-paid.
2 Modern cowboys spend a lot of time:
   a outside on their own.
   b meeting people.
   c on the phone.
3 Blaine and Tyrel Tucker grew up:
   a on a ranch.
   b in the city.
   c in different places.
4 People like Pat Crisswell become cowboys for:
   a the long holidays.
   b the salary.
   c job satisfaction.

Critical thinking **analysing comparisons in a text**

4 The aim of the writer is to help us understand the life of a modern cowboy. He uses several comparisons to do this. Look at the pairs of ideas (1–4). Write words and phrases from the article that describe each idea, and decide if the two ideas are similar or different.

1 a the cowboy in the Hollywood films *freedom, adventure, romantic image*
   b the real life of a cowboy *hard, dangerous, physical, long hours, low pay*
   The two ideas are very different
2 a the life of a cowboy in the past
   b the life of the modern cowboy
3 a cowboys like Blaine and Tyrel
   b cowboys like Pat Crisswell
4 a the advantages of an office job in the city
   b the advantages of working as a cowboy

Word focus *make* or *do*

5 Find phrases in paragraphs 2 and 4 with *make* or *do* and complete these phrases.

1 _____ a job
2 _____ breakfast
3 _____ a call
4 _____ money
5 _____ something different

6 Complete these phrases with *make* or *do*. Use a dictionary to help you, if necessary.

1 _____ your homework
2 _____ a mistake
3 _____ a decision
4 _____ someone a favour
5 _____ well at work/school
6 _____ your bed
7 _____ a noise
8 _____ work

7 Work in pairs. Ask your partner three questions using phrases with *make* and *do*.

*What kind of job do you want to **do** in the future?*
*Is it important to **make** a lot of money?*

Speaking ⟨ my life ⟩

8 Read the last sentence of the article again. Do you think Pat Crisswell was crazy to give up his job in the city, or do you think job satisfaction is more important than money?

9 When you look for a job, what things on this list are most important? Put the items in order of importance from 1 to 8 (1 = most important, 8 = least important).

- learning new skills
- a good salary
- working with a team of people
- making your own decisions
- getting regular promotion
- working outdoors
- opportunities to travel to different places
- long holidays

10 Work in groups. Tell the rest of the group your order and explain why.

I think working with a team is important because it's more interesting than working on your own.

TWENTY-FIRST *century* COWBOYS

▶ **58**

Cowboys have lived and worked in the west and south-west of the United States for over three centuries and they are a famous symbol of the USA. When you watch those old Hollywood cowboy films from the fifties and sixties, you don't see a job; you see a life of freedom and adventure. It's a romantic image which we love to believe in. However, the real job of an American cowboy has always been hard and sometimes dangerous; it's physical with long hours and low pay.

No one knows exactly how many people still do the job of a cowboy in the twenty-first century, but the number is probably between ten and fifty thousand. Life hasn't changed much for cowboys since the early days. The cattle walk across huge plains to eat the grass and the cowboy rides on his horse to bring them home. Like the cowboys of the past, a twenty-first century cowboy still gets up early on freezing cold mornings and makes breakfast over a fire. He can't take days or weekends off and there is no paid holiday. And when you are in the middle of nowhere, your mobile phone doesn't work, so you can't make a call to family or friends when you feel lonely.

So why does a man – because it is usually a man – become a cowboy? For some, it isn't a choice, because they are born into the life; men like Blaine and Tyrel. They are brothers and have worked with cows since they were children. Their mother had a ranch and they rode a horse before they could walk. Both Blaine and Tyrel have large moustaches and wear traditional cowboy clothes with the famous hat and boots. They prefer the traditional cowboy culture: 'It's a real life about you, your horse and the open country.' Last winter, they looked after 2,300 cows. Every day from December until April, they rode across nearly 100,000 acres of land with only the cattle and the horses for company.

Unlike Blaine and Tyrel, some people choose the job later in life. Pat Crisswell had an office job with the US government. He made good money, but he didn't like city life and spending all day inside. He wanted to do something different. So one day, he gave up his job and moved to a ranch in Texas, earning much less money as a cowboy. He remembers his work colleagues in the city on the day he left. They all thought Pat was crazy, but he wanted job satisfaction. And for a cowboy, job satisfaction doesn't come from the money or a comfortable office; it comes from being free to wake up under the sky and being your own boss.

(line numbers: 30, 35, 40, 45)

---

acre (n) /ˈeɪkə(r)/ measurement of land
good money /ɡʊdˈmʌni/ expression meaning 'a lot of money' or 'well-paid'
middle of nowhere /ˈmɪd(ə)l əv ˈnəʊweə(r)/ informal expression meaning a place far away from a town, city or other people
plain (n) /pleɪn/ grassy areas of open land
ranch (n) /rɑːntʃ/ large farm for cattle, horses or sheep

---

my life ▶ PAST EXPERIENCES ▶ GIVING DIRECTIONS ▶ JOB SATISFACTION ▶ A JOB INTERVIEW
▶ A CV

7d A job interview

Vocabulary **job adverts**

1 Look at the job advert. Answer the questions.

1 When does the restaurant need people?
2 Would you apply for this kind of job? Why? / Why not?

WAITERS AND KITCHEN STAFF TO START TODAY!

Full-time and part-time positions available.

Experience is not essential as we will provide training.

To apply, come in and speak to the manager with your CV and contact details.

2 Find words in the advert with these meanings.

1 people who work for a business or company
2 formal word for 'jobs' with a company
3 necessary or needed
4 formal word for 'give'
5 ask for something, e.g. a job, by writing or filling in a form
6 abbreviation meaning Curriculum Vitae (with information about you, your qualifications and experience)
7 information including name, phone number and address

Real life **a job interview**

3 ▶ 59 Hania applied for the job in the advert in Exercise 1. Listen to parts of her interview with the manager. Are these sentences true (T) or false (F)?

1 The interviewer has read her CV.
2 Hania has another job at the moment.
3 She wants a full-time job at the restaurant.
4 She liked her last job because of the customers.
5 Hania doesn't ask any questions.
6 The manager doesn't think she needs much training.

4 Do you think Hania is a good person for the job? Why? / Why not?

5 ▶ 59 Listen again and complete these questions from the interview. Then match five questions with the categories in bold in the box below.

1 _____ long have you been in England?
2 _____ do you want this job?
3 _____ did you like about your last job?
4 _____ did you deal with any difficult situations?
5 _____ you have any questions for me?
6 _____ you give me more information about that?

▶ **A JOB INTERVIEW**

Your current life and job
What are you doing at the moment?
Tell me about your current job.

Reasons for applying
Can you tell me your reasons for applying for this job?
Why have you applied for this job?

Past experience and qualifications
Have you worked in a restaurant before?
What qualifications do you have?

Questions for the interviewer
What are the typical hours?
Can you tell me the salary?

6 Work in pairs. Look at the job advert. You are going to practise an interview for this job.

SHOP ASSISTANTS WANTED IN BUSY SPORTSWEAR SHOP

Full-time and part-time positions available.

Experience is not essential. Must be friendly, polite and good with people. Training provided.

To apply, email your CV and contact details to manager@babamsportswear.com

Student A: You are the manager at the shop. You have five minutes to prepare questions.

Student B: You have applied for the job of shop assistant. Think about answers for any questions the interviewer might ask you and prepare a question to ask the manager.

When you are both ready, begin the interview.

7 Change roles and repeat the interview.

my life ▶ PAST EXPERIENCES ▶ GIVING DIRECTIONS ▶ JOB SATISFACTION ▶ A JOB INTERVIEW
▶ A CV

7e Applying for a job

Writing a CV

1 Complete the CV with these headings.

Address   Date of birth   Education   Home telephone
Interests   References   Skills   Work experience

Curriculum Vitae

Aldo Peterson

Nationality	Swiss and British
1 _____	17 September, 1992
2 _____	Flat 3A, 85 Cadogan Gardens, London SW1
Email	a_peterson@swisstel.com
3 _____	0207 685 74653
Mobile	07759 856 746

4 _____

2013–2014	MA in Events Management, London College of Catering and Hotel Management
2010–2013	BSc in Geography and Economics, London University

5 _____

Current position:	Assistant manager: Helping the general manager, managing staff
2014–2016	Hotel receptionist: Checked in guests, worked in a large team, translated hotel correspondence in French, German and English.
Summer 2013	Group team leader on summer camp in the USA: planned activities for groups of teenagers and organized the schedule.

6 _____

Languages: English and German (bilingual), French (fluent)
Computing: Word, Excel, web design

7 _____

Captain of local hockey team, did most winter sports, acted in student theatre productions

8 _____

Dr Giles McFadden, Dept of Hotel Management, 15 Given Street, London
Alessandra Delfs, Mattenstr. 7, Reinach, 4153, Switzerland

2 How similar is a CV in your country? Would you use these headings? Would you add any other information?

3 **Writing skill missing out words in CVs**

a Compare these full sentences with the sentences in bold from a CV. Which words are missing in the CV sentences? Which verb forms do the CV sentences use?

1 *I am working part-time in a restaurant.* **Working part-time in a restaurant.**
2 *I've worked in a four-star hotel in France.* **Have worked in four-star hotel in France.**
3 *I had to meet guests at reception.* **Met guests at reception.**

b Underline the sentences in the CV starting with verb forms. How would you normally write each sentence?

c Rewrite these sentences for a CV.

1 ~~I am~~ studying mathematics at University. *Studying mathematics at University.*
2 I made pizzas in the student cafeteria.
3 I've competed in athletics competitions for my school.
4 I had to train new employees.
5 I am learning to play the drums.
6 I've given presentations to large groups of people.

4 Think about what you are currently doing (e.g. what job you are doing or where you are studying) and your past work and studies (e.g. what you did or have done). Write six sentences for your CV.

5 Now write your complete CV.

6 Work in pairs. Exchange CVs. Use these questions to check your partner's CV.

- Does it have clear headings?
- Does it use present and past participles?

7f My working life

These Italian actors are working in Istanbul, Turkey.
They are performing *Romeo and Juliet*.

Before you watch

1 Key vocabulary

Read the sentences. The words and phrases in bold are used in the video. Match the words to the definitions (a–f).

1 I only buy **organic** food from supermarkets.
2 We **set up** our **market stall** at seven in the morning.
3 The positive parts of my job **outweigh** the negatives.
4 I like the **variety** in my job. Every day is different.
5 When you have a party, you can **bring together** all your friends in one place.

a prepare
b produced on farms which use no chemicals
c are more important than
d when something has different parts so you don't always do the same thing
e a place for selling things outside
f have everyone in the same place

While you watch

2 You are going to watch three people talking about their jobs. Before you watch, look at the photos and descriptions (1–3), and predict which person says each sentence (a–f).

1 Katy has a market stall and sells organic fruit and vegetables.
2 Virginia is a language teacher.
3 Marcus is an actor.

a 'At the moment I'm in a play called Romeo and Juliet by William Shakespeare.' – *Marcus*
b 'I always have to work at the weekends.'
c 'I like sharing my culture with other people.'
d 'I enjoy working with other people and working in a team.'
e 'Sometimes the weather can be bad because it rains.'
f 'It's a fun job and I enjoy it very much.'

3 ◻ 7.1 Watch the video and check your ideas from Exercise 2.

4 ◻ 7.1 Watch the three people in the video again and complete the notes to answer the three questions.

	What's your typical working day?	What do you like about the job?	Is there anything you don't like about the job?
1	7.30 1 12.00 Lunch 3.00 2	• meet different people • good 3 • good for the environment	• long 4 • the weather (when it rains)
2	4.00 teach at pupil's houses 6.30–8.30 5	• sharing my culture • bringing 6 together	• paperwork and marking can be boring • 7 can be tiring
3	sometimes start first thing in the morning and finish at midnight	• the 8 – no two days are the same • working as a 9 • sense of achievement	• long hours • travel • 10 isn't great

5 ◻ 7.1 Work in groups and compare your notes. Then watch the video again to check your answers.

After you watch

6 ◻ 7.2 **Vocabulary in context**

Watch the clips from the video. Choose the correct meaning of the words and phrases.

7 Complete these sentences about your job or a job you know about. Then tell your partner about the job.

1 The job involves …
2 A typical days starts at … and finishes at …
3 Overall, the positive parts of the job outweigh the negatives because …

8 Which of the three jobs in the video would you prefer? Tell the class your reasons.

Grammar

1 Complete the questions with the present perfect or past simple form of the verbs.

A: How long [1] _____ you _____ (work) here?

B: About three years. I [2] _____ (join) the newspaper when I left university.

A: So, [3] _____ you always _____ (want) to be a journalist?

B: Not particularly. But when I [4] _____ (be) young, I wrote stories.

A: What [5] _____ you _____ (study) at university?

B: Spanish.

A: [6] _____ you ever _____ (live) in Spain?

B: No, but I [7] _____ (spend) a summer in Argentina.

A: Really? That sounds great!

2 **» MB** Work in pairs. Explain why you used the present perfect or the past simple in Exercise 1.

3 **» MB** Write three questions starting *How long have you …?* Then ask and answer your questions with your partner. Use *since* or *for* in your answers.

4 Complete the sentences with these prepositions.

across	at	in	on	opposite	through

1 Walk _____ to the other side of the car park and the factory is there.
2 Can you pass me that book _____ the shelf?
3 I think Paulo is _____ the basement.
4 Go _____ those doors at the end and the photocopier is there.
5 The cafeteria is _____ the top of the building on the fifth floor.
6 We sit _____ each other in the office.

I CAN

use the present perfect and the past simple ☐

use prepositions of place and movement ☐

Vocabulary

5 **» MB** Can you remember the missing part of these compound nouns from Unit 7?

1 sales r *epresentative*
2 fashion d_____
3 shop a_____
4 reception a_____
5 c_____ programmer
6 e_____ exit
7 marketing m_____
8 ground f_____
9 contact d_____

6 Complete the text about the balloon seller with the correct form of *make* or *do*.

Nguyen [1] _____ two jobs. During the day he sells balloons and in the evening he [2] _____ money by working in a restaurant. He helps to [3] _____ food in the kitchen. He works long days, but he is saving so he can complete his studies. If he [4] _____ well at college, he can go to university.

7 Work in pairs. Look at the photo of the balloon seller. Do you think he enjoys this job? Why? / Why not?

I CAN

talk about jobs and places of work ☐

Real life

8 Match these questions at a job interview (1–5) with the responses (a–e).

1 Why have you applied for this job?
2 What are you doing at the moment?
3 Have you worked in a hotel before?
4 What do you like about your current job?
5 Do you have any questions for me?

a Meeting different people.
b No, but I have experience with customers.
c So I can use my language skills.
d Yes, just one …
e I'm working at a café in the city centre.

9 **» MB** Work in pairs. Take turns to ask the questions in Exercise 8 and respond with your own answers.

I CAN

ask and answer questions about a job ☐

Unit 8 Technology

Robots and humans working together

FEATURES

1 Look at the photo and the caption. How do you think the robot and the humans are 'working together'? In what other ways do robots work with humans?

2 ▶ 60 Listen to someone talking about the importance of technology in our lives. Answer the questions.

1 How does technology help us in our everyday lives?
2 Why does technology sometimes make mistakes?
3 Where does the robot in the photo work? What does it do?

3 Look at this list of human actions. Which can robots do?

fall in love   get bored   get hungry   have new ideas
make decisions   make mistakes   sleep   solve problems
speak a language   understand instructions

4 What simple or repetitive jobs do you do at work, at school or at home? Which of these jobs could you give to a robot in the future?

8a Mobile technology

Vocabulary internet verbs

1 Think about how you have used the internet in the last 24 hours. Why have you used it? List the reasons. Then work in pairs and compare your lists.

to find out information on train times, to check my email, to get directions

2 Complete the sentences with these verbs.

connect	download	log in	play	search
~~set up~~	subscribe	upload	write	

1 To ___*set up*___ a new online account, type in your personal details and click 'enter'.
2 I don't buy CDs anymore. It's much easier to _____ music.
3 I _____ a weekly blog with all my family's news.
4 A lot of my friends _____ online games, but I find them a bit boring.
5 When I need to find information, I _____ the internet.
6 I _____ to a daily podcast which gives me all the latest news.
7 My friends and family _____ their photos and share them on social networking sites.
8 I use online banking because it's so easy. You just _____ with a password and your account details.
9 There's no wifi here, so I can't _____ to the internet.

3 Which of the sentences in Exercise 2 are true for you? Change any sentences which are not true or give more details.

I write a blog, but I don't write about my family. I talk about what my friends and I like doing.

Reading

4 Read the blog. Who do you think wrote it? Why did the person write it?

5 Read the blog again and choose the correct option in these sentences.

1 The team had an *easy / hard* journey to the Karimskaya River.
2 The weather was *good / terrible* when they arrived.
3 The blogger says that communication was *fairly similar / very different* for explorers in the past.
4 He thinks social media is *a waste of time / useful* for modern explorers.
5 *The writer / Someone else* touched a strange plant.
6 The writer got a message from a person he *knew / didn't know*.

kamchatka project

▶ 61

Posted July 15, 2:55 PM

After travelling through three international airports and nineteen time zones, we are here at last! We are at the beginning of the Karimskaya River in the region of Kamchatka. It's the middle of nowhere, but I've got a signal on my phone. It's a sunny afternoon and if the weather stays the same for the next few days, everything will go well.

Posted July 16, 8:05 AM

We had a good night's sleep and are about to cook breakfast. I've already connected to the internet and checked my emails. It's funny to think that in the past, explorers couldn't share their news until months after the trip. Nowadays, if anything interesting happens, explorers blog about it before breakfast!

Posted July 18, 7:20 PM

Twitter and Facebook are great if you have a problem. We were working in a forest today and someone in our group touched a strange plant. Suddenly his skin became red, hot and painful. I posted a photo of the plant on Twitter and asked for advice. Minutes later I got a reply from someone who knows this region well. 'It's a pushki plant. It won't kill you if you touch one, but it will hurt!'

Grammar zero and first conditional

> **ZERO and FIRST CONDITIONAL**

Zero conditional
*Twitter and Facebook **are** great **if** you **have** a problem.*
***If** anything interesting **happens**, explorers **blog** about it before breakfast!*

First conditional
***If** the weather **stays** the same, everything **will go** well.*
*It **won't kill** you **if** you **touch** one.*

For further information and practice, see page 170.

6 Look at the grammar box and complete these sentences.

1 We use a *zero / first* conditional sentence to talk about things that are generally true.
2 We use a *zero / first* conditional sentence to talk about a possible future situation.
3 In a *zero / first* conditional sentence we use *if* + present simple + present simple (or present simple + *if* + present simple).
4 In a *zero / first* conditional sentence we use *if* + present simple + *will* (or *will* + *if* + present simple).
5 *If* can come at the beginning of the sentence or in the middle. If it is at the beginning, we *use / don't use* a comma in the middle.

7 Match the beginnings of the sentences (1–6) with the endings (a–f). Then decide if the sentence is zero conditional (0) or first conditional (1).

1 If I get lost on the way to your house, d (1)
2 If you click on this link,
3 You can't read the articles on the website
4 If there's a red sign on the screen,
5 I'll call you from the top of the mountain
6 I only write my blog

a you have a virus.
b it downloads the video for free.
c if you don't subscribe.
d I'll use the satnav in my car.
e if I have something interesting to write about.
f if I can get a phone signal.

8 ▶ **62** Complete the sentences with the correct form of the verbs. Then listen and check your answers.

1 If I _____ (go) on holiday, I take lots of sun cream.
2 We _____ (need) a torch if we go out late tonight.
3 We always get lost if my brother _____ (drive).
4 If we _____ (see) a supermarket, I'll stop and buy some sandwiches for the journey.
5 If that old phone stops working, I _____ (buy) a new one.

6 I can't buy food if the supermarket _____ (not / be) open.
7 You _____ (ring) this number if you have any questions.
8 If you don't try harder, you _____ (not pass) your exam.

Speaking ⟨ my life ⟩

9 Have you ever been on a camping trip? What did you take?

10 Work in groups. You are going to the mountains for two days. The weather forecast is for sun on the first day and rain on the second. Because you are walking and camping, you don't want to take too many items. You have tents, rucksacks and food. Look at the photos. Discuss these items and choose the five most useful. Give reasons for taking them.

A: *If we **take** …, we **won't need** …*
B: *We'**ll need** … if it **rains** …*

camera

mobile phone

gas cooker

hairdryer

hat

laptop

towel

matches

satnav

sun cream

torch

sunglasses

umbrella

8b Invention for the eyes

Speaking

1 Work in groups. Discuss the importance of these inventions. Put the inventions in order from 1 (the most important) to 7 (the least important).

- the aeroplane
- the bicycle
- the camera
- the engine
- the internet
- the telephone and mobile phone
- the washing machine

2 Present your list to the class and compare it with other groups. What other important inventions would you add to the list? Why?

Listening

3 ▶ **63** Listen to a science programme. Answer the questions.

1 What is the problem for more than one billion people in the world?
2 What has Joshua Silver invented?

4 ▶ **64** Listen to the first half of the programme again. Number the instructions on the diagram in the correct order (1–4).

pump with silicone oil inside

pipe

wheel

lens with silicone oil inside

...... The lens changes shape.
__1__ You turn the wheels on each side.
...... The silicone oil moves into the lens.
...... The pump pushes the silicone oil through the pipe.

5 ▶ **65** Listen to the second half of the programme again. Are the sentences true (T) or false (F)?

1 Silver had to do experiments with the glasses before they worked properly.
2 A man in Ghana used the glasses first.
3 The glasses are expensive to produce.
4 The centre is making a big difference in cities around the world.

Grammar defining relative clauses

▶ **DEFINING RELATIVE CLAUSES**

The underlined part of each sentence is a defining relative clause. This clause gives essential information about the noun.
*There is a scientist **who** has solved the problem.*
*Joshua Silver has invented glasses **which** don't need an optician.*
*They live in places **where** there aren't any opticians.*
Note: We sometimes use *that* instead of *who* or *which* (but not *where*): *Joshua Silver has invented glasses **that** don't need an optician.*

For further information and practice, see page 170.

6 Look at the sentences in the grammar box. Which word (*who, which* or *where*) do we use:

    a for people?
    b for things?
    c to talk about what exists or happens in a place?

7 Look at these sentences from the listening. Underline the relative clause.

    1 A man in Ghana was the first person who used the new glasses.
    2 Silver started an organization which is called the 'Centre for Vision in the Developing World'.
    3 The centre works with schools in countries where people can't get glasses easily.

8 Complete these sentences with *who, which* or *where*.

    1 Thomas Edison is the person _____ invented the electric light bulb.
    2 I live in a village _____ there is no public transport.
    3 The Tesla is the first sports car _____ uses electricity.
    4 Silicon Valley is a place _____ many successful technology companies like Apple and Microsoft are based.
    5 In 1800 Alessandro Volta made an invention _____ was the first battery.
    6 Maria Beasley was the inventor _____ made the first life raft.

9 In which sentences in Exercise 8 can you use *that* at the beginning of the relative clause?

10 Look at the photo and the text about another invention, Lifestraw. Complete the text with *who, which* or *where* and these phrases.

> ~~cleans the water~~   like hiking and camping
> there is a lake   can break
> there is no safe
> invented Lifestraw

11 Think of a famous person, an invention, and a place or city. Write a sentence to define or explain each one. Then exchange sentences with your partner. Can your partner guess what they are?

> *It's **a thing which** you use to find information and to contact people. (a mobile phone)*
> *It's **a city where** you can see Big Ben. (London)*

LIFESTRAW

LifeStraw is an invention [1] <u>*which cleans water*</u> while you drink, so it's useful in areas [2] _____ water supply. It's also small, so you can carry it to places [3] _____ or river and it's popular with people [4] _____. *Lifestraw* can turn 1,000 litres into drinking water and it doesn't have any moving parts [5] _____. The people [6] _____ also make other products for cleaning water in 64 countries around the world.

Speaking ⟨ my life ⟩

12 Work in groups. Invent something which will help you, your family or your friends in their everyday life. Discuss these questions and draw a simple design of the invention with any important information on a large sheet of paper.

    • What is the invention for? (e.g. a robot for cleaning the house)
    • Who will use it? (e.g. busy working people)
    • Where can you use it? (e.g. around the office)

13 Prepare a short presentation about your invention. Give your presentation to the class.

> *Our new invention is a machine **which** …*
> *It's for people **who** …*
> *You can use it in a place **where** …*

8c Designs from nature

Reading

1 Photos 1–5 on page 99 show inventions. Photos a–e show the animals and plants which gave the inventors their ideas. Match the inventions (1–5) with the animals and plants (a–e).

2 Read the article and check your answers from Exercise 1.

3 Read the article again. Choose the correct option (a–b) to complete these sentences.

1 Geckos are amazing because they:
  a can walk upside down.
  b can walk on glass and plastic.
2 Engineers, designers and scientists can learn a lot from:
  a how nature copies things.
  b how nature designs things.
3 The wind turbine engineers and the car manufacturer studied:
  a shapes in nature.
  b size in nature.
4 George de Mestral got the idea for Velcro:
  a by studying other types of clothing.
  b by chance.
5 Wilhelm Barthlott got his idea from:
  a the inside of the leaf.
  b the outside of the leaf.
6 The writer thinks designers:
  a will learn a lot from nature in the future.
  b have looked at most of the possibilities.

Wordbuilding **dependent prepositions**

4 These eight words often have prepositions after them. Find the words in the article and write the preposition.

1 problem _____   5 work _____
2 good _____   6 think _____
3 interested _____   7 similar _____
4 depend _____   8 idea _____

> ▶ **WORDBUILDING Dependent prepositions**
>
> Many verbs, adjective and nouns often have a preposition after them. These are called 'dependent prepositions'.
> verb + preposition: *I **agree with** you.*
> adjective + preposition: *I'm **bad at** football.*
> noun + preposition: *I have a **question about** this.*
>
> For further practice, see Workbook page 67.

5 Look at the wordbuilding box. Match the words in Exercise 4 with the categories (verb, adjective, noun).

6 Choose three of the words with a dependent preposition in Exercise 4 and write a sentence with each word. Then work in pairs. Take turns to read your sentences but do not say the preposition. Your partner must say the preposition.

Critical thinking **the writer's sources**

7 To write an article, a writer often uses different 'sources' to find information. Which of these sources (1–6) do you think were most useful for writing *Designs from nature*? Say which parts of the article used information from the sources.

1 photographs
2 interviews with people
3 biographies
4 questionnaires
5 books about the topic
6 articles in magazines

8 Work in pairs. Which sources would you use to write about these topics? Use the sources in Exercise 7 and your own ideas.

1 people's favourite type of everyday technology
2 famous inventors in history
3 new types of technology in the future

Speaking (my life)

9 Work in pairs. Do some research for a short article about different people's favourite technology (e.g. a smartphone). Prepare questions to ask people to find out about these things.

• what their favourite technology is
• how often they use it
• what it's used for
• its design (colour, shape, size)
• its manufacturer
• anything else that's important

10 Work with other pairs and interview them using your questions.

A: *What's your favourite piece of technology?*
B: *Definitely my phone. I love it! I take it everywhere!*

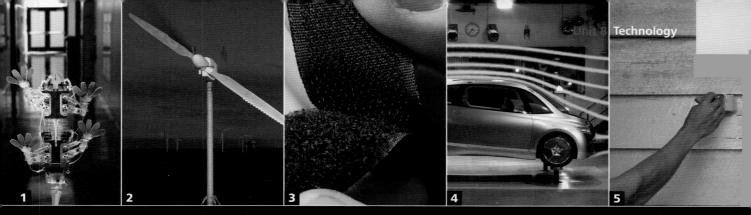

DESIGNS *from* NATURE

When we have a problem, nature often has the answer

▶ 66

In a room at Stanford University, scientists have a problem with their robot. It can walk up and down walls made of glass and plastic, but it can't walk upside down. So today they have a gecko in the room and they are studying how it walks. It's an amazing animal. Like the robot, it's very good at moving up and down trees, but the gecko can also walk upside down. In particular, the scientists are interested in the gecko's feet. They want to learn from its feet and use the same design on their robot.

Animals and plants can teach humans a lot about design and engineering. As a result, many engineers, scientists and designers spend time studying them. When they have a question, nature often has the answer. This science is called biomimetics. *Bio-* means 'living things' and *mimetics* means 'copying'. In other words, these scientists – or *biomimeticists* – depend on animals and plants to help them with design.

Two types of sea animals helped engineers in Canada and Germany. When engineers in Canada were working on improving wind turbines, they studied a whale's flippers because these animals move so easily through water. And when the car company Mercedes-Benz wanted to think of

a new design for a car, they looked at a boxfish. The result was a car that was very similar to the shape of a boxfish and that used less fuel than other cars.

The world of plants helped with the invention of Velcro and a new type of paint. In 1948, the Swiss engineer George de Mestral was walking in the countryside when he pulled a plant's bur from his trousers. He noticed how the bur stuck really well to his clothes, and so he had the idea of Velcro. And in 1982, Wilhelm Barthlott, an inventor who was studying the leaves of a lotus plant, noticed that water always ran off the leaf and it cleaned itself. Barthlott copied the leaf's design and produced a type of paint which stays cleaner than normal paint because the water and dirt run off it.

In conclusion, biomimetics has helped to design the modern world, and there are many more future possibilities. It might take a long time to discover all of them, because after all it has taken nature millions of years to design its animals and plants.

flipper (n) /'flɪpə(r)/ the flat arm or leg of a sea animal, used for swimming
bur (n) /bɜː/ a type of seed from a plant
zip (n) /zɪp/ two rows of metal, teeth-like parts which come together (e.g. on a coat)

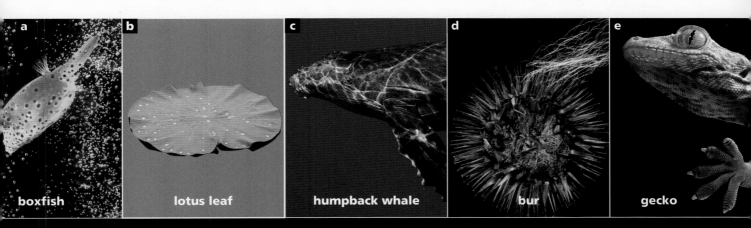

a boxfish
b lotus leaf
c humpback whale
d bur
e gecko

▶ PLANNING A TRIP ▶ A NEW INVENTION ▶ FAVOURITE TECHNOLOGY ▶ HOW SOMETHING WORKS

8d Gadgets

Vocabulary **instructions**

1 When you buy new technology for the first time, do you ever:

- read the instruction manual?
- watch a 'How to' video online?
- ask a friend for help?
- telephone a customer helpline?
- turn it on and see what happens?

2 Match the verbs (1–5) with the phrases (a–e) to make instructions. Then match the instructions with the pictures (A–E).

1	turn on	a	the battery
2	pull	b	the button
3	charge	c	the remote control
4	press	d	the lever forwards
5	push	e	the lever backwards

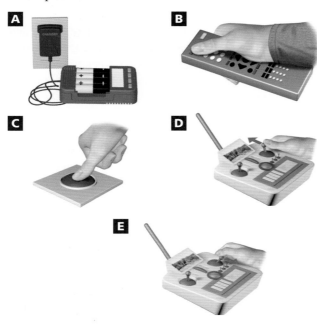

3 Pronunciation linking

a ▶ 67 A word ending with a consonant sound links to the next word if it starts with a vowel sound. Listen and practise saying these instructions.

1 Turn˗it˗on.
2 Charge˗it˗overnight.
3 Press˗it down.
4 Push˗it forwards.
5 Pull˗it back.

b Work in pairs. Think of items you often use at home or at work and make sentences using the verbs in Exercises 2 and 3a. Be careful with linking where necessary.

I turn˗on my mobile˗in the morning and charge˗it˗overnight.

Real life **finding out how something works**

4 ▶ 68 Listen to two people talking about a new gadget called a drone. Number the pictures in Exercise 2 in the order they talk about them (1–5).

5 ▶ 68 Read the list of expressions for finding out how something works. Then listen to the conversation again and tick the questions you hear.

> ▶ **FINDING OUT HOW SOMETHING WORKS**
>
> Can you show me how this works?
> Can you explain the instructions?
> Have you charged the battery?
> How do I turn it on?
> How did you do that? ✓
> What is this (other one) for? ✓
> What does this (one) do?
> What happens if I press this button? ✓
> How do you make it (record / go up)?

6 Work in pairs. Choose objects from the box or gadgets in your bag or in the school. Take turns to ask how they work.

> a computer game   your favourite app
> a mobile phone   a photocopier   a printer
> a tablet   a USB stick   a vending machine

A: *Can you show me how this works?*
B: *Yes. First of all, you need to turn it on, here.*

my life ▶ PLANNING A TRIP ▶ A NEW INVENTION ▶ IMPROVING DESIGN ▶ HOW SOMETHING WORKS
▶ USEFUL TECHNOLOGY

8e An argument for technology

Writing a paragraph

1 Read this paragraph. Where do you think it comes from? Choose the correct option (a–c).

a   an instruction manual
b   a report on energy in the workplace
c   a message to a colleague at work about the lighting

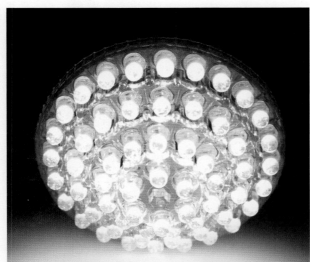

LED lighting is a very efficient form of modern lighting technology. Firstly, LED lighting lasts longer than normal lighting. For example, a normal light bulb lasts for around 5,000 hours. LED light bulbs last 100,000 hours. In addition, LED light bulbs change 80% of electricity into light. Normal bulbs only change 20% into light and the rest is heat. In other words, LED lights need less electricity to produce more light. On the other hand, LED lights are more expensive to buy than normal lights. However, you don't have to change them every year and they use less energy. As a result, they are cheaper over a long period of time.

2 Writing skill **connecting words**

a Look back at the highlighted connecting words in the paragraph in Exercise 1. Match the words with their uses (1–6).

1   to put ideas and sentences in order ___*firstly*___
2   to introduce contrasting information
    _____ , _____
3   to say the same thing in a different way
    _____
4   to add extra information to support your main idea _____
5   to introduce an example _____
6   to introduce a result _____

b Complete this paragraph with connecting words from Exercise 2a. Sometimes more than one is possible.

> Since the late twentieth century, the internet has completely changed our lives. [1] _____ , it has delivered information to every house with a computer. [2] _____ , you can type in any word and find thousands of pages on the subject. [3] _____ , with faster speeds, it can show videos and explain how things work. [4] _____ , some people think it can be dangerous, especially for young people. [5] _____ , if we teach people how to use it safely, then it's like having a library in your home. [6] _____ , I think every home should have internet access.

3 Read these notes for a paragraph about GPS technology. The notes give the main idea of the paragraph and arguments for and against. Write a paragraph using the notes and the connecting words from Exercise 2.

> GPS is a good idea for anyone who travels a lot
> • GPS maps are always up-to-date and correct
> • safer to use when driving
> • more expensive than a normal map
> • saves time (and money on petrol)

4 Choose one of these types of technology. Plan a paragraph about why it is useful. Make notes like the ones in Exercise 3.

> email   mobile phones   music downloads
> wireless technology   your own idea

5 Now write your paragraph. Use connecting words.

6 Exchange paragraphs with a partner. Does your partner's paragraph:

• introduce the main idea of the paragraph?
• give reasons why the technology is useful?
• use connecting words?

8f Ancient languages, modern technology

Using modern technology to record ancient
languages in Arunachal Pradesh, India

Before you watch

1 Look at the photo and read the caption. What kind of technology can you see? How do you think these people are using it?

2 Key vocabulary

Read the sentences. The words in bold are in the video. Match the words with the definitions (a–f).

1 Every two weeks, a language **disappears** and no one ever uses it again.
2 How much **awareness** is there of the problem?
3 Many languages could **die out** in the next few years because no one speaks them.
4 Humans can't **survive** if there isn't any water.
5 In recent years, there's been a **shift** in the way we communicate because of technology.
6 Don't **neglect** your school work over the holidays.

a stops existing
b change in something
c knowledge or understanding of a situation
d become less common and finally disappear
e forget about
f continue to live or exist in a difficult situation

While you watch

3 🎥 8.1 Watch the video and number these actions in the order they happen (1–4).

a The team go to a region in northeast India where there are many different languages.
b The three men leave but they hope that the local communities will use the technology kits.
c The team visit Australia to interview the last speaker of a language.
d The team visit a large village where the older people speak a language called Apatani.

4 🎥 8.1 Watch the video again and decide if the sentences are true (T) or false (F).

1 The aim of the National Geographic's Enduring Voices project is to help save ancient languages which are disappearing and dying out.
2 The Australian man speaks a language which people thought had already disappeared.
3 There used to be seven thousand known languages in the world, but now there are only half that amount.
4 One language disappears every two weeks around the planet.
5 In the end, Greg and David can't make the equipment work, so they don't record the speakers.
6 In the village, the young people aren't interested in learning new languages.
7 No one in the village speaks both English and Apatani.

8 Local people learn to use the technology kits, with a laptop computer, video cameras, and basic recording equipment.
9 The team hope people will keep their old language alive and speak it themselves.

After you watch

5 Vocabulary in context

🎥 8.2 Watch the clips from the video. Choose the correct meaning of the words and phrases.

6 Complete this paragraph about a language using words from the video.

> **National Geographic Enduring Voices Project**
> In North America there are between 150 and 170 ¹ k_____ languages. Many of these are native American languages which are ² d_____. Now, National Geographic Enduring Voices Project is trying to help native speakers save their languages so we don't lose them ³ f_____. They use special recording ⁴ e_____ to interview older people speaking the language, and try to translate some of the ⁵ b_____ words. As a result of this work, the language of Salish, which was dying out, has ⁶ s_____. A few years ago, only about 50 people aged over 75 spoke the language of Salish, but now the tribe offers courses in Salish and the children are ⁷ s_____ in the language.

7 Work in groups. Discuss some or all of these questions.

- Is your country's native language a global or important language? Why? / Why not?
- If your native language is dying out, how can you save it? How can technology help to save it?
- How much is your native language changing? For example, does it use any English words? (e.g. *computer*)
- How important is a global language like English in your country? Do most people speak or try to learn a second language like English?
- How useful is technology for learning and communicating in a new language?
- How do you use technology for learning English?

abandon (v) /əˈbændən/ stop using
hassle (n) /ˈhæs(ə)l/ an annoying or difficult situation
loss (n) /lɒs/ the state of no longer having something

Grammar

1 Complete the sentences with the present simple or *will* form of these verbs.

not call	not go	love	pass	press	work

1 When you _____ this button, the TV comes on.
2 If you put new batteries in, it _____ again.
3 When it's sunny, we _____ to go to the beach.
4 If he _____, we won't know what time to meet him.
5 I _____ hiking if the weather is bad.
6 If you work hard, you _____ the exam.

2 Complete the defining relative clauses with *who*, *which* or *where*.

1 The internet is an invention _____ has changed the modern world.
2 My best friend is someone _____ is always happy to see me.
3 They live in a place _____ there's no internet.
4 A satnav is something _____ tells you where you are.
5 Your teacher is someone _____ helps you learn English.
6 The space shuttle was the first spacecraft _____ travelled to from and to Earth.

3 ▶▶ MB Complete these sentences so they are true for you. Then work in pairs. Explain the sentences to your partner.

1 _____ is someone who is important in my life.
2 _____ is an invention which improves my life.

I CAN	
use zero and first conditionals	
use defining relative clauses	

Vocabulary

4 Complete the sentences with one word.

1 To s *et* up an account, create a password.
2 P_____ the button here.
3 Plug it in here to c_____ the battery.
4 This is a type of t_____ which flies and takes photographs.
5 I'm interested i_____ robots.
6 Use your email to l_____ in.
7 Did you s_____ the problem with your laptop?
8 I have a question a_____ this grammar.
9 We g_____ hungry at midday.
10 Do you like to p_____ video games?

5 ▶▶ MB Choose three more words from the unit. Write a sentence with each word, but miss out the key word. Then work in pairs. Take turns to read your sentences and guess the missing word.

I CAN	
talk about technology	
use dependent prepositions	

Real life

6 Put these words in the correct order to make questions.

1 switch / it / how / do / I / on?
2 if / I / happens / button? / press / this / what
3 can / me / you / how / this / works? / show
4 you / did / that? / do / how
5 charged / battery? / the / you / have
6 this / button / do? / what / does

7 Match these responses (a–e) with the questions (1–6) in Exercise 6. One response matches two questions.

a Sure. First, switch it on.
b Yes, I have. It should work now.
c It restarts it.
d By pressing this.
e You turn it off.

8 ▶▶ MB Work in pairs. Look at these two inventions from Unit 8. Try to describe:

- what they do.
- how they work.
- the different parts.

It's something which …. If you turn this, it …

I CAN	
find out how something works	
give instructions	

Zoltan Takacs is an explorer who studies snakes. This photo is in Micronesia.

FEATURES

1 Look at the photo of Zoltan Takacs. How do you think his holidays are similar to his working life?

2 ▶ 69 Listen to Zoltan and two other people talking. What is similar about their working life and their holidays?

3 ▶ 69 Listen again. Which accommodation and activities does each person talk about? Write the number of the speaker (1–3) with the words they use.

bed and breakfast	camper van	caravan	hotel	tent

camping	clubbing	diving	hiking	sightseeing	skiing
sunbathing					

4 Work in pairs. Ask and answer these questions about your holidays.

1 When was your last holiday?
2 Where did you go?
3 What type of accommodation did you stay in?
4 What activities did you do?
5 What do you think makes a good holiday?

9a Holiday stories

Reading

1 Work in groups. Have you ever had these problems or other problems on holiday? What did you do?

- It rained all the time.
- You missed your plane / train / bus / ferry.
- The hotel wasn't very good.
- You couldn't find your bag at the airport.
- You got lost when you went sightseeing.
- Your family or friends couldn't agree on what to do.

2 Read a story about a holiday. Why wasn't the tourist happy with her room? What did she do?

▶ 70

Holiday Stories

I was in a foreign country for the first time in my life. It had sounded amazing in the brochure: 'Enjoy seven days in one of the most beautiful cities in the world while staying at a luxury hotel.'

I had been excited about the trip, but now I wasn't so sure. I had waited at reception for fifteen minutes before someone checked me in. And my room was small and dark, with a window looking over a car park. I tried to be positive and I unpacked my bags. I decided to have a shower before going sightseeing. However, the shower wasn't working so I called hotel reception.

An hour later, an engineer arrived. He hit the pipes a few times. 'Sorry, but I cannot fix it today. Maybe, tomorrow.' Then he held out his hand. He wanted a tip for doing nothing! I was furious. But suddenly, I had a thought. He hadn't fixed my shower, but I gave him the money anyway. Two minutes later, I was at the reception desk. I explained the problem to the hotel manager and gave him a very large tip.

Fifteen minutes later, I moved into room 405. It was twice the size of room 308, it had a wonderful view of the city, a comfortable bed and, most importantly, there was water in the bathroom.

3 Read the story again. Number the events (a–i) in the order they happened (1–9).

a gave the manager a tip
b arrived at the hotel
c the engineer looked at the shower
d gave the engineer a tip
e booked the holiday
f tried to turn on the shower
g called reception
h moved to room 405
i waited at reception

4 When do people give tips in your country? How much do they give?

Vocabulary holiday collocations

5 Complete the sentences with these verbs.

book	call	check in	give	go	stay	unpack

1 I plan to .... **abroad** next year for the first time in my life.
2 When did you .... **your holiday**?
3 We hope to .... **at a hotel** in the centre of the city.
4 We need to .... **at reception**.
5 Let's .... **our bags** and then go sightseeing!
6 Can you .... **reception** and ask someone to come and clean the room?
7 Do you always .... **the waiter** a tip in this country?

6 Match these verbs to the groups of nouns.

book	get	go	rent	stay

1 .... : on a tour, clubbing, diving
2 .... : at home, on a campsite, out all night
3 .... : a table (in a restaurant), a flight, a ticket
4 .... : a car, an apartment, skis
5 .... : twenty days' holiday per year, sunburned, lost

Grammar past perfect simple

> **PAST PERFECT SIMPLE**
>
> 1 *I **had been** excited about the trip, but now I **wasn't** so sure.*
> 2 *He **hadn't fixed** my shower, but I **gave** him the money anyway.*
> Note: In informal English we often use *'d*.
> (*I'd been = I had been*)
>
> For further information and practice, see page 172.

7 Look at the grammar box. How do we form the past perfect simple?

8 Answer the questions (a–b) for each sentence (1–2) in the grammar box.

   a Which is the main action? Which action happened earlier?
   b Which verb is in the past simple and which is in the past perfect?

9 ▶ **71** Read this conversation between two friends about a holiday. Choose the correct options. Then listen and check your answers.

A: How was your holiday?
B: To be honest, I'm really happy to be home!
A: Why? What ¹ *happened / had happened*?
B: Well, on the first day at the hotel, someone stole my bag at the reception desk.
A: Did you catch the person?
B: No. He ² *ran / 'd run* out of the hotel entrance, so it was too late. The hotel ³ *reported / had reported* it to the police, but I never got it back. Fortunately, I ⁴ *packed / 'd packed* my passport and money in a different bag, so as soon as I ⁵ *bought / 'd bought* some new clothes I went sightseeing.
A: Great.
B: The rest of the holiday went well until the last evening. Suddenly there was no electricity in the hotel. I went to find the manager, but she ⁶ *left / 'd left* for the night. But luckily the assistant manager ⁷ *had / had had* some torches and candles and all the hotel guests sat in the reception area and sang traditional songs from their different countries. That was fun. In fact, that ⁸ *was / had been* probably the best night of the holiday!

10 Complete the sentences with the past simple or the past perfect simple.

   1 We landed late in London, so our connecting flight to Dubai _____ (leave) and we had to stay at the airport hotel.
   2 When my sister reached Rome, her luggage _____ (not arrive) and she spent an hour at lost luggage.
   3 The hotel hadn't expected them until the evening, so they _____ (go) for lunch while the hotel staff prepared the rooms.
   4 We _____ (not eat) for hours, but we finally arrived in the city centre and found a restaurant that was open.
   5 I realized I _____ (lose) my passport as soon as I put my hand in my pocket.
   6 As soon as they had met their friends, they _____ (have) a wonderful time.
   7 We'd had a wonderful meal, so we _____ (give) the waiter a big tip.
   8 I _____ (leave) my passport at home by mistake, so I had to go back.

11 Pronunciation *'d*

   ▶ **72** Listen to sentences 7 and 8 in Exercise 10. Notice the pronunciation of *'d*. Then listen again and repeat.

Speaking ⎯ my life

12 You are going to tell a story about a holiday. You can invent the story or it can be about something that happened to you or someone you know. Prepare five sentences about it using these ideas.

> A few weeks before the holiday, we had …
>
> When we got to the hotel / the airport …, we realized / we remembered that we had …
>
> One day, we'd just visited …
>
> On the last day …
>
> After we got home, we found that …

13 Work in pairs. Take turns to read your story to your partner and decide if your partner's story is real or not.

9b A different kind of holiday

Listening

1 Work in groups. Do you prefer travelling in a group or on your own?

2 ▶ 73 Listen to part of an interview about a different kind of holiday. Answer the questions.

1 What new job does Madelaine have?
2 What is she responsible for?

3 ▶ 73 Listen to the interview again. Are the sentences true (T) or false (F)?

1 Madelaine has done her first tour.
2 Madelaine is going to the Galápagos Archipelago for the first time.
3 Some people on the tour come on their own.
4 You have to do the same activities as other people in the group.
5 Madelaine thinks the holidays are expensive.

4 Would you like to go on one of Madelaine's holidays? Which parts of the world would you like to visit or work in?

Wordbuilding *-ed/-ing* adjectives

> ▶ **WORDBUILDING *-ed/-ing* adjectives**
>
> *I know that you're very **excited** about your new job.
> My first tour is very **exciting**.*
>
> For further practice, see Workbook page 75.

5 Look at the wordbuilding box. Answer these questions. Then find other *-ed* and *-ing* adjectives in the audioscript on page 187.

1 Which adjective describes how a person feels?
2 Which adjective describes a place, person or thing?

6 Choose the correct adjective.

A: So, how was your holiday?
B: I had an ¹*amazed / amazing* time. I'm so ²*bored / boring* to be back at work.
A: I'm sure. Where did you go exactly?
B: We went hiking in Patagonia! It's a ³*fascinated / fascinating* place.
A: Yes, I watched an ⁴*interested / interesting* TV programme about it once. The mountains there are enormous. It looked like a ⁵*frightened / frightening* place to climb.
B: Well, we had a fantastic guide so I wasn't ⁶*worried / worrying*. Though there was one man who was ⁷*annoyed / annoying* about all the climbing. He kept complaining and saying he was ⁸*tired / tiring* all the time.
A: Sounds like he booked the wrong holiday!

7 **Pronunciation number of syllables**

▶ 74 Listen to the sixteen adjectives from Exercise 6. Write the number of syllables you hear in each word. Then listen again and repeat.

1 *amazed (2), amazing (3)*

8 Work in pairs. Use *-ing* and *-ed* adjectives formed from these verbs to talk about the topics (1–6).

amaze	bore	excite	fascinate	interest
tire	worry			

1 a place you visited recently
2 a project you are working on
3 the last book you read
4 a person you met recently for the first time
5 a TV programme you saw last week
6 a present you received recently

*I recently visited London. I was **excited** because it was the first time I'd ever been, but in fact the trip was a bit **boring**.*

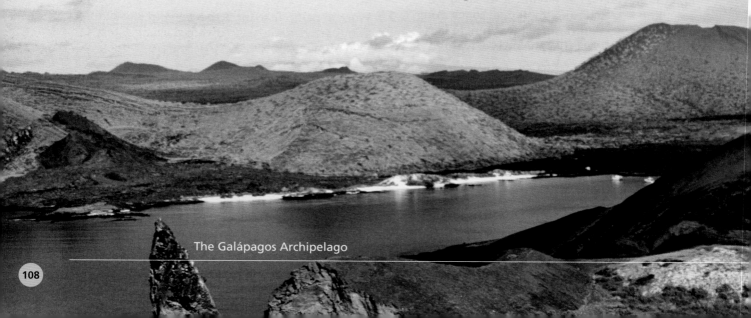

The Galápagos Archipelago

Grammar subject questions

> ▶ **SUBJECT QUESTIONS**
>
> **Subject questions**
> *Who books these types of holidays?*
> *How many people go on the tour?*
> *Who has been here before?*
> *What happened next?*
>
> **Other questions**
> *How much does it cost?*
> *When did you go on holiday?*
> *Where have you been today?*
> *Why did you choose this holiday?*
>
> For further information and practice, see page 172.

9 Look at the grammar box. Complete the rules (1–2).

1 In *subject questions / other questions*, the question word replaces the subject.
2 In subject questions, *we use / we do not use* the auxiliary verb *do* or *did*.

10 Choose the correct option to complete the questions.

1 How many students *study / do study* English in your class?
2 How many days *you stayed / did you stay* in the hotel?
3 Which artist *painted / did paint* the 'Mona Lisa'?
4 Where *you lived / did you live* when you were young?
5 What *happened / did happen*? I thought you were on holiday!
6 Which places *I should visit / should I visit* in Brazil?
7 Who *can you help / can help* me with my homework?
8 How much money *you take / did you take* with you?

11 ▶ 75 A group of four friends are planning their next holiday together. Complete their questions with the words in brackets and listen to check your answers.

Ryan: OK, so first of all, how much money
¹ _____ (we / want) to
spend this year?

Maggie: Not much! It needs to be cheap. How about going camping?

Ryan: Good idea. Who ² _____
(want) to go camping?

Adriana: Only if we can go somewhere hot!

Maggie: But we'll have to fly to go somewhere hot, and flying is expensive.

Peter: Who ³ _____ (have) a car? We could drive somewhere with the tents. That's cheaper than flying.

Ryan: I can probably borrow my brother's car. I drove to Spain last summer. It was really hot.

Adriana: Which cities ⁴ _____
(you / visit)?

Ryan: Barcelona and Madrid. I don't mind going again.

Maggie: Great. How many people
⁵ _____ (agree) with
going to Spain?

Speaking (my life)

12 Work in a group. Imagine you have won $1,000 from a travel magazine to spend on a group holiday, lasting a week. Ask each other questions about:

• the type of holiday you want to go on.
• the accommodation and places you want to visit.
• the types of activities (daytime and evening) you want to do.

Try to agree and plan a holiday which everyone in the group will enjoy.

9c Two sides of Paris

Reading

1 What tourist attractions is Paris famous for?

2 Read the article. What two parts of Paris is it about?

3 Read the first two paragraphs again and complete these notes about what a tourist can do in Paris. Use words from the article.

1 see famous art and ___*architecture*___
2 go up _____
3 visit _____
4 eat some of the best _____
5 go _____
6 choose from _____
7 visit tunnels called _____
8 walk down steps to see _____

4 Read the rest of the article. Choose the correct option (a–c) to answer these questions.

1 Are tourists allowed to go underground?
   a Yes, nowadays they can go everywhere.
   b It depends on where they want to go.
   c No, never.
2 Why are the tunnels dangerous?
   a They might fall down.
   b There are criminals down there.
   c The writer doesn't say.
3 How have people used other parts of the tunnels?
   a For somewhere to live.
   b For studying the architecture.
   c For fun and entertainment.
4 Why is it difficult to find Dominique and Yopie's room?
   a They never take anyone there.
   b The tunnels are very small and dark.
   c It isn't on a map.

Critical thinking **the author's purpose**

5 Work in pairs. Tick the three sentences which describe the author's purpose. Give reasons for your answers.

1 to compare and contrast two sides of Paris
2 to support the people who use the unofficial part of the tunnels
3 to suggest visiting some of the tunnels
4 to support the police in their work to stop people entering the tunnels
5 to inform the reader about something they don't know about
6 to criticize people who use the unofficial tunnels

Word focus *place*

6 Read these sentences from the article. Match the phrases in bold in the sentences (1–3) with the uses and meanings (a–c).

1 After a busy morning, it's time to find **a good place to** eat.
2 It's **no place for** anyone who is frightened of the dark or small places.
3 Theatre performances sometimes **take place** here.

a to advise certain people not to go somewhere
b to say something happens
c to recommend somewhere

7 Work in pairs. Ask and answer these questions about your town or city.

1 Is it a place where there are lots of things for tourists to do? Why? / Why not?
2 Where are the best places for tourists to go sightseeing and shopping?
3 What special events take place every year?

Speaking ⟨ my life ⟩

8 Work in pairs. Plan a two-minute presentation for a group of tourists about the place you live or a place you know well. List what tourists can see and do there, using some of these ideas.

- art galleries
- cafes and restaurants
- good places for sightseeing
- museums
- nightclubs
- places with a good view (e.g. a tower)
- shopping
- special events
- theatres

9 Work with another pair. Take turns to give your presentation. Try to convince the other pair to visit your place.

It's a place where there are lots of things to do for tourists. For example, lots of different festivals take place here …

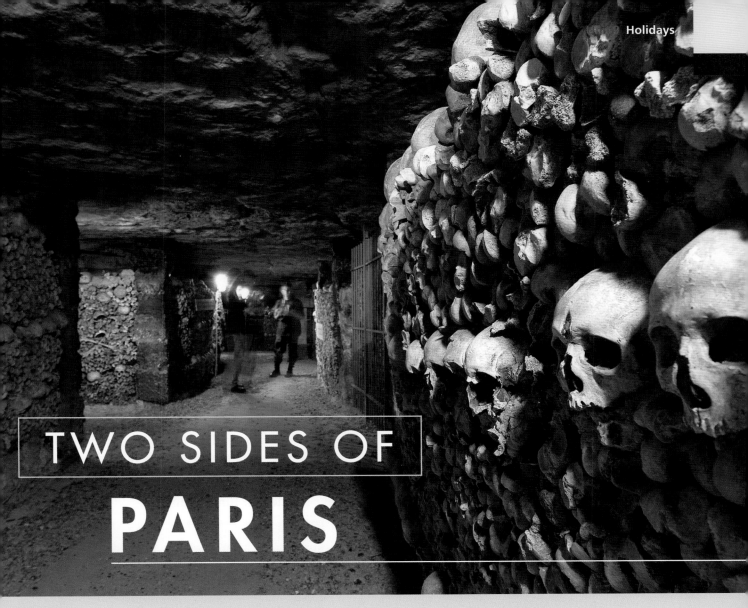

TWO SIDES OF PARIS

▶ 76

When tourists visit Europe, Paris is usually top of their list. It's a city where you can see some of the most famous art and architecture in the world. Most tour groups start by going up the Eiffel Tower for a view of the city, or they
5 visit a museum or art gallery. After a busy morning, it's time to find a good place to eat. There's nothing better than sitting outside a café or restaurant in Paris, watching people walking by, and eating some of the best food in the world. The city is also famous for its fashion, so after
10 lunch it's time for some shopping. And in the evening, there's a huge number of theatres and nightclubs to choose from.

That's the city that most tourists see when they visit Paris. But there is another amazing part of Paris you
15 could visit – and it's underground. Paris has hundreds of kilometres of tunnels. Tourists can visit part of these tunnels called the catacombs, where over six million people were buried in the nineteenth century. 'Normal' tourists are allowed here, but you have to walk down two
20 hundred steps and through long, dark corridors to see the bones and skeletons. Some tourists have even paid to stay down here overnight.

However, this public part of the tunnels is quite small. There are another 250 kilometres of the tunnels which are
25 closed to the public. They are dangerous and the police don't want people to go down there. Nevertheless, a lot of people find their way into these tunnels through secret entrances. The police often search the area and once they found a cinema down here. It's well known that art shows and theatre
30 performances sometimes take place in the tunnels, and that they are popular with university students for parties.

There are 'unofficial' tours of the tunnels with tour guides like Dominique and Yopie (not their real names). If you pay, they will take you deep underground. It's no place for anyone who
35 is frightened of the dark or small places. The stone tunnels are small and it's easy to hit your head on the ceiling. After two hours you arrive in a room which isn't on any official map. Yopie and his friends built it. It's comfortable and clean with a table and chairs, and a bed. Yopie says there are many other
40 rooms like this under Paris. 'Many people come down here to party, some people to paint. We do what we want here.'

skeleton (n) /'skelɪt(ə)n/ the bones of a human or animal

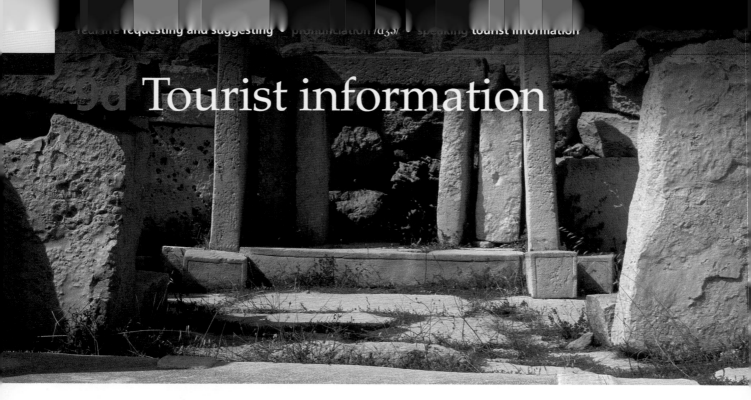

Tourist information

Real life requesting and suggesting

1 Work in pairs. Look at the information brochure for the Tarxien temples. Would you visit this kind of place on holiday? Why? / Why not?

2 There is information missing in the brochure. What questions can you ask to get the information (1–5)?

1 What days is it open? / Is it open today?

3 ▶ 77 Listen to a conversation at the tourist information office. Complete the information about the Tarxien temples.

4 ▶ 77 Look at the expressions for requesting and suggesting. Listen to the conversation again and tick the expressions you hear.

> ▶ **REQUESTING AND SUGGESTING**
>
> **Requesting information**
> I'm interested in visiting …
> Do you know the opening times? / What time does it open / close?
> Could you tell me the price? / How much is it?
> Is there any public transport? How often does the bus go?
> Are there any … ?
>
> **Suggesting options**
> How about … -ing
> You can also …
> Another option is to …
> Or you could take …

5 Pronunciation /dʒə/

a ▶ 78 Listen to these two questions. How does the speaker pronounce the first two words?
Do you know the opening times?
Could you tell me the price?

b ▶ 78 Listen again and repeat the questions.

6 Work in pairs. Take turns to be a tourist and a person at tourist information.

Student A: Turn to page 155.

Student B: Turn to page 154.

The Tarxien Temples in Malta

Information for visitors

This is a UNESCO World Heritage Site. The four Tarxien temples are around 5,000 years old.

Address: Neolithic Temple Street, Tarxien

Opening times: Open from [1] _____ to Sunday, from 10 a.m. to [2] _____ p.m. (Last admission at 4.30 p.m.)

Tickets: Book in advance or buy at the entrance

Adults: € 6.00
12 to 17-year-olds, seniors (over 65) and students: € [3] _____
Children (6–11): €3.00
Infants (5 and under): Free

Official guided tour: €20.00 with tour guide and lasts [4] _____ hours

Transport to the site: Buses every hour from the [5] _____

112

my life ▶ A HOLIDAY STORY ▶ THE HOLIDAY OF A LIFETIME ▶ A PLACE YOU KNOW ▶ **TOURIST INFORMATION** ▶ A FORMAL EMAIL

9e Requesting information

Writing an email requesting information

1 When you want to go on holiday, how do you find out information about the holiday? (e.g. online, from a travel agent, by email or phone)

2 Read the email and answer the questions.

1 What is the writer's reason for writing?
2 What two things does he want to know?

> Dear Sir or Madam,
>
> I am writing to request more information about the 'Explorer's Holidays' on your website. In particular, could you provide me with more details of your next tour to Alaska?
>
> Currently, the website says that you will confirm the exact dates of tours for next year in the near future. I would be grateful if you could inform me as soon as they become available.
>
> My second question is about accommodation. It seems to include camping and staying in hotels, but the information on the site is not very clear. I would like to receive more details about this.
>
> Thank you in advance for providing this information.
>
> I look forward to hearing from you.
>
> Best regards,
>
> William P Faversham

3 Writing skill **formal expressions**

Find formal expressions in the email that have a similar meaning to these informal expressions.

Starting
1 Hi
2 It's about …

Requesting more information
3 Can you send me …?
4 Please tell me …
5 when you have them
6 I'd like to get …

Ending
7 Thanks for the information.
8 Hope to hear from you soon.
9 All the best

4 Circle any contracted forms (e.g. *I'm, it's, you're*) in the email and in Exercise 3. Do we use contracted forms more in formal or informal writing?

5 Choose the more formal option.

1 *I'm writing to ask for / I am writing to request* more information about your product.
2 *I would be grateful if you could / Can you* send an up-to-date price list.
3 *I would also like / I also want* a copy of the holiday brochure.
4 *Thanks / Thank you* for your *help / assistance*.
5 *I'll tell / I will inform* you when they are *ready / available*.
6 *Could you confirm / Please let me know* when *I will receive / I'll get* the payment.
7 *Hope to hear / I look forward to hearing* from you soon.

6 You have looked at a holiday website for cruises around the coast of South America. Write an email to the tour company and request information about:

1 how long the cruise lasts (in weeks).
2 when and where the cruise starts and ends.
3 the cost of a cabin.

7 Exchange emails with your partner. Has your partner used formal expressions?

Living in Venice

For tourists in Venice, Italy, a
gondola is the best way to travel

Before you watch

1 Work in pairs. Look at the photo of Venice and answer the questions.

1 Why do you think Venice is popular with tourists?
2 What do you think it's like to live and work in Venice?

2 Key vocabulary

Read the sentences. The words in bold are used in the video. Match the words with the definitions (a–g).

1 The **traders** at the market have lots of different food and local products.
2 Young people have to **face the challenge** of finding their first job.
3 My father is a **gondolier.** He takes tourists round Venice.
4 You can't buy a place to live because **property** costs a lot of money.
5 Many young people **move away** to more modern cities.
6 Did you ever **get to** meet anyone famous?
7 Good health is a **gift** in life – especially as you get older!

a a person who sails a traditional boat in Venice called a 'gondola'
b leave one place to live in another
c buildings that people own (e.g. houses, apartments)
d people who buy and sell things
e deal with the difficulties
f a present or something you are lucky to have
g have the opportunity to

While you watch

3 ▭◀ 9.1 Watch the video. Number these things (a–f) in the order you see them (1–6).

a a trader preparing vegetables
b early morning in the Piazza San Marco
c sunset in Venice
d musicians playing violins
e a gondola
f a man jogging

4 ▭◀ 9.1 Watch the video again and answer these questions about living in Venice.

1 When is the best time of day for shopping in the outdoor markets?
2 How does Fabrizio Copano describe Venice?
3 What is happening to the population?
4 What is particularly expensive in Venice?
5 What does Giovanni dal Missier say about the tourists?
6 What sort of jobs do most people do in Venice?
7 How does Gino Penzo describe the cities of Florence and Rome?

After you watch

5 ▭◀ 9.2 Vocabulary in context

Watch the clips from the video. Choose the correct meaning of the words and phrases.

6 Work in pairs. Ask and answer these questions about a town or city you know well.

1 Is it clean and easy to live in, with a high quality of life?
2 How expensive is property and housing?
3 Is it difficult to earn a living there?
4 Do you think young people are moving away? If so, why?

7 Work in pairs. You are going to practise a conversation between a tourist and a tour guide.

Student A: You are a tour guide showing a visitor your town or city. Make notes about these things.

• the best places to see
• good places to eat
• good places for shopping and entertainment

Student B: You are a tourist visiting your partner's town or city. Find out what it's like to live there. Look at these ideas and prepare questions to ask your tour guide.

• the best places to see
• the advantages of living in the town or city
• the disadvantages of living in the town or city

8 Change roles and have another conversation.

---

advantages (n) /əd'vɑːntɪʤɪz/ good things
crowd (n) /kraʊd/ many people in the same place
disadvantages (n) /'dɪsədvɑːntɪʤɪz/ bad things
huge (adj) /hjuːʤ/ very big
increase (v) /ɪn'kriːs/ get bigger

UNIT 9 REVIEW AND MEMORY BOOSTER

Grammar

1 Complete the conversation with the past simple or the past perfect simple.

A: How was your holiday?
B: It was fine, in the end.
A: Why? What ¹_____ (happen)?
B: Well, when we ²_____ (arrived) at the hotel they were full and so we ³_____ (not / have) a room.
A: Oh no! Why ⁴_____ you (not / book) the hotel?
B: I had! But someone ⁵_____ (make) a mistake with the reservation. Anyway, they ⁶_____ (got) us rooms in another hotel, but it was in another town.
A: So what ⁷_____ you (do)?
B: Well, I was really angry after everything that ⁸_____ (happen), but the manager ⁹_____ (paid) for a taxi to the other hotel.
A: That was nice.

2 ▶▶ MB Work in pairs. These phrases are from the Holiday Story on page 106. Try to remember and tell the story using them.

> one of the most beautiful cities in the world
> waited at reception for 15 minutes
> was small and dark   decided to have a shower
> wasn't working   an engineer arrived
> 'I cannot fix it'   a tip for doing nothing
> explained the problem to the hotel manager
> moved into room 405

3 Choose the correct option to complete the questions. Which are subject questions?

1 How many tourists *visit / do visit* your town or city every year?
2 What places *photograph they / do they photograph*?
3 Where *they usually stay / do they usually stay*?
4 Who *shows / do show* the tourists round the city?
5 How much *costs a tour / does a tour cost*?

I CAN	
use the past perfect	
use subject questions and other questions	

Vocabulary

4 Complete each sentence with a pair of verbs.

check in + get	pay + give	call + book	unpack + go

1 When you _____ the bill, remember to _____ the waiter a tip.
2 Can you _____ the restaurant and _____ a table?
3 Let's _____ our bags and _____ sightseeing.
4 First, _____ at the airport and then _____ on the plane.

5 Complete the adjectives with *-ing* or *-ed*.

1 What's the matter? Do you feel bor_____?
2 This book is very interest_____ .
3 We had an amaz_____ time in Peru.
4 Stop being annoy_____ and leave me alone!
5 This film is so excit_____ !
6 I'm really frighten_____ of the dark!

I CAN	
talk about holidays	

Real life

6 ▶▶ MB Work in pairs. Look at the photos. What can you remember about these places? Discuss the questions.

1 Where are these places?
2 What do you think you can you see there?

7 Put these words in the correct order.

1 interested / caves / the / in / visiting / I'm
2 know / do / you / opening / the / times?
3 another / is / to / a / option / take / taxi
4 tell / could / you / the / me / price?
5 about / tour? / a / taking / how / sightseeing
6 bus / often / how / does / the / go?
7 you / could / family / ticket / buy / a

8 ▶▶ MB Work in pairs. Practise a conversation.

Student A: You are the tourist. Ask about a museum.

Student B: You work at tourist information. Answer the questions and suggest options.

I CAN	
request information	
suggest options	

Unit 10 Products

Selling baskets in Hung Yen, Vietnam

FEATURES

1 Look at the photo. What products is the man selling? What do you think they are used for?

2 ▶ 79 Listen to part of a radio programme about the man in the photo. Answer the questions.

   1 Where does he make his baskets?
   2 Who are his customers? Why do they buy them?
   3 Where does he sell the baskets?

3 Do you usually buy things from small local producers and sellers? Or do you normally buy products from big, international companies?

4 Work in pairs. Tell your partner about the last things you bought, e.g. clothing, a book, something online. Answer these questions for each product.

   • What was it?
   • Where did you buy it?
   • Why did you buy it?
   • Do you know what company made it?
   • Do you know where it was made?

10a A lesson in logos

Reading

1 Look at the product in the photo. Do you recognize the logo on the laptop? What is wrong with it? Read the article and check your ideas.

▶ 80

A LESSON IN LOGOS

A logo is how people recognize your company. When you see a tick logo on an advertisement, for example, you know it's Nike sportswear. The gold 'M' on red says 'McDonalds'. And everyone knows who made the technology you are using when it has an apple on it.

The Apple logo is one of the simplest but most successful logos in the world. Apple products are used in millions of homes and offices. Over five hundred iPhones are sold every minute and the company makes more than two hundred billion dollars a year. An Apple product is recognized by people all over the world because of its design and the famous logo.

However, when the first Apple laptops were produced in 1999, Apple realized they had a problem with their logo. When the laptop was put on a table, the customer saw the Apple logo on the top of the laptop. But when the laptop was open, the logo was upside down. This wasn't a problem for the person using the laptop, but it didn't look good to other people. In the end, the logo was turned round so that the logo was seen correctly by other people.

Why was it so important to Apple? Because when you see other people using a product, you are more likely to buy it.

2 Read the article again. Are these sentences true (T) or false (F)?

1 The writer thinks everyone knows about Apple products.
2 On the first laptops, the company didn't use the Apple logo.
3 When you closed the first laptops, you saw the logo upside down.
4 On modern Apple laptops, other people can see the logo correctly when you are using it.
5 If we see other people doing something, we often copy them.

3 Discuss these questions as a class.

1 Do you agree with the last sentence in the article? Is it true for you? Why? / Why not?
2 How important do you think logos are? Do they make you buy products?

Wordbuilding word forms

4 Match these word forms with the definitions (1–5).

advert   advertise   advertisement   advertiser
advertising

1 (verb) to tell the public about a product, job or service
2 (noun) short for the word *advertisement*
3 (noun) a person or company that advertises
4 (noun) a notice, picture or film telling people about a product, job or service
5 (noun) the activity of telling the public about a product, job or service

> ▶ **WORDBUILDING word forms**
>
> When you learn a new word, try to learn its other forms. Use a dictionary to help you.
> *produce* (v), *product* (n), *productive* (adj), *production* (n), *producer* (person / company)
>
> For further practice, see Workbook page 83.

5 Look at the wordbuilding box. Complete these sentences with the correct form of *produce*.

1 I work for Mercedes and we _____ cars and other vehicles.
2 Coca-cola is one of the most famous _____ in the world.
3 Wine _____ in France are worried about low sales this year.
4 My brother works in video _____ . He makes videos for online advertising.
5 I've had a very _____ day and I've finished all my work.

6 Pronunciation stress in different word forms

a ▶ 81 Listen and underline the stressed syllables in these words. Notice how the stress sometimes changes in the different word forms.

> advert   advertise   advertiser   advertising
> advertisement   product   produce   producer
> productive   production

b ▶ 81 Listen again and repeat the words.

Grammar the passive

> ▶ **THE PASSIVE**
>
> **Present simple passive**
> 1 *An Apple product **is recognized** by people all over the world.*
> 2 *Apple products **are used** in millions of homes.*
>
> **Past simple passive**
> 3 *The first Apple laptops **were produced** in 1999.*
> 4 *The logo **was turned** round.*
>
> For further information and practice, see page 174.

7 Look at the sentences in the grammar box. Answer these questions.

   a In a passive sentence we use the past participle of the main verb. What other verb do we use?
   b Compare sentence 1 with this active sentence:
      People all over the world recognize an Apple product.
      In which sentence is *people* the subject and in which sentence is *an Apple product* the subject?
   c Sentences 2, 3 and 4 don't say who does the action. Why is this?
   d Sentence 1 says who does the action. Which word introduces this?

8 Complete the information about YouTube with the present simple passive and the past simple passive form of the verbs.

> ## YouTube in numbers
>
> • Six billion hours of YouTube video
>   ¹ _____ (watch) every month.
> • Four hundred hours of video ² _____ (uploaded) every minute.
> • The first YouTube video ³ _____ (call) 'Me at the zoo'. It ⁴ _____ (make) by Jawed Karim in 2005.
> • Ten years ago, the site ⁵ _____ (visit) by 20 million people per month. Today, the YouTube website ⁶ _____ (used) by 1.3 billion people per month.
> • YouTube ⁷ _____ (sell) in 2006 and now it ⁸ _____ (own) by Google.

9 Read about another logo. Choose the correct option.

> In the world of business, logos ¹ *design / are designed* very carefully. Millions of dollars ² *spend / are spent* on them, because logos ³ *put / are put* on every advertisement and often on products too. Customers often ⁴ *prefer / are preferred* products with a famous logo.
> So when companies ⁵ *try / are tried* to change their logo they have to be very careful. Gap is a good example of how companies sometimes ⁶ *make / are made* mistakes with logos. Gap clothes ⁷ *buy / are bought* all over the world and the simple blue logo ⁸ *recognize / is recognized* on every high street. However, in 2010, the company ⁹ *decided / was decided* to change the logo.
> Many of its customers ¹⁰ *complained / were complained*, and a week later, the company ¹¹ *changed / was changed* the logo back. The company hadn't realized how much its logo ¹² *loved / was loved* by its customers.

10 Complete these sentences so they are true for you. Use the passive form of the verb.

   1 My bag _____ (make) in _____ . (which country?)
   2 My favourite film _____ (direct) by _____ . (who?)
   3 My home _____ (build) in _____ . (when?)
   4 My favourite book _____ (write) by _____ . (which author?)

Speaking ⟨ my life ⟩

11 Work in pairs. Take turns to choose a type of product from the list. Think of a famous product or a product you often buy. Your partner has to ask a maximum of ten questions and guess the company. Use the ideas below or your own ideas.

> a drink   a car   clothes   furniture   technology

> Was it invented in this country?
> Where is it made?
> How is it normally sold? (e.g. in shops, online)
> Can you describe the logo?
> Is the product a fizzy drink?

A: **Was it invented** *in this country?*
B: *No,* **it was invented** *in the USA.*

10b Product design

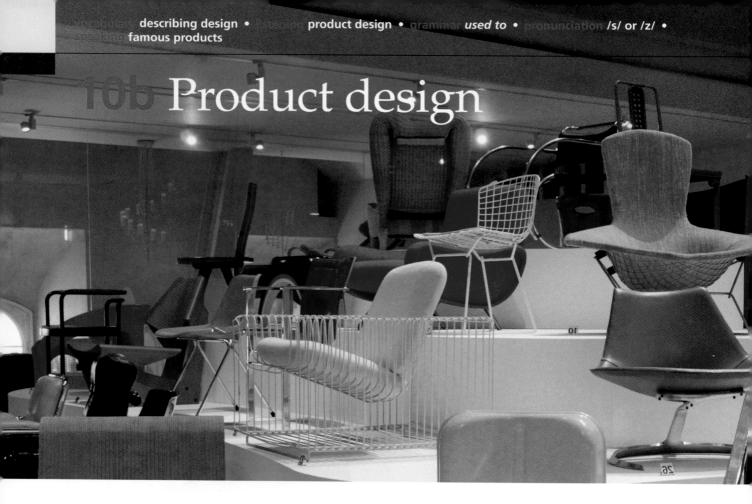

Vocabulary describing design

1 Read the sentences (1–7). Match the adjectives in bold to the definitions (a–g).

1 You don't need to read the instructions because it's so **user-friendly**.
2 I know my clothes are **old-fashioned**, but I can't afford anything new.
3 I still use the same phone I had five years ago. It looks very **basic** but it works.
4 I can sell you this one now, but a more **up-to-date** model comes out in three weeks.
5 That style of dress is very **fashionable** this summer. Everyone's wearing it.
6 I like her taste in clothes. She always wears **classic** designs.
7 My mother gave me this bag. It's very **useful** because it holds everything.

a simple, not complicated
b it does a good job
c easy to learn how to use
d simple and traditional but always in fashion
e out-of-date, not modern
f the latest or newest
g popular at the moment

2 Work in pairs. Use the adjectives from Exercise 1 to describe the designs of objects:

- in the photo.
- in your bag.
- in your classroom.

Listening

3 How do you listen to music? Do you use:

1 records?
2 cassettes?
3 CDs?
4 downloads?
5 streaming?

4 ▶ 82 Listen to a radio programme about a famous product called the Sony Walkman. Which things from Exercise 3 did it play?

5 ▶ 82 Listen again. Read the questions and choose the correct option (a–c).

1 What does the speaker say about listening to music in the seventies?
   a People didn't listen to as much music as they do now.
   b You couldn't listen to music on your way to school or work.
   c Music wasn't as good and it's better nowadays.
2 What showed that the Sony Walkman was successful, according to the speaker?
   a Lots of people bought it.
   b Other companies copied it.
   c It was in the English dictionary.
3 Why did some people think the Sony Walkman was a crazy idea?
   a It didn't look very stylish.
   b It didn't do lots of different things.
   c It was too small.

Grammar *used to*

> ▶ **USED TO**
>
> People **used to buy** music on vinyl records.
> My mother **used to have** a Sony Walkman.
> We **didn't use to download** music.
> **Did** you **use to buy** CDs?
>
> For further information and practice, see page 174.

6 Look at the grammar box. What form of the verb follows *used to*?

7 Compare this sentence with the sentences in the grammar box. Answer the questions (1–2).
He bought his first record in 1973.

1 Which form do we use to describe a single action at a specific time in the past?
2 Which form do we use to describe a habit in the past which is not true now?

8 Underline the best option.

1 I *used to / use to* buy CDs but now I download all my music.
2 We *used to go / went* to our first music concert when we were fourteen.
3 Musicians *used to play / played* live all the time but nowadays they spend more time in recording studios.
4 My brother *didn't use to / didn't use* have long hair, but he grew it when it became fashionable.
5 I *didn't use to learn / didn't learn* the guitar until I was twelve years old.
6 My parents *didn't use to take / didn't take* me to concerts, but I go every week now.
7 Did you *use / used* to like this song?
8 When did you *move / use to move* to England?

9 Pronunciation /s/ **or** /z/

a ▶ 83 Listen and read the sentences. Notice the pronunciation of the words *use* and *used*. Which words have the sound /s/ and which have the sound /z/?

I **used** to buy CDs but I didn't **use** to buy records. Nowadays, I **use** my mobile phone to download music.

b ▶ 83 Listen again and repeat the sentences.

10 Complete the sentences with *used to*, *didn't use to* or *did you use to* and the verb given.

1 My family _____ (spend) every summer on a boat. It was great.
2 I _____ (eat) vegetables when I was a child, but I love them now.
3 _____ (you / have) a camera before you got that mobile phone?
4 My sister _____ (play) the guitar in a rock band when she was younger. They sounded terrible, but she loved it!
5 He _____ (earn) much money compared to what he earns nowadays. His current job is really well-paid.
6 _____ (you / write) letters before email was invented?

Speaking ⟨ my life ⟩

11 Write five true sentences about your past with *used to* or *didn't use to*. Then write the question form.

*I **used to** play the guitar. **Did** you **use to** play the guitar?*
*I **didn't use to** like vegetables. **Did** you **use to** like vegetables?*

12 Work in pairs. Ask and answer your questions from Exercise 11. Find similarities and differences between you and your partner.

A: *Did you use to play the guitar?*
B: *No, I didn't use to play the guitar, but I used to play the piano.*
A: *Did you use to like vegetables?*
B: *Yes, I did.*

10c Is stuff winning?

Reading

1 Read this conversation between two people. Answer the questions.

1 Where do you think it is happening?
2 Who is the conversation between?

> A: This room is so untidy. There's too much **stuff** everywhere.
> B: I know. I'll tidy it but I don't have anywhere to put some of these **things**.
> A: Well let's throw some of it away. For example, what's this **thing**?
> B: No, don't throw that away. I like to keep **stuff** like that, just in case.

2 Look at the words *stuff* and *thing* in the conversation. Which is countable? Which is uncountable?

3 Look at the photo on page 123. Is your home full of stuff like this? Or is it very tidy with only a few things?

4 Read the article quickly. What is the article mainly about? Choose the best option (a–c).

a Some people are buying too much stuff and need to spend less.
b Some people are bored because they have nothing to do.
c Some people are trying to have less stuff in their lives.

5 These sentences are missing from the ends of the paragraphs in the article. Read the article again and match the sentences with the paragraphs (1–5).

a They buy more stuff in order to avoid getting bored.
b All these people are interested in how they can also have a 'minimalist' life.
c Maybe one way to begin is by going offline for fifteen minutes a day and seeing if you feel better!
d And by the end of the month, you have thrown away lots of your stuff.
e I also need to reply to a few text messages from work.

Critical thinking **fact or opinion?**

6 Look at the sentences (1–6) from the article. Which sentences:

a give facts?
b give the author's opinion?
c report other people's opinion?

1 The email inbox shows 243 unread emails.
2 The good news is that now there is an excellent website to help people like me.
3 When Ryan Nicodemus and Joshua Fields Millburn set up this website, they had 52 visitors in the first month.
4 Some people also think that there is a problem with having lots of stuff in our heads.
5 People said they were bored of watching TV.
6 We should also have less stuff in our heads.

7 Work in pairs. Underline the words in Exercise 6 which helped you to answer. Which types of words or phrases did you underline:

1 for factual information?
2 for opinions and reporting opinions?

8 Look at the article again. Which statement (a–c) do you agree with? Give reasons for your answer.

a On the whole, the article is based on facts and results.
b On the whole, the article is based on the writer's opinion and the opinions of others.
c On the whole, the article is a good balance of fact and opinion.

Speaking ⟨ my life ⟩

9 Work in pairs. Prepare a short presentation to convince other people to have less stuff in their homes or to spend less time online. Use ideas from the article and add your own opinions. Include these points.

• Present the problem.
• Present the reasons.
• Present the solutions.

10 Work with another pair. Take turns to give your presentations and convince the other pair of your opinions.

Today we'd like to talk to you about the stuff in your home. Do you spend time every day at the shops or online buying more things?

IS STUFF WINNING?

▶ 84

I bought another book today and have put it on a pile of unread books on my new coffee table. There's no more space on the table, which also has digital devices, coffee cups, and some socks I need to put away in my bedroom. But my bedroom is also full of stuff. I pick up my phone. The email inbox shows 243 unread emails. I've already missed three calls this morning.

I know that I want less stuff in my life, but at the moment the stuff is winning. I seem to spend all my time buying things, and then putting them away, when really I'd like more time for family, friends and hobbies. The good news is that now there is an excellent website to help people like me, called The Minimalists. When Ryan Nicodemus and Joshua Fields Millburn set up this website, they had 52 visitors in the first month. Two years later, it has over two million visitors a month.

Ryan Nicodemus explains how it began. He was working between sixty and eighty hours a week and spending his free time buying more products to make himself feel better. One day, he decided to start working fewer hours and to get rid of all his stuff. After a while, he realized he was much happier and he wanted to share his ideas with others. So he set up the website with Joshua to give advice to other people about how to become 'minimalist'. On the website there are blog posts and lots of practical ideas. One of their ideas is to play the thirty-day minimalism game. On day one you throw out, sell, recycle or give away one object in your life. Then on day two, two objects. On day three, three objects.

In the same way that stuff can fill the space in our homes, some people think that there is a problem with having lots of stuff in our heads. Often people go online because they don't want to be doing nothing, so they keep their brains busy with unnecessary activities. According to a recent survey, most people born between 1980 and 2000 use their phones when they have nothing else to do: 46% check their social media, 43% play games, and a fifth do some online shopping.

In the same survey, some people said they were bored with their screens and online life; for example, 27% of them said they were bored of watching TV and 14% were bored of social media. So perhaps we need more time without all these devices and, like Nicodemus and Milburn who have less stuff in their homes, we should also have less stuff in our heads.

---

minimal (adj) /ˈmɪnɪm(ə)l/ very small in size or number
minimalist (n) /ˈmɪnɪməlɪst/ a person who uses a small number of things or simple ideas in their work and life

10d Website design

Vocabulary websites

1 Complete the sentences with these words.

> about us   adverts   contact   content   home
> links   search

1 The _____ page is the first page you see on a website.
2 Good websites have _____ to other pages and to other websites.
3 You can send a message on a website using the _____ page.
4 The _____ page has information about the company or the person who has the website.
5 Some websites have _____ which appear on the top or the side of the screen. They can be really annoying!
6 Visitors want to read and watch up-to-date _____ on a website.
7 The _____ box helps you find specific information more quickly.

2 Work in groups. Discuss the questions.

1 Which websites do you visit when you want to do these things?

  - search for information
  - listen to music
  - find the translation of a word into English
  - buy clothes, books or music
  - find out the latest news

2 Why do you prefer these websites?
3 What do you think makes one website better than another?

Real life giving your opinion

3 ▶ 85 Sergio and Rachel own a shop called Retake Records, which sells second-hand records and CDs. They are planning a new website for online customers. Tick the topics they discuss (1–8).

1 the name of the website
2 the home page
3 the contact page
4 a search box
5 product information
6 links to other sites
7 the 'about us' page
8 ways of paying

4 ▶ 85 Listen again and complete the sentences.

1 Great. I think we _____ buy it today.
2 Let me show you. What do you _____?
3 I see what you _____, but we can have a photo of the shop at the top.
4 In my _____ it's more important that people see the records for sale.
5 R: Also it needs a search box so they can find the record they want.
  S: Yes, you're _____.
6 R: Lots of other websites have an 'about us' page. _____ you could put the text there?
  S: Good _____.
7 S: Also, I think we could have a video of the shop on the page, with both of us talking about who we are and what we do.
  R: Yes, I _____.
8 I'm not _____ about that. Regular customers will want to call or email us …

5 Look at the expressions for discussing opinions and check your answers from Exercise 4.

> ▶ **DISCUSSING OPINIONS**
>
> **Asking for an opinion**
> What do you think?
> What's your opinion?
>
> **Giving your opinion**
> I think we should …
> In my opinion …
> I'm not sure about …
>
> **Agreeing and disagreeing**
> I agree. / You're right. / Good idea.
> I see what you mean, but …
> I disagree. / I don't agree.
>
> **Making suggestions**
> Maybe you could …
> I suggest you …

6 Work in groups. You are going to plan a new website. Discuss these questions. Use the expressions for discussing opinions.

1 What are you going to sell from your website?
2 What is the name of your business?
3 What pages do you need?
4 How will you show your product on the page?
5 What else will you have (e.g. videos)?

7 Present your plans to the rest of the class.

▷ **my life** ▶ PRODUCTS I BUY ▶ HABITS IN THE PAST ▶ USING LESS STUFF ▶ **DISCUSSING OPINIONS**
▶ A REVIEW

10e A review

Writing a review

1 Read the review of a website and answer the questions.

1 What is the purpose of the website?
2 Why does the writer like the website?
3 What is one problem with the site?
4 What is the writer's conclusion about the site?

One of my favourite websites is a free photo-sharing site called www.photoshowme.com. It's a great place for photographers to show their photos to other people.

The site has quite a few good features. Firstly, it's easy to find photographs that you are interested in. They are organized into different categories like 'travel', 'food' or 'people' so you can search for things you want to look at. Another good point is that you can comment on each other's photos, and every month a professional photographer is invited to make comments. In my opinion, you learn a lot from this person's comments.

The only problem is that it has too much advertising. I think that's how the site makes money, but when you are looking at beautiful photographs, it's annoying when an advert appears on the screen.

On the whole, it's a useful website for anyone who loves taking photographs and communicating with other people about them.

2 Writing skill giving your opinion

a Write down any useful phrases in the review that:

a give positive opinions
One of my favourite ... is...
b give negative opinions
c sum up the writer's main opinion

b Match these phrases to the uses (a–c) in Exercise 2a.

1 One thing I really like is that …
2 In general, …
3 Another bad point is that …
4 One big advantage is that …
5 To sum up …

3 Think of a website you often use. Make notes to answer the questions and plan a review of the website.

Paragraph 1:
What is the website? What is it for?
Paragraph 2:
In your opinion, what are the good points about the website?
Paragraph 3:
Are there any bad points or problems with the site?
Paragraph 4:
On the whole, what do you think about the site?

4 Write your review. Use the useful phrases in Exercise 2.

5 Exchange reviews with your partner. Use these questions to check your partner's review.

• Does it explain the purpose of the website?
• Does the review give positive opinions?
• Does it give negative opinions?
• Does it sum up the writer's main opinion?

10f Wind turbines

Wind turbines can save money and
save the environment

Before you watch

1 Work in pairs. Look at the photo and answer the questions.

1 Do you have wind turbines in your local area?
2 How do wind turbines work? What do they produce?

2 Key vocabulary

Read these sentences. The words in bold are used in the video. Match the words with the definitions (a–g).

1 The land is very **flat** in this area.
2 I **paid off** the loan on this car.
3 This tower can **withstand** very strong wind.
4 My electricity comes from the **national grid**.
5 The price can be **anywhere between** one hundred and two hundred dollars.
6 This lorry weighs **a ton**.
7 The farmer grows **crops** on the land.

a gave all the money back
b a system of cables across the country which sends electricity
c not be damaged by something
d a unit of weight equal to 1,000 kilograms
e with no hills or mountains
f plants for food
g a phrase used when you don't have the exact figure

While you watch

3 [▶ 10.1] Watch the video and match the numbers and years to the information (1–8).

a 6,000
b 2
c 81,530
d 180
e 130
f 257
g 1993
h 140,000

1 The number of wind turbines at the schools in Spirit Lake: _____
2 The year the first wind turbine was built: _____
3 The amount of money the smaller turbine has saved the district: $ _____
4 The height of a wind turbine: _____ feet
5 The total amount that the two turbines save the schools: $ _____
6 The amount of money Charles Goodman will make in a year from his wind turbines: $ _____
7 The number of wind turbines in this area of countryside: _____
8 The speed of wind that the turbine can withstand: _____ miles per hour

4 [▶ 10.1] Watch the video again and answer the questions.

1 Why was the second turbine built?
2 How are the turbines fixed in the ground so they don't fall over?
3 Where is the power sent from the two turbines?
4 What do the farmers sell?
5 Why does Charles Goodman smile when the wind is blowing?
6 Why are the wind turbines useful in class?
7 What does Jan Bolluyt say the wind turbines are good for?

After you watch

5 Vocabulary in context

[▶ 10.2] Watch the clips from the video. Choose the correct option to complete the sentences.

6 Work in pairs. List the different reasons in the video why wind turbines are good for the area of Spirit Lake.

7 With your partner, prepare a short, two-minute presentation about building wind turbines near your local town. Explain:

• how wind turbines work.
• the different reasons why turbines are good.
• why the town needs to build one.

8 Work with another pair and take turns to give your presentations. How similar were your reasons for building wind turbines?

Grammar

1 Choose the correct options.

IKEA furniture
[1] *sells / is sold* by the company from nearly 400 different shops around the world, and from its online store. However, the company [2] *didn't used / didn't use* to make furniture. It [3] *started / was started* in 1943 in Sweden by Ingvar Kamprad. Ingvar [4] *use to / used to* sell small objects like watches and pens by post. As the company grew, it [5] *produced / was produced* larger household furniture and today around 12,000 different products [6] *make / are made*, including chairs, beds, cupboard, and pictures.
IKEA is famous for changing the way we buy products. In the past, furniture [7] *finished / was finished* in the factory and customers [8] *were bought / used to buy* it ready-made from a shop. But modern IKEA furniture [9] *builds / is built* by the customer after they buy it. Also, furniture shops [10] *used to / didn't use to* be in the centre of cities, but IKEA [11] *built / was built* its shops outside the city centre. This idea was popular with customers and nowadays you often see large shops outside the centre of cities.

2 **》》 MB** Look at the text in Exercise 1 again and answer these questions

1 Which of the verb forms are passive?
2 Why do we use these passive forms?

I CAN
use the passive form of the present simple and past simple
use *used to*

Vocabulary

3 Complete this table of words.

verb	adjective	noun	another noun	person
advertise			advertising	
produce		product		

4 Reorder the letters to make adjectives about products.

1 suer-rifelndy
2 casib
3 hashionfable
4 slacsic
5 lufuse
6 lod-asfihoned
7 pu-ot-tade

5 **》》 MB** Work in pairs. Write five products or brands from Unit 10. Match them with the adjectives in Exercise 4 or think of other adjectives.

Gap clothes — *classic, fashionable*

1 _____ — _____
2 _____ — _____
3 _____ — _____
4 _____ — _____
5 _____ — _____

6 Which part of the website (a–e) do you click to do these things (1–5)?

a about us   d search
b contact   e link
c home

1 to go to a different website
2 to send a message to the person or company who has the site
3 to look for specific information on the site
4 to return to the main page
5 to find out about the person or company who has the site

I CAN
talk about products and advertising
talk about websites

Real life

7 Read part of a discussion between three people about the colour of a new logo for the front of a shop. Write the missing words in the phrases.

A: The designers have sent the new logo in three different colours. [1] W_____ d_____ y_____ t_____ is the best colour?
B: [2] I_____ m_____ o_____, the black and white logo is the best. It's easy to see.
C: I [3] d_____. Black and white is boring.
A: I [4] s_____ w_____ y_____ m_____. It isn't very interesting.
B: OK, let's look at the other two. [5] M_____ we c_____ use the yellow logo.
C: No, I [6] d_____ a_____. Yellow is very difficult to see in the street.
A: Yes, [7] y_____ r_____. So I suggest we use the blue logo.
B: [8] G_____ i_____. I think we should do that.

8 **》》 MB** Underline the phrases in Exercise 7 for:

• asking for an opinion.
• giving an opinion.
• agreeing and disagreeing.
• making suggestions.

I CAN
ask for and give opinions
agree, disagree and make suggestions

Unit 11 History

Captain Scott's hut was left with all its contents in 1917, and only found again in 1956.

1 The hut in the photo is about one hundred years old. Where do you think it is? What do you think Captain Scott did?

2 ▶ 86 Listen to a historian talking about the hut and check your ideas from Exercise 1. Then answer these questions.

1 What objects can you see inside the hut?
2 Why is it important to look after the hut?
3 The historian says, 'the hut has become a time capsule'. What do you think he means by a *time capsule*?

3 Work in groups. Plan your own time capsule with five objects, which you will bury under the ground. Discuss which five objects will be most useful for future historians. Use these examples or your own ideas.

> a clock   a copy of today's newspaper   drawings and diaries
> a memory stick with music and films   a menu from a restaurant
> money (coins and notes)   a popular novel   a tin of food

4 Present your final list for the time capsule to the class and explain the reasons for your choices.

11a The history of video gaming

Reading

1 Work in pairs. Look at the photo in the timeline of video gaming and discuss the questions.

1 What can you see in the photo?
2 When do you think it was taken?
3 How many differences can you think of between the game in the photo and modern video games?

The game in the photo is black and white …

2 Read the timeline of video gaming. Answer the questions.

1 Which video games does it mention?
2 Do you remember or know about any of the games?
3 Does anyone still play these games today?

3 Read the article again. Are these sentences true (T) or false (F)?

1 When Pong came out, it was a new kind of game.
2 Pong was a competitive game.
3 Only boys enjoyed playing Space Invaders.
4 A Game Boy only had one type of game.
5 People couldn't stop playing Tetris.
6 The Wii had a different type of game and attracted new players.

Wordbuilding verb + preposition

> ▶ **WORDBUILDING verb + preposition**
>
> Many verbs are often used with a preposition. When you learn a new verb, try to also learn the different prepositions you can use with it.
> *play with (someone), play against (someone), play for (a team), play in (teams)*
>
> For further practice, see Workbook page 91.

4 Complete the questions with these prepositions.

| about   for   on   with (x3) |

1 Do you often play video games _____ friends?
2 Which video games are most people talking _____ these days?
3 How much do you normally pay _____ a video game on your phone?
4 How much do you spend _____ video games every month?
5 When you leave the house, what do you always take _____ you?
6 Some people think video games are bad for you. Do you agree _____ them?

5 Work in pairs. Take turns to ask and answer the questions in Exercise 4.

▶ 87

A timeline of UIDEO GAMING

1970

The first video games appeared in the 50s and 60s but the first really successful game was 'Pong', which came out in 1972. People said that they had never seen anything like it before. It was one of the first home video games that you played against another person for points.

1980

When people remember playing video games in the late 70s and early 80s, they often think of Space Invaders. That's because everyone was talking about it at the time – people of all ages said they loved it.

1990

Much smaller video game devices became available in the 90s. For example, you could take the Game Boy with you anywhere. It had lots of different games, including Tetris, which was the most popular. Many gamers said they played Tetris for hours and weren't able to stop!

130

Grammar reported speech

> ► **REPORTED SPEECH**
>
> We use reported speech to report what someone said in the past.
> 1 *People said that they **had** never **seen** anything like it.*
> 2 *People of all ages said they **loved** it.*
> 3 *Nintendo said they **were working** on a new type of gaming device.*
> 4 *They said they **would** produce games for the whole family to play.*
> Note: After the reporting verb *said*, you can use *that* but you don't have to.
>
> For further information and practice, see page 176.

6 Look at the grammar box. Match the sentences with reported speech (1–4) to these sentences with direct speech (a–d).

    a People of all ages said, 'We love it.'
    b Nintendo said, 'We are working on a new type of gaming device.'
    c Nintendo said, 'We will produce games for the whole family to play.'
    d People said, 'We've never seen anything like it.'

7 Underline the verbs in the direct speech in Exercise 6 and in the reported speech in the grammar box. Then complete this table.

Direct speech	Reported speech
Present simple	1
2	Past continuous
Present perfect or past simple	3
4	*Would*

At the beginning of the 21st century, Nintendo said they were working on a new type of gaming device and that they would produce games for the whole family to play. The device was called a 'Wii' and – unlike other video games – the games were active, and you could do exercise in your living room. The Wii became popular with a new group of people – the over fifties.

2000

8 Read the first sentence and complete the second sentence with the correct verb form.

  1 The boy said, 'I love the game Super Mario.'
     The boy said that he _____ the game Super Mario.
  2 She said that she wanted a new Xbox.
     She said, 'I _____ a new Xbox.'
  3 When I phoned, Mum said the children were playing tennis on the Wii.
     When I phoned, Mum said, 'The children _____ tennis on the Wii.'
  4 The company said, 'We are planning a new version of the game.'
     The company said they _____ a new version of the game.
  5 Their message said they had gone to the cinema.
     Their message said, 'We _____ to the cinema'.
  6 My father said, 'I bought my first Game Boy in 1990.'
     My father said he _____ his first Game Boy in 1990.
  7 Julian said he would play against us later.
     Julian said, 'I _____ against you later'.
  8 One scientist said, 'Computer games will change people's brains.'
     One scientist said that computer games _____ people's brains.'

9 ► **88** Listen to a short conversation between Jack and Sonia. Write down what they say.

  1 Jack: *I need the TV for my game.*
  2 Sonia: _____
  3 Jack: _____
  4 Sonia: _____
  5 Jack: _____

10 Rewrite the conversation from Exercise 9 as reported speech.

  1 Jack said that he   *needed the TV for his game.*
  2 Sonia said that she _____
  3 Jack said that he _____
  4 Sonia said that he _____ and that she _____
  5 Jack said that _____

Speaking ⟨ my life ⟩

11 Work in pairs. Ask and answer these questions. Write your partner's answers.

  1 What sort of games (e.g. board games, computer games) are popular in your country?
  2 Do you often play any of these games?
  3 What type of games do you prefer?
  4 Will people play board games in the future? Or will they only play computer games?

12 Change partners. Report what your partner said.

Aniko said that chess was very popular in her country.

11b Messages from the past

Vocabulary **communication**

1 Put these types of communication into the two categories in the table. Can any words go in both categories?

> an advert   an email   a Facebook page
> a letter or card   a newspaper
> a phone conversation   a presentation
> a sticky note on the fridge
> a radio programme   a text message
> a Whatsapp message

Personal (with family and friends)	Public (with lots of people)

2 Work in pairs. Which types of communication in Exercise 1 are normally used for these messages (1–6)? Give reasons for your answer.

1 to tell someone you are getting married
2 to say there is a new president
3 to thank someone who lives in another country for a present
4 to ask your brother to feed the cat while you are on holiday
5 to share some family holiday photos
6 to tell a group of people about a new product

Listening

3 Work in pairs. Look at the newspaper headline and photo. Who do you think wrote the message? What do you think the message says? Tell the class your ideas.

4 ▶ 89 Listen to the news story about the message in the bottle. Number the three parts of the story (a–c) in the order you hear them (1–3).

a the history of messages in bottles
b how someone found the message in a bottle
c why someone sent the message in a bottle

Fishing captain finds one-hundred-year-old message in a bottle at sea

5 ▶ 89 Listen to the news story again. Choose the correct option (a–c).

1 How did the captain feel when he saw the bottle in the sea?
   a surprised
   b disappointed
   c curious
2 Why had someone written the message?
   a as a love letter
   b because they were lost at sea
   c as part of a scientific experiment
3 Why is this a world record?
   a It's the longest message in a bottle which anyone has found at sea.
   b It's the oldest message in a bottle which anyone has found at sea.
   c It's the oldest message in a bottle which anyone has written.
4 Why did the ancient Greeks put bottles in the sea over two thousand years ago?
   a to find out if the Mediterranean Sea and the Atlantic Ocean were connected
   b to send messages to ships in the Mediterranean Sea and the Atlantic Ocean
   c to help sailors who were lost in the Mediterranean Sea and the Atlantic Ocean
5 In 1915, why did the sailor send the message to his wife?
   a to say he was coming home
   b to say that he loved her
   c to say where he was

132

Grammar **reporting verbs** (*say* and *tell*)

▶ **REPORTING VERBS (*SAY* and *TELL*)**

1 He **told news reporters** that he had been very curious when he had seen the message.
2 The message **said** that his boat was sinking and that he loved her.

For further information and practice, see page 176.

6 Read the sentences in the grammar box and answer these questions.
1 Which verbs report the words of someone?
2 Which reporting verb is followed by an object (e.g. *you, her, them, reporters*)?
3 Which reporting verb is not followed by an object?

7 Choose the correct options to complete the conversation.
A: Did I ¹ *say / tell* you there was a great TV programme on last night?
B: No, what was it about?
A: Space travel in the next one hundred years. They ² *said / told* that humans would soon land on Mars.
B: Really? When did they ³ *say / tell* that would happen?
A: The presenter didn't ⁴ *say / tell* exactly, but probably in the next thirty years.
B: OK. I read an article that ⁵ *said / told* there would be a hotel on the moon soon.
A: Yes, but someone ⁶ *said / told* me a few years ago that there were going to be space hotels orbiting the Earth soon, and nothing's happened yet.

8 Work in pairs. Report these messages using *say* or *tell*.
1 'Your lunch is in the fridge.'
She _____ him that his _____ .
2 'I'm lost in the middle of the city.'
He _____ that he _____ .
3 'I've loved you for years.'
Maria _____ Joel that she _____ .
4 'We're waiting for you at the café.'
They _____ that they _____ .
5 'I'll call you back later.'
Dave _____ me that he _____ .
6 'You need to phone this number.'
The message _____ that I _____ .

Writing and speaking ⟨ my life ⟩

9 Write a message to put in a bottle in the sea. Include information about who you are and why you are writing the message. Use one of these suggestions or your own idea.

• you are lost at sea
• you are stuck on a desert island
• you are doing an experiment

10 Exchange your message with a partner. Imagine someone has found the message one hundred years in the future. Write a short news report about your partner's message. What did the message say?

Today, a person found a message in a bottle. It was written 100 years ago. The message said …

11 Read your news report to your partner.

A fishing boat near the Shetland Islands, Scotland

11c Stealing history

Vocabulary ancient history

1 You are going to read an article which includes these words. Match the people (1–4) with the definitions (a–d) and the objects (5–8) with the photos (e–h).

People	Objects
1 archaeologist	5 tomb
2 soldier	6 statue
3 robber	7 painting
4 collector	8 pot

a someone who buys a certain type of object (e.g. coins, paintings)
b someone who is in the army and wears a uniform
c someone who steals from others (and breaks the law)
d someone who studies the buildings and objects of people who lived in the past

Reading

2 Look at the title of the article. What do you think it is about? Why will it talk about the four types of people in Exercise 1?

3 Read the article and check your answers from Exercise 2. Then answer these questions.

1 What was the name of Abu Sir al Malaq in the past?
2 Why was it famous?
3 What sort of people work at Abu Sir al Malaq?
4 Why do criminals come to Abu Sir al Malaq?
5 What is Amal Farag trying to do?
6 The robbers take some objects to sell. What do they often do with the other objects?
7 In the past, who else has stolen from Egypt?
8 Why does the problem continue?

Critical thinking emotion words

4 Look at these sentences and compare them with the sentences in the article. What extra words does the author use in the article?

1 These people are here to discover more about Egypt's history. (paragraph 2)
2 Her team are trying to save the history at Abu Sir al Malaq. (paragraph 3)
3 It continues to be big business. (paragraph 4)

5 Why does the writer use these words? What do they tell us about the writer's opinion?

Word focus *one*

6 Read these sentences from the article. Match the use of *one* in the sentences to the explanations a–e.

1 Busiris was **one of** ancient Egypt's largest cities.
2 There is only sand and stone, with **one or two** small villages nearby.
3 They are moving the ancient objects **one by one** to museums and safe places.
4 **One day** in 2012, she was working here.
5 Maybe **one day** the problem will be solved.

a to talk about a particular day in the past
b to talk about a careful process
c to talk about one in a group of people or things
d to talk about a small number of people or things
e to talk about some point in the future

Speaking [my life]

7 Work in groups. You would like to open a new museum about your local town or city. Make notes about the following.

• what your town was famous for in the past
• what historical objects you can show in the museum
• what you can tell visitors about

8 Work with another group. Present your ideas and try to convince the other group that your idea is the best. Use emotion words.

*This town **desperately** needs a new museum for a number of reasons. Firstly, …*

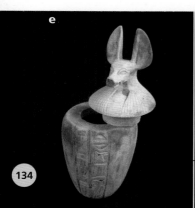
e

f

g

h

STEALING HISTORY

▶ 90

Abu Sir al Malaq is a place about one hundred kilometres south of Cairo in Egypt. In ancient times it was called Busiris. Busiris was one of ancient Egypt's largest cities and it was famous for its architecture and buildings. Nowadays, there is only sand and stone with one or two small villages nearby. But the area of Abu Sir al Malaq is still famous because of its history.

When you arrive at Abu Sir al Malaq you meet a lot of archaeologists from museums. These hard-working people are here to discover more about Egypt's history. Inside the old tombs they can find pots and paintings which tell us more about this period of history. Surprisingly, there are also soldiers with guns, who protect the archaeologists and the ancient tombs. That's because robbers often come to Abu Sir al Malaq and try to steal things. They can sell these historical items for large amounts of money to collectors around the world.

Amal Farag is one person who wants to protect the area from the robbers. She works for the government and her team are desperately trying to save the ancient objects at Abu Sir al Malaq. They are moving them one by one to museums and safe places. However, it's almost impossible to save everything. She shows me a tomb on the hillside. One day in 2012, she was working here with a colleague when she suddenly met three men. They were stealing some historical objects from a tomb. When they saw Amal and her colleague, they quickly ran away. Typically, robbers take the good pieces and throw away the rest. 'For every nice piece', says Amal, 'they destroy hundreds.'

It's wrong to think that stealing historical objects is a modern problem in Egypt. History books describe how people stole from tombs over three thousand years ago. When Roman armies arrived in Egypt, they took gold and valuable objects back to Rome on their ships. And from the 16th to the mid-20th century, different countries controlled Egypt and took away statues and beautiful art. Nowadays, there are laws controlling the movement of historical objects to and from Egypt. Maybe one day the problem will be solved, but in the meantime, it continues – sadly – to be big business.

25

30

35

40

desperately (adv) /ˈdesp(ə)rət(ə)li/ without thinking about your own safety

11d A journey to Machu Picchu

Real life **giving a short presentation**

1 Do you ever give talks or presentations in your own language (or in English)? What are they about? Why would people give talks or presentations in these situations?

- at work
- at school or university
- at the meeting of a local club or town council
- at a special occasion (e.g. a wedding)

2 ▶ 91 Listen to parts of a presentation about Peru and Machu Picchu. Which of the topics (a–f) does the presenter talk about?

a the people in Peru and their customs
b the history of Machu Picchu
c the history of the Incas
d the capital city of Peru
e his own journey
f the food in Peru

3 ▶ 91 Listen again and complete the expressions for giving a short presentation.

▶ GIVING A SHORT PRESENTATION

Good morning and ¹_____ all for coming.
Today I'd like to ²_____ about …
Let me ³_____ by telling you about …
So, that's everything I wanted to ⁴_____ about …
Now, let's ⁵_____ at …
The ⁶_____ part of my presentation is about …
I'd like to ⁷_____ you some of my photos.
To sum ⁸_____ …
Are there any ⁹_____ ?

4 Pronunciation **pausing**

a ▶ 92 Presenters often pause at the end of a sentence, the end of a phrase, or before and after important words they want to emphasize. Listen and read the first part of the presentation. Notice the first four pauses (/) and write in the other pauses.

Good morning / and thank you all for coming. / Today / I'd like to talk about my holiday in Peru / and in particular, about my journey to Machu Picchu. It's also called 'The Lost City of the Incas'. Let me begin by telling you about the history of Machu Picchu.

b Work in pairs. Try reading the same part of the presentation with similar pauses.

5 Prepare a short presentation for your partner. Think about a historical place you have visited and make notes for these questions. Then give your presentation.

- Where is it?
- Why is it important?
- Who lived there in the past?

11e The greatest mountaineer

Writing a biography

1 Think of three pieces of information you would expect to find in a biography. Work in pairs and compare your ideas.

2 Read the biography of Reinhold Messner. Does it include your ideas from Exercise 1? Which paragraphs (1–4) mention these topics (a-f)?

a when and where he was born
b facts about his childhood and early life
c why he became well known
d something he said
e what other people think or have said about him
f what he is doing now

3 Writing skill punctuation in direct speech

a The biography of Messner includes direct speech. Underline three examples of direct speech in the text.

b Answer these questions about punctuation rules for direct speech.

1 Where do you put the two quotation marks?
2 Do you always put a full stop at the end of the quotation or only if it ends the sentence?
3 Where do you use a comma? What does it separate?

c Complete these sentences with the missing punctuation to show direct speech.

1 My grandfather always told me you should follow your dreams
2 Yes we can said Barack Obama when he campaigned to become the US President
3 Film critics said she's the greatest actress of her generation
4 Education is the most powerful weapon said Nelson Mandela

4 Write a short biography (100–140 words) about someone famous or someone you admire. Try to include all the topics in Exercise 2 and remember to use the correct punctuation with quotations or direct speech.

5 Exchange your biography with a partner. Use these questions to check your partner's biography.

- Which topics in Exercise 2 has your partner included?
- Is the punctuation in direct speech correct?

The world's greatest mountaineer

Reinhold Messner has been described as the greatest mountaineer in history. He's famous for being one of the first men to climb Mount Everest without oxygen in 1978. But he was also the first man to climb all fourteen of the world's mountains over eight thousand metres.

Messner was born in 1944 in a small village in the mountains of northern Italy. When he talks about the area he still says, 'it's the most beautiful place in the world.' His father was a climber and took his son up a mountain when he was only five. As a teenager, Messner climbed with his younger brother Günther.

In their twenties, the two brothers started climbing in the Himalayas, but Günther died in an accident and Reinhold lost six toes. Nevertheless, Reinhold continued climbing and he became a legend among other mountaineers. The climber Hans Kammerlander believes Reinhold changed climbing. 'Reinhold had so many new ideas,' says Kammerlander. 'He found new ways, new techniques.'

Nowadays Messner spends more time at home with his family and he has written over sixty books. In 2006 he opened the first Messner Mountain Museum, where people can find out more about the world he loves.

1 foot = 0.3048 metres

11f The Golden Record

Voyager 1 and the planet Jupiter

Before you watch

1 Key vocabulary

You are going to watch a video about Voyager 1. Read these sentences. The words in bold are used in the video. Match the words with the definitions (a–b).

1 The **spacecraft** Voyager 1 was **launched** on the 20th August, 1977.
   a sent on a journey (e.g. a boat or a rocket)
   b a vehicle used for travel in space
2 It is leaving our **solar system** and going further into **space.**
   a a collection of planets (and their moons) which go round one sun
   b the area away from earth, where the planets and stars are
3 Voyager 1 has completed its first **mission** successfully but it still has an important **function**.
   a a particular job or task
   b a general role or purpose
4 There's **classical** music from Europe, and **jazz** recordings by Louis Armstrong.
   a type of music written in the eighteenth and nineteenth century in Europe.
   b type of music that started in the early twentieth century, originally by the African American communities of New Orleans.
5 Voyager carries a message for other **life forms** in the **universe**.
   a all of space and everything in it
   b any living thing

2
Look at the photo. Do you think it's important for humans to learn more about space with spacecraft like Voyager 1? Why? / Why not?

While you watch

3
🎥 **11.1** Watch the video about Voyager 1 and make notes about these questions.

1 Why did Voyager 1 go into space?
2 Where is The Golden Record?
3 What is on The Golden Record?

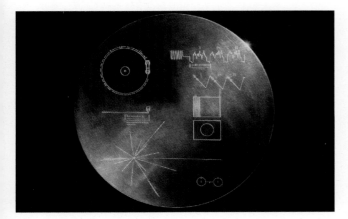

4
🎥 **11.1** Watch part 1 of the video again (00.00–01.26). Are the sentences true (T) or false (F)?

1 A child is speaking on the first message in the video.
2 Voyager 1's first mission was to photograph Jupiter and Saturn.
3 The Golden Record has information about the Earth in the year 2000.
4 A team of six people spent a year deciding what to include on the Golden Record.
5 Voyager 1 is travelling back to Earth with its information.

5
🎥 **11.1** Watch part 2 of the video (01.27–04.37) and answer the questions.

1 How many photos are on the record? What do they show?
2 Number these sounds (a–e) in the order you hear them (1–5).
   a a human heart
   b crying
   c birds and frogs
   d wind and rain
   e a volcano
3 Which language is each message recorded in?
   a 'Hello everybody.' ....
   b 'Hello? How are you?' ....
   c 'Greetings to our friends in the stars. We hope that we will meet you someday.'

   ....
   d 'Hope everyone's well. We are thinking about you all. Please come here and visit when you have time.' ....

After you watch

6 Vocabulary in context

🎥 **11.2** Watch the clips from the video. Choose the correct meaning of the words and phrases.

7
Work in groups. Imagine you work for NASA and you are going to send information about the Earth today into space. You can use a memory stick with lots of digital memory. Discuss what to put on the stick.

• What types of photos, videos, sounds and music will you include?
• What recorded message will you include for other life forms? (e.g. a greeting)
• What else can you include which represents the Earth in the twenty-first century?

8
Join another group. Take turns to present your plans.

Grammar

1 Rewrite the direct speech as reported speech.

1 'I want to fly in space.'
He said he _____.
2 'I'm driving home.'
She said she _____.
3 'We visited the pyramid in Giza.'
They said they _____.
4 'He's gone to the museum.'
You said he _____.
5 'One day I'll go on holiday to Rome.'
Matt said one day he _____.

2 Complete the sentences with *say* or *tell*.

1 I _____ him to hurry up!
2 Did she _____ what time she was coming?
3 Don't _____ me the answer. I'll work it out.
4 Who _____ we'd find the tomb here?
5 Did the archaeologist _____ who built this house?
6 Sarah _____ she'd be a bit late.

3 ≫ MB Work in pairs. Tell your partner:

- something about the story of this bottle
- something the news reader on the TV or radio said this morning.
- something your English teacher told you.

I CAN

use reported speech ☐

Vocabulary

4 Choose the correct option.

In 2010, everyone was talking ¹ *on / about* a new video game called Angry Birds. Everyone was playing ² *in it / it* on their mobile phones because – unlike other types of video games – you didn't have to spend much money ³ *at / on* the app and you could take it ⁴ *with / on* you everywhere. For a few months, it was the most popular video game in the world. There were even Angry Birds toys and clothes, TV shows and adverts. There is even an Angry Bird park in Finland where you can play ⁵ *for / against* other people using large Angry Birds.

5 Complete the text with these words.

| paintings | archaeologists | statue | tomb | pots |

The Inca civilisation was the largest civilisation of South America in the 13th and 14th century. Today, you can visit the huge pyramids that the Incas built, and ¹ _____ are still finding objects such as ² _____ for cooking or ³ _____ showing pictures from their past. For example, the small ⁴ _____ on the left of the photo is a llama. It was found in the ⁵ _____ of an important person from an ancient Inca city.

I CAN

use verbs + prepositions ☐
talk about ancient history ☐

Real life

6 Match the beginnings of the sentences (1–7) with the endings (a–g).

1 Good morning everyone _____
2 Today I'd like to talk _____
3 Let me begin by telling _____
4 So, that's everything I wanted to _____
5 Now, let's look _____
6 That's the end _____
7 But before I finish, _____

a you a bit about the city of Pisa.
b of my talk.
c and thank you for coming.
d are there any questions?
e about my visit to Italy.
f say about Pisa.
g at my next stop which was the city of Florence.

7 ≫ MB Work in pairs. Look at the sentence beginnings (1–7) in Exercise 6. Complete the sentences to make your own presentation.

I CAN

give a short presentation ☐

Unit 12 Nature

Chasing a tornado in Kansas, USA

FEATURES

1 Look at the photo and describe what you can see. Use some of these words to help you.

bright	cloud	dark	evening	fall	light	move
rain	shine	storm	sun			

I think it's the afternoon. There's a tornado and it's moving.

2 ▶ 93 Listen to part of a documentary about storm chasers and answer the questions.

1 What do most people do when a tornado is coming?
2 What type of people are storm chasers?
3 What do storm chasers do?
4 What is a common time of day to see a tornado?
5 Why are tornadoes dangerous?

3 Think about your answers to these questions. Then tell the class.

1 Why do you think people want to be storm chasers?
2 Would you like to be a storm chaser? Why? / Why not?

12a What if …?

Vocabulary **extreme weather**

1 Match these weather words with the photos (a–d).

> flood   hail   snowstorm   thunder and lightning

2 Discuss the questions.

  1 Which parts of the world often have the extreme weather in Exercise 1?
  2 Which types of extreme weather do you have in your country? Do you have extreme weather at certain times of the year?
  3 What's the weather like today? Is it normal for this time of year?

Reading

3 Read the article. What kind of questions does Randall answer on his blog?

4 Read the article again and answer these questions with *yes* or *no*.

  1 Does Randall work for NASA?
  2 Do people send in questions about things that really happened?
  3 Does Randall use scientific facts to answer the questions?
  4 Are you safer from lightning on a submarine than on a boat?
  5 Can the electricity from lightning move across water?
  6 Can hail break a car windscreen?

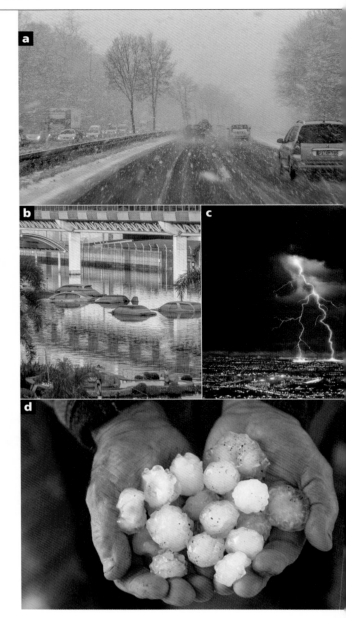

▶ 94

WHAT IF …?

Randall Monroe is a scientist and he used to work for NASA. One day he started a blog called *What if …?* Every week people send Randall questions about unlikely or impossible things, and Randall gives scientific answers.

Here are some *What … if …?* questions about weather and nature.

What would happen if lightning hit you in a submarine? What if you were in a boat?
If you were in a submarine, you'd be safe because you'd be underwater. However, lightning usually hits the tallest thing, so if you were on a flat surface, like in a boat on the sea, you wouldn't be as safe.

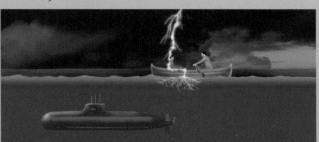

Would I be safe if I was in a swimming pool during a thunderstorm?
You wouldn't be safe if your head was above the water. Lightning might hit you. And if the lightning hit the water near you, the electrical energy would spread outwards across the water.

If it was raining, how fast would you have to drive to break the car windscreen?
The rain would break the glass if you drove at the speed of sound. But if you did that, the car would take off! Rain wouldn't break the glass if you drove at a normal speed.

But in freezing temperatures, hail would break the windscreen if you drove fast. In fact, that sometimes happens in some parts of the world.

Grammar second conditional

> **SECOND CONDITIONAL**
>
> *If you **were** in a submarine, you'**d be** safe.*
> *If you **were** in a boat, you **wouldn't be** as safe.*
> *You **wouldn't be** safe if your head **was** above the water.*
> *The rain **would break** the glass if you **drove** at the speed of sound.*
> ***Would** I **be** safe **if** I **was** in a swimming pool during a thunderstorm?*
> ***What would happen if** lightning **hit** you in a submarine?*
>
> For further information and practice, see page 178.

5 Look at the grammar box. Then choose the correct option (a–b) to complete these sentences.

1 We form the second conditional with:
   a *if* + past simple + *would* + verb.
   b *if* + present simple + *will* + verb.
2 We use the second conditional to talk about:
   a real situations.
   b impossible or unlikely situations.
3 The second conditional refers to situations in:
   a the past.
   b the present or future.
4 A comma separates the two clauses when:
   a the first clause begins with *if*.
   b the second clause begins with *if*.

6 Put these words in the correct order to make second conditional sentences. The first word is correct.

1 If / time, / I / had / you / help / I / with / your / 'd / homework / .
2 You / need / help / wouldn't / listened / class / if / you / in / .
3 Would / you / for / ask / friends / your / money / if / didn't / you / have / any / ?
4 I / ancient / Rome / 'd / visit / if / time / travel / possible / was / .
5 They / use / translator / a / wouldn't / English / they / if / spoke / .
6 If / business, / a / new / started / you / would / produce / what / you / ?

7 Complete the text with the correct form of the verbs.

8 Complete the second sentence using the second conditional. Describe the opposite situation to the first sentence.

1 It doesn't rain here so the land is very dry.
   If it _____*rained*_____, the land _____*wouldn't be*_____ as dry.
2 The river never floods, so we don't have to leave our homes.
   If the river _____, we _____ leave our homes.
3 We don't get hot temperatures in my country, so people don't need air conditioning.
   If we _____ hot temperatures in my country, we _____ air conditioning.
4 We need to check the weather forecast every day because there are sudden tornadoes at this time of year.
   If there _____ sudden tornadoes at this time of year, we _____ check the weather all the time.
5 It doesn't snow here in winter, so we are able to drive to work every day.
   If it _____ here in winter, we _____ drive to work every day.

9 Pronunciation *would / wouldn't / 'd*

a ▶ 95 Listen to a short conversation. How many times do you hear the words *would*, *wouldn't* or *'d*?

b Look at the audioscript on page 189 and check your answers. Then work in pairs. Practise reading the conversation.

Speaking ⟨ my life ⟩

10 Work in pairs. Discuss these questions.

1 Would you live in another country if you could? Where would you move to? Why?
2 If you could meet someone famous, who would it be? What would you ask him or her?
3 If you won a lot of money, would you stop working / studying? How would you spend the money?

*I'**d** like to live in another country if I **could**. I'**d** probably move to Canada, because it has beautiful places.*

What would happen if there wasn't a Gulf Stream?

The Gulf Stream is a stream of warm water which begins in Florida and travels across the Atlantic Ocean. As a result, countries on the west coast of Europe have warmer climates. If the Gulf Stream [1] _____ (stop) flowing, Europe [2] _____ (be) very different. Countries like Great Britain [3] _____ (become) much colder, especially in winter. If the sea was colder, spring and summer [4] _____ (not / last) as long. Farmers [5] _____ (not / be able to) produce certain types of food and heating costs [6] _____ (go up). So if we [7] _____ (not / have) the Gulf Stream, a lot of Europeans [8] _____ (have to) change the way they live.

12b Nature in one cubic foot

Vocabulary nature

1 Work in pairs. Discuss the questions.

 1 Do you like taking photos? What kinds of photos do you take?
 2 Do you ever take photos of nature? Why? / Why not?

2 Look at the photos (A–D). Which of these places (1–8) can you see in the photos? Which three places are man-made?

1	forest	5	garden
2	mountain	6	ocean
3	field	7	park
4	river	8	desert

3 Work in pairs. Which of the places in Exercise 2 do you:

 • see every day?
 • see when you go on holiday?
 • never see?

Listening

4 ▶ 96 Listen to a documentary about David Liittschwager, the photographer. Why does he take photos of wildlife in the green metal frame?

> **cube** (n) /kjuːb/ a shape like a box that has six equal square sides (cubic = adj)

5 ▶ 96 Listen to the documentary again. Are these sentences true (T) or false (F)?

 1 Many people think they don't live near nature.
 2 David Liittschwager wants people to notice the wildlife near them.
 3 David took his green metal frame to different parts of the world.
 4 He spent three weeks taking photos around the world.
 5 He only photographed living things that are smaller than one millimetre in size.

Grammar *anywhere, everyone, nobody, something, etc.*

▶ **ANYWHERE, EVERYONE, NOBODY, SOMETHING, etc.**

Affirmative
1 *David Liittschwager wants to show us that everyone can find nature.*
2 *Plants and animals are always somewhere nearby.*

Negative
3 *There's nowhere to look at nature.*
4 *You don't see anything except people walking their dogs.*

Question
5 *Have you photographed anything interesting?*
Note: *-body* and *-one* mean the same:
everyone / everybody can find nature.

For further information and practice, see page 178

6 Look at the grammar box. Look at the parts of the words highlighted in yellow. Then complete these rules with *-thing, -where, -body* or *-one*.

1 We use _____ or _____ to talk about people.
2 We use _____ to talk about places.
3 We use _____ to talk about objects.

7 Look at the parts of the words highlighted in blue in the grammar box. Complete the sentences with *any-, every-, some-* or *no-*.

1 _____ body loves taking photos. It's very popular.
2 _____ body likes that photo. We all look terrible in it.
3 'Did _____ body take a photo of me?' 'No, I don't think _____ body did.'
4 _____ body took my photo. It's in today's newspaper.

8 Read about the places in the photos A–D. Choose the correct options.

9 Complete the questions and answers in four different conversations. Use the highlighted words from the grammar box.

A: Did you go [1] _____ where interesting yesterday?
B: No, I stayed in. I wanted to watch [2] _____ thing on TV about plants and animals in South Africa.

A: Sorry I'm late. Has [3] _____ one phoned for me?
B: [4] _____ body phoned but [5] some _____ left this letter at reception.

A: I'm starving, I've had [6] _____ thing to eat all day.
B: Well why don't we go and get something to eat? There are cafés [7] _____ where in this part of town.

A: Have you seen my pen? I left it [8] some _____ on my desk.
B: No, I haven't. And [9] no _____ moved [10] any _____ when you were out.

Speaking 〈 my life 〉

10 Work in pairs. Complete the questions with words starting with *any-*. Then take turns to ask the questions and answer in your own words. Try to use words with *any-, every-, some-* or *no-* in your answers.

1 Are you going _____ nice on holiday this year?
2 Did you do _____ interesting last weekend?
3 Have you ever met _____ you know while you were on holiday?

Central Park, New York

Some people think that there isn't [1] *anywhere / anyone* to see nature in New York. But Central Park is a quiet place with a forest full of plants and animals, and you can always find [2] *somewhere / nowhere* to sit and watch and listen to nature.

Monteverde Reserve, Costa Rica

There's probably [3] *nowhere / nothing* else in the world with so many different plants. There are plants of all sizes and colours [4] *everywhere / somewhere* you look.

Duck River, Tennessee

[5] *Everybody / Somebody* in Tennessee who likes fishing knows about the Duck River. It's one of the best rivers in the USA for different kinds of fish.

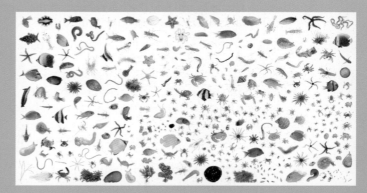

Coral reef, French Polynesia

[6] *Everything / Everybody* looks bright and colourful on a coral reef and there's always [7] *anything / something* beautiful to look at, from the multi-coloured coral to the orange, green and yellow sea life.

12c Living with chimpanzees

Reading

1 What are your favourite animals? Explain why.

2 Read the article about Jane Goodall quickly. Which paragraphs (1–5) describe:

a her early life in Africa?
b how she became well known?
c her current life and work?

3 Read the article again. Put these events in the order they happened and write the year or decade.

a The human population in the region increased.
b She became a doctor.
c A war started in Gombe.
d She saw her first chimpanzee. *1 – 1960*
e She started writing a diary.
f She goes back to Gombe every year.
g She published her first book.
h She left Gombe to travel and give talks.

4 Match the words from the article (1–5) with the definitions (a–e).

1 tool (line 17)
2 natural habitat (line 34)
3 survive (line 35)
4 lecture (line 42)
5 conservation (line 48)

a an object for making and doing things
b the protection of nature and wildlife
c a place where you find a certain type of animal or plant
d a formal talk to people about a specific subject
e continue to live

Critical thinking **close reading**

5 Read the article again. Are these sentences true (T) or false (F)? Or is the information not in the article (N)?

1 Jane and her mother hadn't enjoyed life back in England so they moved.
2 They didn't arrive with many possessions.
3 Jane had studied chimpanzees at university.
4 No one knew that chimpanzees ate meat before Jane discovered it.
5 Some scientists didn't believe Jane's research at first.
6 During the seventies and eighties, humans caused the problems in Gombe.
7 For a while, Jane stopped helping chimpanzees.
8 Jane has retired from her job.

Word focus *start*

6 Look at the words in bold in the sentences. Match the uses of the word *start* to the forms (a–d).

1 Jane Goodall and her mother **started their new life** in Africa on July 14, 1960.
2 She **started to write** in her diary every day
3 During the seventies a war **started**.
4 Jane **started running** towards the forest

a verb + *to* + infinitive
b verb + *-ing* form
c verb + noun phrase
d verb (not followed by an object or verb)

7 Match the questions (1–4) with the answers (a–d).

1 Why did you start to learn Chinese?
2 What time does the football match start?
3 If you started a new life, what would you do?
4 Why did you start working here?

a I had a part-time job in the summer and then they offered me a full-time job.
b I thought it would be useful in the future.
c I don't know. Maybe I'd go and work with animals somewhere.
d At three.

Speaking ⟨ my life ⟩

8 Work in pairs. Imagine you are Jane Goodall. Answer these questions with the information from paragraphs 1 and 2 of the article.

1 When did you first arrive in Africa?
2 What possessions did you have with you?
3 When did you see a chimpanzee for the first time?
4 What three discoveries did you make about chimpanzees?

9 With your partner, write four more questions for Jane Goodall using the information in paragraphs 3, 4 and 5.

10 Work with another pair and take turns to ask and answer your questions.

A: *What happened to you in 1966?*
B: *I became a Doctor.*

11 Write down five important dates in your life. Give them to your partner. Ask and answer questions about your dates.

▶ 97

Jane Goodall and her mother started their new life in Africa on July 14, 1960. They arrived on the east shore of Lake Tanganyika in the Gombe National Park. A group of men met them and carried their luggage. They didn't have very much: a tent, a few clothes and a cup. Later on the same day, somebody said they had seen a chimpanzee. Straight away, Jane started running towards the forest, where she saw a chimpanzee for the first time.

Jane had always dreamed of visiting Africa and studying chimpanzees, but she didn't know much about them and she had no scientific qualifications. However, after she arrived in Gombe, she spent many months watching groups of these animals and learning about them. She started to write about them in her diary and after many months of difficult work, she made three important and new discoveries: chimpanzees ate meat, they used tools to get food and they also made tools.

She began to publish articles in journals such as *National Geographic* magazine. After a while, scientists started reading her articles and Jane was offered a place at university. Finally, in 1966, she became Doctor Jane Goodall. Her work also made her famous. There was a film documentary, *Miss Goodall and the Wild Chimpanzees* (1963) and then the first of many books, called *My Friends the Wild Chimpanzees* (1969).

During the seventies, there was a war in the region and Gombe became a dangerous place. Many foreigners left, but Jane stayed. Eventually the war ended, but there was another problem at the start of the 1980s. As the human population increased in Gombe, more trees were cut down. With fewer trees, the chimpanzees lost their natural habitat and it became difficult for them to survive. By the end of the decade, only about a hundred chimpanzees were living in Gombe. At this time, Jane started working with local people to grow more trees in the region. 30 35

After 1989, Jane left Gombe and started travelling to other parts of the world. She gave lectures about her work and she organized safe places for young chimps whose parents had died or been killed. Now in her eighties, she spends about three hundred days a year giving interviews, talks and lectures, meeting with government officials about animal conservation and raising money for the Jane Goodall Institute which continues her research. And she still spends part of every year in the forest in Gombe, watching her chimpanzees. 40 45 50

The life of Jane Goodall

12d Discussing issues

Real life finding a solution

1 Look at the photo of the tiger in a zoo and answer the questions.

  1 How do you think the tiger feels? How do the girls feel?
  2 Do you ever visit zoos? Why? / Why not?

2 Read the newspaper extract below. Answer the questions.

  1 Is it certain that the zoo will close?
  2 What problem does the council need to solve?
  3 What would happen to the animals if it closed?

Animals have nowhere to go

The city's zoo is going to close in six months' time if the city council cannot solve the problem of low visitor numbers and lack of money. The zoo manager is worried about the animals at the zoo. 'If the zoo closed, they wouldn't be able to go back into their natural habitat. We'd have to find them a new home.'

3 ▶ 98 Listen to a conversation between the leader of the city council and the zoo manager. Are the sentences true (T) or false (F)?

  1 If the zoo doesn't receive more money, it will close.
  2 Lots of people visit the zoo.
  3 The zoo manager thinks zoos help some animals to survive.
  4 The zoo manager likes the suggestion about advertising.
  5 The zoo manager likes the suggestion about sponsorship.

4 ▶ 98 Complete the sentences with these phrases. Then listen again and check.

But if we don't	I'm sorry but	that isn't
we can't	How about	What if you
why don't you	You might	

  1 _____ giving us more money?
  2 _____ the council doesn't have any more money for the zoo.
  3 _____ find a solution soon, then we'll have to close it.
  4 _____ advertised the zoo more?
  5 But if we don't have any money, _____ advertise.
  6 Well, _____ try sponsorship?
  7 Actually, _____ a bad idea.
  8 _____ be right!

5 Match the sentences in Exercise 4 with the correct category in expressions for finding a solution.

> ▶ **FINDING A SOLUTION**
>
> **Stating and explaining the problem**
> The problem is that …
>
> **Making suggestions**
> We could also …
>
> **Responding positively**
> That's a good idea.
>
> **Responding negatively**
> Yes, but …
> No, that won't work.

6 Work in groups of four. Have a meeting to discuss the zoo's problems.

Student A: Turn to page 153.

Student B and Student D: Turn to page 155.

Student C: Turn to page 154.

12e The Eden Project

Writing an article

1 Read the article about a place called *The Eden Project* and answer the questions.

1 What can you see at the Eden Project?
2 Why do people visit the Eden Project?

A 'Biome' at the Eden Project

The Eden Project

Since it opened in 2001 in the south-west of England, millions of people have visited the Eden Project and learned about the natural world. It is one of England's most important tourist destinations.

As soon as you arrive, you see the huge plastic domes called 'biomes'. The two biggest biomes are the Rainforest Biome and the Mediterranean Biome. The Rainforest Biome has a warm climate, with plants from parts of Asia, Africa and South America. The Mediterranean Biome has over 1,000 different plants from countries around the Mediterranean Sea and from California and South Africa.

In addition to the biomes, the Eden Project also has outdoor gardens with plants and flowers you can use for medicine, fuel and food. There are also art exhibitions, theatre performances, and outdoor concerts throughout the year. Groups of school children regularly visit and there are courses for adults about plants and nature.

So the Eden Project is not just a tourist attraction. It aims to educate people about the importance of plants in our lives and to protect plants which are in danger of disappearing from the Earth.

2 Writing skill planning an article

a Work in pairs. The writer used the Eden Project website to research and plan this article. Think of three more ways to research an article.

b When you plan an article, it's useful to write questions and organize the information from your research using a mind map. Match the questions (a–f) to the information (1–6) in the mind map.

a What is the place?
b When and where did it open?
c What else is there?
d Why is it important?
e What's the most interesting thing about the place?
f Who visits it?

c Look at the mind map and read the article again. How does the writer organize his information? Match the information (1–6) to these parts of the article.

- the introduction (paragraph 1)
- paragraph 2
- paragraph 3
- the conclusion (paragraph 4)

3 Plan and write an article about a place you know or would like to visit. Write 120–140 words. Follow these steps.

1 Decide where you can research the information.
2 Write questions you want to answer and find the information.
3 Plan the article with a mind map. Write the questions and information on your mind map.
4 Decide which information will go in which paragraph.
5 Write the article using the mind map.

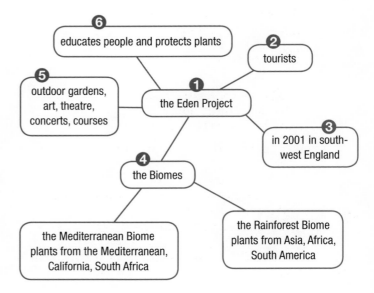

6 educates people and protects plants

2 tourists

5 outdoor gardens, art, theatre, concerts, courses

1 the Eden Project

3 in 2001 in south-west England

4 the Biomes

the Mediterranean Biome plants from the Mediterranean, California, South Africa

the Rainforest Biome plants from Asia, Africa, South America

12f Cambodia animal rescue

At the Phnom Tamao Rescue Centre in Cambodia there is one thing many of the animals have in common ...

Before you watch

1 You are going to watch a video about an animal rescue centre in Cambodia. Look at the photo and answer the questions.

1 What kinds of animals can you see?
2 What do they 'have in common'?
3 How do you think the rescue centre helps them?

2 Key vocabulary

Read these sentences from the video. Match the words in bold with the definitions (a–h).

1 Many animals at the centre are brought in by a special team called the 'Wilderness **Protection** Mobile Unit'.
2 **Poachers** can make a lot of money.
3 Matt Young works for Wild Aid, a US group that **sponsors** the MU and the rescue centre.
4 Once we're sure they're nice and healthy again, we can get them out to Kirirom and **release** them.
5 Dara, and the other animals at the Phnom Tamao Rescue Centre, are all **victims** of the **illegal** poaching of wild animals in Cambodia.
6 In some Asian countries, certain parts of the tiger are **ground into powder**.
7 The MU can help stop more wild animals from becoming **endangered**.

a people or animals that are affected by a bad situation
b not allowed by law
c put them back into the wild
d in danger
e made into very small pieces
f keeping something safe
g people who kill or capture animals illegally for money
h gives money to

While you watch

3 ▶ 12.1 Watch the video. Number these animals in the order you see them (1–8).

a scorpions
b eagle
c tiger
d crocodile
e monkey
f gibbon
g bear
h elephant

4 Match the animals (1–5) with the correct phrases from the video (a–e).

1 The tiger
2 The eagles
3 The gibbon
4 The bear
5 The elephants

a was found in a birdcage in a petrol station.
b is called Mimi and was someone's pet.
c need special care and are given food by hand.
d are called Lucky and Sima.
e is called Dara and loves to play.

5 ▶ 12.1 Watch the video again and answer the questions.

1 What do the letters MU stand for?
2 What does the MU do?
3 What do the government of Cambodia and the MU want to stop?
4 What does the American group Wild Aid do?
5 Where did the little gibbon live before the rescue centre?
6 Which organization sponsors Mimi?
7 Why did the family take Mimi to the rescue centre?
8 How many animals does the Rescue Centre care for?

After you watch

6 Vocabulary in context

a ▶ 12.2 Watch the clips from the video. Choose the correct meaning of the words and phrases.

b Complete this summary of the video using words from Exercise 6a.

The animal rescue centre gives special [1]c_____ to many different animals. With [2]s_____ from the government, the centre looks after [3]r_____ animals. Sometimes the animals have been kept as pets which people found too hard to [4]h_____. But many of them are also in danger from poaching because parts of their body are in [5]d_____ and are sold for a lot of money.

7 Discuss these questions as a class.

1 Why are places like the Phnom Tamao Rescue Centre important? Do you have similar organizations in your country?
2 Does animal poaching exist in your country? What animals do the poachers catch? Why?
3 What can governments do to stop poaching? What else can we do to protect animals from poaching?

Grammar

1 Complete the second conditional sentences with the correct form of the verbs.

1 If it was hotter, we _____ (go) to the beach.
2 The grass would be much greener if it _____ (rain).
3 Hurricanes would be more common if you _____ (live) in the southern USA.
4 We _____ (not / need) air conditioning if we moved to a colder climate.
5 They wouldn't eat my cooking if they _____ (not / like) it!

2 Complete the sentences for you. Then compare your sentences with a partner.

1 If I had a million dollars, I'd …
2 If I could go anywhere in the world, I'd go to …
3 If I lived in another country, I'd live in …

3 Complete the sentences with these pairs of words.

> anyone + anywhere   everyone + anything
> nobody + everybody   nowhere + everywhere
> someone + somewhere   something + nothing

1 _____ is as beautiful as this region. _____ you look, there are trees.
2 _____ told me there's a snake _____ in the grass, so be careful.
3 Has _____ seen Michelle? I can't find her _____.
4 _____ is hungry. Is there _____ in the fridge?
5 I left a message but _____ called me back. Is _____ on holiday?
6 I'd like _____ special to eat but _____ on the menu looks very interesting.

4 **>> MB** Work in pairs. Can you remember why the photographer used this green cube? Complete the sentences.

• The photographer thinks everyone lives near …
• He took the green cube to …
• He photographed anything …

I CAN	
use the second conditional	
use words starting with *any-, every-, no-, some-*	

Vocabulary

5 **>> MB** Work in pairs. Look at the photos from the unit and answer the questions for each photo.

1 What time of day is it?
2 What's the weather like?

6 Work in pairs. Look at these words for places in nature. Compare the two places in each pair and say one similarity and one difference.

forest / park
They both have trees, but a forest has a lot more trees.

> mountain / desert   river / ocean   park / garden
> river / park   field / forest   ocean / desert

I CAN	
talk about the weather	
talk about places in nature	

Real life

7 Put these words in the correct order to make phrases for finding a solution.

1 opening / about / what / a new zoo?
2 help? / why / ask for / don't / we
3 won't / we / sell any products / if / advertise / we don't /
4 the / that / many people / don't / problem is / recycle plastic
5 but / work / that / I'm sorry / won't
6 good / a / idea / that's

8 **>> MB** Work in pairs and look at these problems. Make suggestions to solve the problems.

• animals have nowhere to go if we close the zoo
• a school has no money to buy new technology
• a restaurant doesn't have many customers

I CAN	
find a solution to a problem	

UNIT 1a Exercise 3, page 10

How well do you sleep?

Mostly A answers:
The average human needs around eight hours of sleep per night. You probably get this because you usually sleep very well. You have regular routines and you are hardly ever tired.

Mostly B answers:
You sleep fairly well. Maybe you wake up once or twice a night and that's normal. But you have a busy life, so you need extra hours in bed. Try to go to bed early during the week and sleep an extra hour at the weekend.

Mostly C answers:
You work hard and get home late, and sometimes work in the evening at home, so you probably don't get the sleep you need. Try to relax in the evening and go to bed early.

Unit 5b Exercise 12, page 61

Pair A

Write questions for these answers or use your own ideas (e.g. write questions about your own country).

Buckingham Palace

Dubai

Easter Island

the Sphinx

Facebook

UNIT 5d Exercise 6, page 64

Student A

1 You ordered some clothes online. You received an email from the company. The clothes are not in stock. Telephone the customer service helpline.

- Say why you are calling.
- Your order number is EI3304A.
- Spell your surname.
- Find out how long you have to wait for the clothes.
- Ask for a refund. The price was $149.50.

2 You are a customer service assistant for a book supplier. Answer the telephone.

- Ask for the customer's order number and the title of the book.
- The book isn't in stock. You don't know when the book will arrive.
- Offer the caller a second-hand copy of the same book. It's £3.50.

UNIT 12d Exercise 6, page 148

Student A

You are the zoo manager and will lead the meeting. Here are two possible suggestions. You can also make more suggestions.

- Ask companies to sponsor different animals. Their company name will be on a sign near the animal.
- Organize an open day where everyone in the city can visit the zoo for free to learn more about their zoo.

When you are ready to begin the meeting, explain the problem and then discuss each suggestion. Start your meeting by saying: *Hello, everyone and thank you for coming. Today we are going to discuss the zoo. The problem is that …*

Unit 5b Exercise 12, page 61

Pair B

Write questions for these answers or use your own ideas (e.g. write questions about your own country).

the Sun

the Great Wall of China

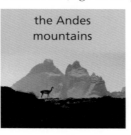
the Andes mountains

Twitter

Lake Titicaca

UNIT 5d Exercise 6, page 64

Student B

1 You are a customer service assistant for a clothing company supplier. Answer the telephone.

- Ask for the customer's order number and his/her surname.
- The clothes aren't in stock but they will be in two weeks.
- Offer some different clothes at the same price.

2 You ordered a book online called *Learn Spanish in One Week*. You received an email from the company. The book is not in stock. Telephone the customer service helpline.

- Say why you are calling.
- Your order number is AZE880.
- Find out how long you have to wait for the book.
- Ask for the price of the second-hand copy.
- Buy the second-hand book.

Unit 9d Exercise 6, page 112

Student B

1 You work at tourist information. Look at the information about the Caves of Lascaux. Answer the tourist's questions and make suggestions.

The Caves of Lascaux

The Caves of Lascaux are in the Dordogne region of France. The paintings there are over 17,000 years old.

Opening times: 9 a.m. to 5 p.m.
Ticket price: Adults: 8 euros, Children: 5 euros
Transport: Buses leave every 15 minutes from the city centre. Taxis also available.
Tours: Free tours are available but please book in advance.

UNIT 12d Exercise 6, page 148

Student C

You work for the zoo. Here are two possible suggestions to make at the meeting. You can also make your own suggestions.

- Start a zoo shop which sells T-shirts, posters, hats, etc.
- Invite newspaper and TV journalists to a special day where you explain the importance of the zoo and its conservation work.

2 Now you are the tourist. Look at the information about the Catacombs of Rome. Ask questions and complete the information.

The Catacombs of Rome

Opening times: 9 a.m. to _____ and 2 to 5 p.m. It's open six days a week but closed on _____ .
Tickets: Adults: 8 euros   Children: _____
Public transport: There is _____ .

UNIT 12d Exercise 6, page 148

Student B

You work for the zoo. Here are two possible suggestions to make at the meeting. You can also make your own suggestions.

- Offer special tickets with discounts such as a 'family ticket' or cheaper prices for children.
- Ask people to buy an animal but it lives at the zoo.

UNIT 1e Exercise 3b, page 17

1 DOB = Date of birth, No. = number,
e.g. = for example, etc. = et cetera
2 Mr is used before the name of any man.
Mrs is used before the name of a married woman.
Ms is used before the name of a woman when we don't know if she is married or single.
Dr means Doctor.
3 Form B: It says 'Please use capital letters' at the top.

UNIT 4c Exercise 2, page 50

The riddle: the answer is 'your name'.
The matchstick puzzle: move two matches.

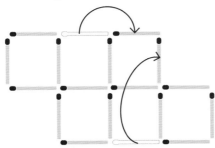

The numbers memory challenge: most people remember up to the seven numbers in 7430673 but it's more difficult to remember eight numbers or more.

Unit 9d Exercise 6, page 112

Student A

1 You are the tourist. Look at the information about the Caves of Lascaux. Ask questions and complete the information.

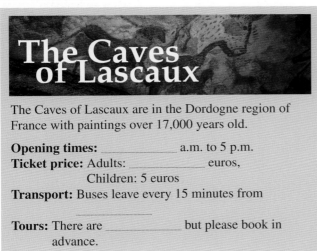

The Caves of Lascaux

The Caves of Lascaux are in the Dordogne region of France with paintings over 17,000 years old.

Opening times: _____ a.m. to 5 p.m.
Ticket price: Adults: _____ euros,
Children: 5 euros
Transport: Buses leave every 15 minutes from
_____
Tours: There are _____ but please book in advance.

Unit 5b Exercise 11, page 61

1 the river Amazon
2 the president
3 the moon
4 Google
5 the Pacific Ocean

Unit 7a Exercise 1, page 82

According to a report in *The Telegraph*, these are the jobs employers find most difficult to fill in the UK.

1 computer programmer
2 nurse
3 engineer
4 accountant
5 marketing manager

UNIT 12d Exercise 6, page 148

Student D

You work for the zoo. Here are two possible suggestions to make at the meeting. You can also make your own suggestions.

- Contact other zoos and exchange animals so people will come back to look at different animals.
- Have a parade with costumes and food through the city centre with some of the animals.

2 Now you work at tourist information. Look at the information about the Catacombs of Rome. Answer the tourist's questions and make suggestions.

The Catacombs of Rome

Opening times: 9 a.m. to 1 p.m. and 2 to 5 p.m. Open six days a week. Closed on Wednesdays.
Tickets: Adults: 8 euros   Children: 5 euros
The tour lasts 40 minutes.
Public transport: There is the underground (Metro A line) or bus 174 or 118 from outside tourist information.

GRAMMAR SUMMARY UNIT 1

Present simple and adverbs of frequency

Use

We use the present simple:

- to talk about habits and routines.
  *I **play tennis** every week.*

- to talk about things that are always true.
  *Sleep **is** really important for health.*

Form

We form the present simple with the infinitive form of the verb. To make negative sentences, we add *don't* before the verb. To make questions, we add *do* before the subject.

After *he, she, it*, etc. we add *-s* to the verb. We use *doesn't* in negative sentences, and *does* in questions.

	+	–	?
I/you/we/they	I **eat**.	You **don't eat**.	**Do** you eat?
he/she/it	She **eats**.	He **doesn't eat**.	**Does** he/she/it eat?

The verb *be* is different from other verbs.

	+	–	?
I	I**'m** fit.	I**'m not** fit.	**Am** I fit?
you/we/they	We**'re** fit.	They **aren't** fit.	**Are** you fit?
he/she/it	She**'s** fit.	She **isn't** fit.	**Is** he fit?

▶ **Exercise 1**

Adverbs and expressions of frequency

We use adverbs and other expressions in present simple sentences to talk about how often we do things.
*Mike **usually** goes for a run in the evening.*
*I'm **often** late for work.*
*I have a hot drink **five or six times a day**.*
*We go on holiday **two or three times a year**.*

Some common frequency adverbs are:

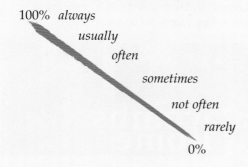

100% *always*
  usually
    often
      sometimes
        not often
          rarely
    0%

Position

Frequency adverbs and expressions of frequency go in different places in a sentence.

- Adverbs of frequency go before the main verb, but after the verb *to be*.
  *They **never** <u>eat</u> out.*
  *She'<u>s</u> **always** out at the weekend.*
  *I **don't often** <u>do</u> sport.*

- Expressions of frequency normally go at the beginning or end of a sentence.
  *I go out with friends **three or four times a week**.*
  ***Once a week**, I go for a run.*

▶ **Exercises 2 and 3**

Present continuous

Use

We use the present simple to talk about things we do or that happen regularly. We use the present continuous to talk about something in progress in the present. This can be:

- something actually in progress at this moment.
  *I can't answer the phone because **I'm driving**.*

- something happening around now, but not necessarily at this moment.
  I'm looking for a new job.

- a changing situation.
  *More and more people **are changing** their diet.*

Form

We form the present continuous with *be* + verb + *-ing*.

	+	–	?
I	I**'m writing**.	I**'m not writing**.	**Am** I writing?
you/we/they	We**'re writing**.	They **aren't writing**.	**Are** you writing?
he/she/it	He**'s writing**.	She **isn't writing**.	**Is** she writing?

Some verbs describe states (for example, *agree, believe, hate, know, like, love, prefer, want*). We don't use these verbs with the continuous.
~~He's owning a really nice car.~~
*He **owns** a really nice car.*

▶ **Exercises 4, 5 and 6**

Exercises

1 Complete the sentences with the present simple form of the verbs in brackets.

1 Sam _____ (not live) near me.
2 Sofia _____ (drive) to work.
3 _____ she _____ (speak) any other languages?
4 I _____ (not like) waking up early.
5 _____ they _____ (see) each other at the weekends?
6 We _____ (be) very tired.
7 Some people _____ (not need) a lot of sleep.
8 _____ (be) your bus late?
9 He _____ (have) a big house in the country.

2 Look at the sentences. There are five mistakes with the position of frequency adverbs and time expressions. Find and correct the mistakes.

1 I often am tired at work.
2 We twice a week eat out in a restaurant.
3 Do you often check your phone for messages?
4 She is never late to my lesson.
5 I have two or three times a day a cup of coffee.
6 They don't play often board games.
7 Does usually she take public transport?

3 Complete the text with words from the boxes. Use a verb from box A or a phrase from box B in each gap. You do not need all the words in the boxes.

A
always   every day   never   often   rarely
two or three times a month   usually

B
eat   get up   go   have   leave   make
meet

I ¹_____ ²_____ at about 7.30 a.m. and get ready for work. I ³_____ ⁴_____ breakfast because I don't feel hungry in the mornings. I start work at 9 a.m. and at 12 I have a lunch break. I ⁵_____ ⁶_____ my friend for lunch – normally two or three times a week. At 1.30 I start work again and finish at 5.30 p.m. I like to keep fit, so I ⁷_____ to the gym ⁸_____ . I get home at about 8.00 p.m. and make dinner, but I also ⁹_____ at restaurants ¹⁰_____ . I'm always tired in the evenings so I go to bed early. And that's my day!

4 Complete the sentences with the present continuous form of these verbs.

become   build   go   not work   talk   wait
write

1 I _____ for the bus.
2 A: Where _____ you _____ ?
   B: To the supermarket. We need milk!
3 She _____ this week because she's on holiday.
4 A: What are you doing?
   B: I _____ an email to my friend.
5 A: Where's Michael?
   B: He _____ to someone on the phone.
6 They _____ a new house on my road.
7 More and more people _____ vegetarian.

5 Complete the pairs of sentences with the verb in brackets. Use the present simple form in one sentence and the present continuous form in the other.

1 I _____ my lunch very early today. I normally _____ at 1 p.m. (eat)
2 Tina rarely _____ to work. But today she _____ because of the rain. (drive)
3 She _____ to her brother on the phone right now. They _____ at this time every day. (talk)
4 It's 6 p.m. and I _____ hard in the office. I normally _____ only until 5 p.m. (work)
5 I _____ the shopping now. I always _____ the shopping at this time. (do)

6 Complete the text with the present simple or present continuous form of the verbs.

The Mediterranean diet

People in countries like Italy, Spain, France and Greece ¹_____ (live) longer than people from many other countries. This is probably because of their diet – they ²_____ (eat) lots of food like vegetables, fruit, nuts, beans, fish and olive oil, and people often ³_____ (say) that this diet ⁴_____ (be) good for your heart. But the traditional Mediterranean diet ⁵_____ (change) because more and more people ⁶_____ (eat) junk food. So, in the future the Mediterranean diet might be very different.

Verbs for rules

Use

To talk about rules, we use the verbs *must*, *have to* and *can*.

* To say that something is obligatory, we use *must* or *have to*.
  *You **have to** train hard to do a Marathon.*
  *Runners **must** arrive twenty minutes before the race.*

* To say that something is allowed, we use *can*.
  *Members **can** use the swimming pool for free.*

* To say that something is not obligatory but allowed, we use *don't have to*.
  *You **don't have to** be fit to join the club.*

* To say that something is not allowed, we use *can't* or *mustn't*.
  *You **can't** touch the ball in football.*
  *You **mustn't** leave any bags in this area.*

The verbs *must* and *have to*, and *can't* and *mustn't*, have very similar meanings. In general, we prefer to use *have to* and *can't* in spoken English to talk about rules. In formal, written English, we prefer to use *must* and *mustn't*.
  *You **have to** pay $40 to do the race. (spoken)*
  *Competitors **must** pay $40 to enter the race. (formal, written)*
  *You **can't** go near the pool with shoes on. (spoken)*
  *Customers **must not** go near the pool with shoes on. (formal, written)*

But remember that *mustn't* and *don't have to* have completely different meanings – *mustn't* means 'don't do it!', while *don't have to* means 'it's not necessary to do it'.

Form

We normally use these verbs before a main verb.
  *You **can** <u>borrow</u> my running shoes.*

The verbs *must* / *mustn't* and *can* / *can't* don't work like normal verbs. They never change – we use the same form for all persons (*I, you, he/she/it* etc.). We don't use *do*, *does* or *did* to make questions or negatives.

	+	–	?
I/you/we/they	*I **can** swim.*	*I **can't** swim.*	***Can** you swim?*
he/she/it	*She **can** swim.*	*He **can't** swim.*	***Can** he swim?*

The verb *have to* works like a normal verb. It changes for *he/she/it* in the present simple, and we form questions and negatives in the past and present using *do, does* or *did*.

	+	–	?
I/you/we/they	*I **have to** go.*	*I **don't have to** go.*	***Do** you **have to** go?*
he/she/it	*He **has to** go.*	*She **doesn't have to** go.*	***Does** she **have to** go?*

▶ Exercises 1, 2 and 3

-ing form

We use the *-ing* form of a verb after *be* to form the present or past continuous:
  *I'm **getting** ready to go out.*
  *I was **watching** a film.*

However, we also use the *-ing* form in some other ways.

-ing form as the subject of a sentence

We can make a verb the subject of a sentence. When we do this, we usually use the *-ing* form.
  ***Playing sport** is great for your health.*

-ing form after prepositions

When a verb comes after a preposition, it is always in the *-ing* form.
  *I'm not very good <u>at</u> **swimming**.*

-ing form after some verbs

We sometimes put two verbs together in a sentence. The form of the second verb depends on the first verb. After the verbs *like, dislike, love, hate, can't stand, enjoy* and *don't mind*, the second verb is in the *-ing* form.
  *Jan <u>loves</u> **watching** sport.*
  *I <u>don't mind</u> **running** in the cold.*

▶ Exercises 4 and 5

Exercises

1 Match the rules (1–6) with the meanings (a–c).

  a Do this.
  b Don't do this.
  c This is allowed.

  1 You must wear your seat belt in a car.
  2 You can't hit the ball with your hand in football.
  3 Boxers have to wear special gloves.
  4 You can walk in a marathon.
  5 The students can't use their mobile phones during the exam.
  6 We can take photos during the tennis match.

2 Choose the correct form to complete the sentences. In one case, both answers are possible.

  1 You *mustn't / don't have to* kick the ball when you play basketball. You can only use your hands.
  2 We *mustn't / don't have to* go to the football game. We can watch it on television.
  3 If the fire alarm rings, you *must / don't have to* go straight outside. It's important to be quick.
  4 In many countries, you *must / mustn't* wait until you are 18 to drive. It's not possible if you're younger.
  5 Visitors *must / have to* go to reception when they arrive.
  6 You *don't have to / mustn't* come tonight. Stay at home if you prefer.

3 Choose the correct options to complete the email.

How are you? I'm doing well. You asked me in your email about the gym I go to, so here's some information for you. You [1] *have to / must* pay for a whole month – you [2] *don't have to / can't* pay for one visit. When you pay, they give you a gym card. You [3] *don't have to / mustn't* forget this card because you need it to get in the gym.

I like to use the bikes in the gym. I usually cycle for about an hour, but when there are a lot of people, you [4] *can't / mustn't* use the bikes for a long time. I also do a yoga class once or twice a week. You [5] *don't have to / mustn't* book before, so I usually decide when I arrive. One last thing – you [6] *have to / can't* remember to bring a towel with you because the gym doesn't give them to you.

Why don't you come with me to the gym next week? I can show you everything. Let me know!

4 Complete the sentences with the *-ing* form of a verb from the box.

do	fail	play	help	watch	wake up
read					

  1 She's really good at _____ the piano.
  2 I don't like _____ TV – it's so boring!
  3 _____ exercise is very good for your health.
  4 He hates _____ early at the weekends.
  5 I'm worried about _____ my exam.
  6 _____ a book is a great way to pass the time on a train.
  7 Thank you for _____ me with my work.

5 Choose the correct form to complete the dialogue.

A: Why are you [1] *cleaning / clean* the house?
B: It's dirty. Why?
A: It's such a nice day – why don't we [2] *doing / do* something outside? [3] *Staying / Stay* at home is so boring.
B: OK. What do you think about [4] *go / going* for a run?
A: I hate [5] *run / running*!
B: OK, how about [6] *going / go* for a walk in the mountains?
A: That's a good idea. We could [7] *taking / take* a picnic with us.
B: Great! I love [8] *eat / eating* outside on a sunny day.
A: Good – you can [9] *making / make* the picnic for us, then!

Comparatives and superlatives

Form

Adjective	Comparative	Superlative
slow	slower	(the) slowest
easy	easier	(the) easiest
difficult	more difficult	(the) most difficult
good	better	(the) best

For most **one-syllable adjectives**, we add **-er** to form the comparative and we add **-est** to form the superlative.

> fast → fas**ter** / fas**test**   old → old**er** / old**est**

For most adjectives that have **two syllables or more**, we use **more** + adjective to form the comparative and we use **most** + adjective to form the superlative.

> useful → **more** useful / **most** useful
> expensive → **more** expensive / **most** expensive

For **some two-syllable adjectives** (often adjectives that end in -y, -le, -ow and -er), we can either use -er or more to form the comparative, and -est or most to form the superlative. We sometimes use one form more than the other (e.g. narrower is more common than more narrow, whereas friendlier and more friendly are both common).

> friendly → friendlier or more friendly
>   friendliest or most friendly
> simple → simpler or more simple
>   simplest or most simple
> narrow → narrower or more narrow
>   narrowest or most narrow

Spelling rules

Note the following spelling rules when adding -er or -est to adjectives.

* For adjectives that end in -e, we just add -r or -st.
  nice → nice**r** / nice**st**
* For adjectives that end in -y, we change the y to i and add -er or -est.
  busy → bus**ier** / bus**iest**
* For one-syllable adjectives that end in consonant-vowel-consonant, we generally double the final consonant.
  big → bi**gger** / bi**ggest**   wet → we**tter** / we**ttest**
  However, we do <u>not</u> double w, x or y.
  slow → slo**wer** / slo**west**

Irregular forms

There are three common irregular adjectives.

> good → better / best
> bad → worse / worst
> far → further or farther / furthest or the farthest

Less and *the least*

To make a negative comparison, we use *less* + adjective to form the comparative and *the least* + adjective to form the superlative.

> fun → **less** fun / **least** fun
> popular → **less** popular / **least** popular

Use

We use comparative adjectives to compare things. We often use it with *than*.

> A taxi will be **quicker than** a bus.
> We could get a bus, but a taxi will be **quicker**.
> This one's **more expensive than** the others.
> They're **less popular than** they used to be.

We use superlative adjectives to compare one thing with other things in a group. We usually use *the* before a superlative.

> What's **the easiest** way to get to the town centre?

We can also use a possessive form (*the company's, New York's, my*, etc.) and words such as *the second, the third, the next*, etc.

> Waterloo is **London's busiest** underground station and King's Cross is **the second busiest**.

▶ **Exercises 1 and 2**

as ... as

We use *as* + adjective + *as* to say things are the same.

> Cycling there is **as quick as** going by bus.
> It's **as old as** I am.

To say things are not the same, we use *not as* + adjective + *as*. The thing we mention first is smaller or less busy / heavy, etc.

> The UK is **not as big as** Italy.
> The town is**n't as busy as** it used to be.

▶ **Exercises 3 and 4**

Comparative modifiers

We use comparative modifiers when we say there is a big or small difference between things that we are comparing.

To say there is a **big difference**, we can use *a lot* or *much*.
To say there is a **small difference**, we can use *a bit* or *a little*.

> Public transport is **much more expensive** than it used to be.
> Lucy's house is **a bit nearer** than Sue's.
> We usually fly from Manchester if possible – Heathrow is **a lot less convenient**.

▶ **Exercises 5 and 6**

Exercises

1 Complete the sentences with the comparative or superlative form of the adjective in bold.

1 I've driven lots of **nice** cars, but this one is the _____ .

2 Sheffield is quite **far** from here, but Leeds is _____ .

3 Today's lecture was **interesting** but I think last week's was _____ .

4 I've flown with some **bad** airlines, but SpeedAir has to be the _____ ever!

5 I agree that Budapest is **beautiful,** but in my opinion Prague is _____ .

6 The exhibition is **busy** today, but yesterday was _____ . In fact, I think yesterday was the _____ day so far since it opened.

7 I'm pretty **good** at tennis, but my friend Alex is _____ . Actually, he's probably the _____ in the club.

8 Peru, Colombia and Bolivia are **big**, but Argentina is _____ . In fact, I think Argentina is the second _____ country in South America, after Brazil.

2 Complete the transport facts. Use the comparative or superlative form of the adjectives. Add *the* or *than* if you need to.

¹ _____The fastest_____ (fast) time to visit all the world's countries by public transport is 4 years and 31 days.

The world's ² _____ (long) and ³ _____ (deep) rail tunnel, the Gotthard tunnel in Switzerland, opened in 2016. It is 57 km long and is about 3 km ⁴ _____ (long) the Seikan rail tunnel in Japan.

The Dover Strait between the UK and France is ⁵ _____ (busy) shipping lane in the world – 500–600 ships a day pass through it.

The country with ⁶ _____ (high) number of train passengers is China with over 17 billion rail journeys per year. This is much ⁷ _____ (high) India with 8 billion.

3 Write sentences using *as … as* and an adjective from the box.

big	fast	heavy	~~high~~

1 Height: Mount Fuji 3,776 m, Mount Kilimanjaro 5,895 m
   Mount Fuji isn't as high as Mount Kilimanjaro.

2 Area: USA 9,833,634 km², Canada 9,984,670 km²

3 Top speed: Kangaroo 71 kmh, Horse 71 kmh

4 Weight: Jumbo Jet 180,000 kg, Dreamliner 120,000 kg

4 Rewrite the sentences using *as … as* so that the meaning is the same.

1 Travelling by car is safer than travelling by motorbike.
   Travelling by motorbike isn't as safe as travelling by car.

2 Cycling and driving are both dangerous. They have the same number of accidents.

3 Heathrow Airport is more convenient for us than Gatwick Airport.

4 Usually, the beach is less busy during the week.

5 Going by car is no quicker than taking the bus.

5 Complete the sentences using the words in the box and any other words necessary.

a lot / busy	a bit / interesting	much / cheap
~~a bit / economical~~	a little / big	
much / popular	a lot / quiet	

1 The new model is *a bit more economical* than the old one.

2 Booking in advance can be _____ than paying on the day of travel.

3 Well, yesterday's lecture was _____ than last week's, I suppose.

4 The station is generally _____ in the afternoons and _____ when people are travelling to and from work.

5 Cycling is generally _____ with younger people, especially in student towns.

6 Our new car is _____ our old one. There's a bit more room in the back seat.

6 Complete the text about travel in Indonesia. Use the comparative or superlative form of the adjectives. Add any other words you need.

¹ _____ (good) way to travel around Indonesia depends on where you are. On major islands, getting around is generally ² _____ (much / easy). Away from the tourist areas, it can be ³ _____ (bit / difficult).

Buses are ⁴ _____ (convenient) and popular means of transport. Between tourist centres, the routes are usually ⁵ _____ (little / direct) and the journeys are generally ⁶ _____ (quick). However, prices can be ⁷ _____ (lot / high) the slower local buses.

Trains run only in Java and in parts of Sumatra. They're ⁸ _____ (bit / expensive) the bus but are ⁹ _____ (much / quick) and it's definitely worth paying extra for a ¹⁰ _____ (comfortable) class.

Past simple

Use

We use the past simple to talk about finished actions, events or situations in the past.

> I **visited** the Taj Mahal last year.
> We **saw** a great film at the weekend.

Form

Past simple forms can be regular or irregular.

- We form the past simple of regular verbs by adding -ed to the infinitive form.
  want → want**ed**   look → look**ed**

- If the verb ends in -e, we just add -d:
  like → lik**ed**   hope → hop**ed**

- We form the past simple of verbs ending in consonant + -y by changing -y to -ied.
  study → stud**ied**   try → tr**ied**

- We don't form the past simple of irregular verbs with -ed.
  go → went   hear → heard   see → saw

For a list of common irregular past simple forms, see page 180.

To form negatives in the past simple, we use *didn't* + infinitive.

	+	−
I/you/we/they	I **watched.**	I **didn't watch.**
he/she/it	He **watched.**	She **didn't watch.**

The verb *be* is different from other verbs. Its past simple form is *was* or *were*. We don't use *did* to form negatives.

	+	−
I/you/we/they	I **was tired.**	You **weren't tired.**
he/she/it	She **was tired.**	He **wasn't tired.**

▶ **Exercises 1 and 2**

Past simple questions

We make questions in the past simple with *did* + infinitive.

> Why **did** you **choose** to visit Turkey?
> **Did** she **have** fun on holiday?

When we make questions in the past simple with the verb *be*, we use *was* and *were*. We do not add *did*.

> **Were** you tired after your trip?
> Where **was** your hotel?

▶ **Exercise 3**

Past continuous and past simple

Use

We use the past continuous to talk about an action in progress at a moment in the past.

> I **was watching** TV at eight o'clock last night.
> Tony **was living** in Madrid in 2015.

Form

We form the past continuous with *was/were* and the -ing form of the main verb.

	+	−	?
I/you/ we/they	I **was reading.**	I **wasn't reading.**	**Were** you **reading?**
he/she/it	She **was reading.**	She **wasn't reading.**	**Was** he **reading?**

We often use the past continuous and the past simple together. We use the past continuous for a longer, continuing activity and the past simple for a shorter, finished action.

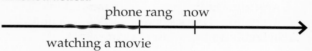

Jack **was watching** a movie when his phone **rang**.
I **met** my husband when I **was travelling** around India.

We often use *when* and *while* to join the two parts of a sentence with past continuous and past simple together. We use *when* before a past simple or a past continuous verb. We normally only use *while* with a past continuous verb.

> I met Matteo **when** I was studying at university.
> Someone stole my camera **while** I was eating in a restaurant.

When we use *when* with the past simple, it can also mean 'after'.

> I called Sylvia **when** I read her message.

If the part of the sentence with *when* or *while* comes first, we put a comma after it.

> **When** I met Matteo, I was studying at university.

Remember that we don't use verbs that describe states (e.g. *believe, like, love, prefer*) with a continuous tense.

▶ **Exercises 4, 5 and 6**

Exercises

1 Complete the second sentence in each pair with the past simple form of the verb.

1 She wants to travel the world.
  She _____ to travel the world.
2 It isn't easy to get a job.
  It _____ easy to get a job.
3 People don't have a lot of money.
  People _____ a lot of money.
4 He doesn't like travelling by plane.
  He _____ travelling by plane.
5 My train is late again.
  My train _____ late again.
6 They study at the university.
  They _____ at the university.

2 Complete the text with the past simple form of these verbs.

| ask | be | be | book | can | decide | drive |
| not know | have | take | not want | | | |

An island holiday … with a difference

Last summer, my husband and I [1] _____ a holiday on the island of Sicily, in Italy. We love the sea, but we [2] _____ to spend every day on the beach. So, we [3] _____ to visit Mount Etna, a live volcano! We [4] _____ to the mountain from our hotel early in the morning. When we arrived, we [5] _____ where to go so we [6] _____ a guide to help us. She [7] _____ very good and told us about the history of the volcano. When we got near the crater, there was a strong smell and we [8] _____ see smoke. The views at the top [9] _____ amazing. We [10] _____ a lot of photos and after that we went back to the hotel and [11] _____ a delicious lunch there. It was a fantastic experience!

3 Write past simple questions with these words.

1 how / be / your hotel?
  ....
2 when / you / get back?
  ....
3 they / get the train home?
  ....
4 what / your / favourite experience?
  ....
5 you / call me / this morning?
  ....
6 How much / our / plane tickets cost?
  ....

4 Complete the sentences with the past continuous form of the verbs.

1 We _____ (wait) for the bus.
2 He _____ (not eat) his food.
3 _____ you _____ (talk) to your friend?
4 What _____ those people _____ (say) to each other?
5 It _____ (not rain) when we left the house.
6 Where _____ she _____ (fly) to?

5 Choose the correct option to complete the sentences.

1 Jack *arrived / was arriving* while I *was watching / watched* TV.
2 When the taxi *arrived / was arriving*, we *got / were getting* in.
3 It *was starting / started* snowing while we *climbed / were climbing* the mountain.
4 He *wasn't playing / didn't play* on his computer when I *was seeing / saw* him.
5 *Did she ski / Was she skiing* when she *had / was having* the accident?
6 I *knew / was knowing* he had a problem when I *heard / was hearing* him shout.

6 Complete the text with the past simple or past continuous form of these verbs.

| can not | come | eat | know | sit | start |
| travel | wait | | | | |

I had an amazing surprise while I [1] _____ around India last year. I [2] _____ dinner in a restaurant in Delhi when someone [3] _____ in and sat at the table next to me. I [4] _____ her face but I [5] _____ remember who she was. We [6] _____ talking and then I realized – it was Maggie, my best friend from primary school!

But the story didn't end there. When I got to the airport on the last day of my holiday, who [7] _____ in the airport? Maggie, of course. She [8] _____ for the same flight and her seat was in front of mine on the plane!

GRAMMAR SUMMARY UNIT 5

Quantifiers

We use quantifiers with nouns to talk about quantity. The choice of quantifier depends on:

- if the noun is countable or uncountable.

- if we are talking about small or large quantities.

Some nouns are countable. This means they can become plural, for example *computer, bag, box, magazine*. Other nouns are uncountable. This means they cannot normally become plural, for example *rubbish, plastic, paper, metal*.

Quantity	Countable	Uncountable
large quantity	a lot of / lots of	a lot of / lots of
neutral quantity (not large or small)	some	some
small quantity	not many	not much
small quantity	a few	a little
no quantity (zero)	not any	not any

We use *a lot of* or *lots of* with countable and uncountable nouns to talk about large quantities. The meaning of *a lot of* and *lots of* is the same.
> There was **a lot of** rubbish on the streets after the party.
> We have **lots of** great shops in my neighbourhood.

We use *some* with both countable and uncountable nouns. It does not refer to a specific amount – we use it to talk about quantities that are not large and are not small.
> I found **some** really useful books in the library.
> (= not a lot)

In more formal English, we use *many* + plural noun to talk about large quantities.
> There are **many** interesting places to visit in the city.

We also use *many* and *much* in questions.
> Are there **many** good shops where you live?
> Do you have **much** free time?

We don't normally use *many* and *much* in affirmative sentences in spoken English. We use *a lot of* or *lots of* instead.

We use *not much* and *not many* to talk about small quantities. We use *not much* with uncountable nouns and *not many* with plural countable nouns.
> There weren't **many** people at the party.
> They don't have **much** money.

Note that *not* always goes with the verb in the sentence.

We also use *a few* and *a little* to talk about small quantities. We use *a few* with plural countable nouns and *a little* with uncountable nouns:
> I have **a few** really good friends.
> There's **a little** milk in the bottle.

We use *not any* with countable and uncountable nouns to talk about zero quantity (when there is nothing).
> I don't have **any** money.
> There weren't **any** shops open when we arrived.

Note that *not* always goes with the verb in the sentence.

We also use *any* with countable and uncountable nouns to ask questions:
> Are there **any** good beaches in the area?
> Do you have **any** orange juice?

▶ Exercises 1, 2 and 3

Articles (*a/an*, *the* or no article)

We use *a/an*:

- to talk about something that isn't specific.
> Have you got **a** pen? (not a particular pen)

- the first time we mention something.
> I saw **a** beautiful painting in the museum.

We use *the*:

- the second time we mention something.
> A man and a woman were waiting for us at the airport. **The** man helped us with our suitcases.

- when something is unique.
> **The** sun looked really beautiful from the top of the mountain.

- with superlatives.
> It was **the best** holiday of my life.

- with the names of some places, such as oceans (e.g. **the** Atlantic Ocean), deserts (e.g. **the** Sahara Desert) and mountain ranges (e.g. **the** Himalayas).

We use no article:

- to talk about plural or uncountable nouns in general.
> I never stay in (–) hotels because they're so expensive. (–) Tourism brings a lot of money to the area.

- the names of most places, for example the names of continents, countries, cities and lakes.

▶ Exercises 4, 5 and 6

Exercises

1 Choose one quantifier from the pair to complete each sentence.

1 many / much
  a There wasn't _____ cheese in the fridge.
  b There weren't _____ apples left.
2 a little / a few
  a There was _____ space for me on the seat.
  b We have _____ recycling bins outside our house.
3 many / much
  a How _____ tea do you drink in a day?
  b How _____ tourists visit the national park?
4 some / any
  a The car park didn't have _____ space for my car.
  b _____ people prefer shopping online.

2 Choose the correct option (a–c).

1 I can't go travelling this year because I don't have _____ money.
  a much   b a lot   c few
2 The hotel doesn't have _____ free rooms.
  a some   b any   c a little
3 I have _____ clothes I don't wear.
  a a lot   b lots of   c much
4 He made _____ coffee for me.
  a any   b many   c some
5 There weren't _____ people at the party.
  a many   b some   c much
6 There was _____ rubbish left in the bin.
  a a few   b a little   c little
7 The shop had _____ things that I liked.
  a much   b a little   c a few

3 Choose the correct quantifiers to complete the dialogue.

A: Wait! Don't throw your coffee cup in the bin.
B: Why not?
A: Well, if ¹ *a lot of / a little* people throw away their coffee cups, it makes ² *a few / lots of* rubbish.
B: I only drink ³ *a little / a few* coffees in the week. That's not ⁴ *much / many* coffee cups.
A: Yes, but I read in an article that people throw away 7 million coffee cups every day in the UK!
B: That is ⁵ *a lot / a little*!
A: I know. The article says that ⁶ *some / any* businesses now have new recycling bins for coffee cups.

B: Were there ⁷ *much / any* recycling bins in the café we were in?
A: No, there weren't … oh look! Here's one! You can recycle your cup here.
B: Great! Now every time I have a coffee I have to come back here to recycle the cup!

4 Choose the correct option to complete these facts.

Surprising facts about our world.
1 Redwood trees are *the / –* tallest trees in the world.
2 *– / The* Lake Superior is the largest lake in the USA.
3 China built *the / an* amazing bridge over the Dehang Canyon. *The / A* bridge is the highest in the world.
4 Mercury is the closest planet to *– / the* Sun.
5 *– / The* honey bees only live for five to six weeks.
6 Until around 4,000 years ago, *the / –* Sahara Desert was green and animals probably lived there.

5 Complete the dialogue with *a, the* or no article (–).

A: I watched ¹ *an / the* interesting documentary last night about ² *the / –* flowers.
B: Really?
A: Yeah, ³ *the / a* documentary showed where in ⁴ *– / the* world they grow ⁵ *the / a* flowers and how they arrive here in the UK.
B: And what did you learn?
A: Well, they grow the flowers in countries like ⁶ *– / the* Kenya and then they transport them round the world.
B: That's not great for ⁷ *a / the* environment. Did you learn anything else?
A: Yeah, most of our flowers come from ⁸ *the / a* big market in the Netherlands. It's ⁹ *a / the* biggest flower market in the world!
B: That's amazing.

6 Choose *the, a* or no article (–) in the text below.

In ¹ *a / the* small town called Rjukan in ² *the / –* Norway, there is no sunlight for six months a year. People in ³ *the / –* Rjukan live without ⁴ *the / a* sun from September to March. But this is changing thanks to Martin Andersen – a local man who had the clever idea to use ⁵ *a / the* mirror to bring sunlight to the town. ⁶ *The / a* mirror is on top of a mountain next to the town and it reflects light from the sun onto ⁷ *a / the* town's main square. ⁸ *The / –* people love coming to the main square and sitting in the sun.

GRAMMAR SUMMARY UNIT 6

to + infinitive

We use the *to* + infinitive form of the verb in different situations.

verb + to + infinitive

Sometimes, two verbs appear together in a sentence. The form of the second verb depends on the first verb. After many verbs (e.g. *decide, help, hope, intend, learn, need, plan, pretend, promise, want, would like*) the second verb has the form *to* + infinitive.

> I **need to go** to the shops.
> We **decided to move** abroad.

adjective + to + infinitive

When a verb appears after an adjective, it often has the form *to* + infinitive:

> It's **exciting to visit** new places.
> It's **nice to see** you again.

▶ Exercise 1

infinitive explaining the purpose of an action

We also use the *to* + infinitive form to say why we do something.

> I went to the library **to look** for a book.
> She's going to Paris **to visit** a friend.

We don't use *for* + verb to give reasons.

> ~~I called Jan **for invite** her to my party.~~
> I called Jan **to invite** her to my party.

Note that the negative of *to* + infinitive is *not to* + infinitive.

> I promise **not to do** that again.
> It's important **not to work** too hard.

See Unit 2 for when we use the *-ing* form of the verb.

▶ Exercises 2 and 3

future forms

Present continuous

We use the present continuous to talk about a fixed arrangement in the future, for example when we have agreed something with other people or when we have already spent money. We normally mention a specific time.

> We're **getting** the train at 11.20 a.m.
> I'm **going** to the theatre with Michele tonight.

be going to

We use *be going to* + infinitive to talk about general plans and intentions.

> I'm **going to travel** around Asia this summer.
> We're **going to go** to the cinema this weekend.

We form questions and negatives with *going to* in the same way as in the present continuous.

> I'm **not going** to have time to see you.
> Are you **going** to drive to the party?

will

We use *will* + infinitive (without *to*) when we make a decision while we're speaking.

> A: *What can I bring you?*
> B: *I'll have the tuna salad, please.*

We also use *will* to make promises and offers.

> We'll **meet** you at the train station.
> I'll **pay** for your ticket.

▶ Exercises 4, 5 and 6

Exercises

1 Complete the text with the *to* + infinitive form of the verbs in the box.

> go   learn   organise   start   stay   study

Yesterday was a special day for Michael Sanders. At the age of 75, he finished his university studies. 'I always intended [1]_____ to university,' says Michael. 'But when I finished school, I decided [2]_____ my career, not study.' However, Michael always had his dream, and he didn't give up. He was 80 when he started his university course, and it wasn't easy. 'I found it hard [3]_____ after such a long time. But the other students were great. They helped me [4]_____ my studies so I always finished my work on time.' And Michael's not finished – he hopes [5]_____ at the university for another year and do another course. 'It's exciting [6]_____,' he says. 'I really enjoy it.'

2 Match the beginnings of the sentences (1–8) with the endings (a–h).

1   I'm saving money
2   She went to the university library
3   Let's go to a café
4   He called me
5   We went to the park
6   I looked out of the window
7   He turned on his computer
8   You need to work hard

a   to buy a new car.
b   to check his email.
c   to get some lunch.
d   to have a walk.
e   to pass your exam.
f   to see the weather.
g   to study.
h   to tell me his news.

3 Choose the correct option to complete the sentences.

1   I can't stand *staying / to stay* inside all day.
2   I think it's easy *learning / to learn* a new language.
3   Jack helped me *to fix / fixing* my car.
4   I would like *to visit / visiting* China one day.
5   I'm not very good at *to paint / painting*.
6   I went to the shop *for buying / to buy* some milk.
7   *Eating / To eat* vegetables is good for your health.
8   I was happy *hearing / to hear* about your new job.

4 Complete the sentences with the *going to* form of these verbs.

> come   not get   not go   have   miss   see
> spend   start

1   I _____ that new crime drama tonight.
2   _____ you _____ to our party tomorrow?
3   Tanja _____ a baby in December.
4   Mathieu _____ six months in Australia later this year.
5   I'm _____ married until I'm at least 40!
6   _____ we _____ our train?
7   We _____ on holiday this summer.
8   I'm _____ university in September.

5 Choose the best option to complete the dialogues.

1   A: This bag's heavy.
    B: *I'll help / I'm helping* you to carry it!
2   A: The coffee's finished!
    B: Oh no! *I'll go / I'm going* to the shop and get some.
3   A: Where's Sarah?
    B: She's not here yet. Her train *is arriving / will arrive* at 16.32.
4   A: Do you have plans for tonight?
    B: *I'm going to go / I will go* to the cinema. I just booked my tickets.
5   A: I can't wait until the exams are finished.
    B: I know. *I'm going to have / I'll have* a holiday after they finish.

6 Choose the best explanation (a–b) for the sentences (1–5).

1   I'm visiting my friend John in Manchester this weekend.
    a   We planned this together and I already have my train ticket.
    b   This is an idea but I'm not totally sure.
2   I'm going to go travelling when I finish my university course.
    a   I've already decided where to go and I've booked some hotels.
    b   This is my idea, but I haven't booked anything.
3   It's raining. I'll take you to the shops in my car.
    a   I just decided this now.
    b   We organised this earlier.
4   I'm getting a new computer this week.
    a   I'm going to look in the shops for a good one.
    b   I already paid for it and I'm waiting for it to arrive.
5   I'm going to join a gym this month.
    a   I made an appointment at a gym for this Friday at 10 a.m.
    b   This is my idea, but I haven't organised anything yet.

Present perfect and past simple

Present perfect: form

We form the present perfect with *have / has* + past participle.

	+	–	?
I/you/ we/they	*I've arrived*	*They haven't arrived*	*Have you arrived?*
he/she/it	*Has she arrived?*	*He hasn't arrived.*	*Has he arrived?*

Regular past participles end in -ed and are the same as regular past simple forms (e.g. *change → changed, live → lived*).

Many past participles are irregular. Some irregular past participles are the same as the irregular past simple form:

> *make* (infinitive), *made* (past simple), *made* (past participle)

Other irregular past participles are different from the irregular past simple form:

> *write* (infinitive), *wrote* (past simple), *written* (past participle).

See page 180 for a list of irregular past simple and past participle forms.

▶ Exercise 1

Present perfect and past simple: use

We can use both the present perfect and the past simple to talk about events in the past.

We use the **present perfect**:

- to talk about events and experiences, when we don't know when something happened, or we don't say because it's not important.
  I've visited over fifty countries.
  He's written some really important books.

- to ask about people's experiences, using *ever*.
  Have you ever worked abroad?
  Has Jeanne ever seen this film?

- for something that started in the past and continues now.
  I've always loved working with numbers. (= I loved it in the past, and I still love it.)

We use the **past simple** when we know the exact time something happened:

> *I saw Max this morning.*
> *I visited our Los Angeles office last year.*

When we have conversations about experiences in our life, we often start with the present perfect to talk about the experience in general, and then use the past simple to give details.

> A: *Have you ever been skiing?*
> B: *Yes, I have. I tried it in California last year.*

▶ Exercises 2 + 3

Present perfect with *for* and *since*

We use the present perfect with *for* and *since* to talk about a situation that started in the past and continues now.

We use *for* with a period of time.
> *I've worked here for three years.*

We use *since* with a point in time (when the situation started).
> *I've known Taylor since 2005.*

We never use *from* with present perfect in this way.
> ~~I've lived in Manchester from six months.~~
> *I've lived in Manchester for six months.*

▶ Exercise 4

Prepositions of place and movement

Prepositions can tell us where something or someone is or the direction something or someone moves.

Prepositions of place

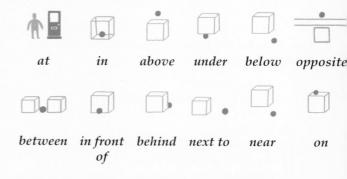

| at | in | above | under | below | opposite |

| between | in front of | behind | next to | near | on |

We use *at* to talk about where we work, live and study:
> *at home, at work, at school, at university.*

We use *in* with towns, cities, countries and continents:
> *in London, in Mexico, in Asia*

We use *on* to say where on a road places are:
> *The bank is on the left. My house is on the right.*

We also use *on* with floors in a building:
> *on the first floor, on the second floor.*

▶ Exercise 5

Prepositions of movement

We use prepositions of movement after a verb that describes a movement (e.g. *go, come, walk, climb*)

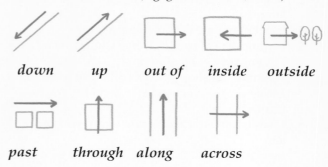

| down | up | out of | inside | outside |

| past | through | along | across |

▶ Exercise 6

Exercises

1 Write present perfect sentences using the words.

1 I / see / that film / five times.
2 you / ever / go / Australia?
3 they / always / live / in the countryside.
4 she / ever / visit / you?
5 I / not finish / my work.
6 why / you / apply / for this job?

2 Choose the correct option to complete the sentences.

1 *I've started / I started* my new job last week.
2 *Have you ever been / Did you ever go* to the USA?
3 *They've always loved / They always loved* playing basketball – they play three times a week!
4 *Jill has spoken / Jill spoke* to her boss last night.
5 *I worked / I've worked* in a café when I was a student.
6 *I've never been / I never went* to a concert in my life.

3 Complete the conversations with the present perfect or past simple form of the verbs in the boxes.

finish	have	get

A: ¹ _____ you _____ work yet?
B: Yes – I ² _____ home an hour ago.
A: ³ _____ you _____ a good day?
B: It was OK.

tell	hear	send

A: ⁴ _____ you _____ about the new job at Max's company?
B: Yes, ⁵ I _____ already _____ my CV. You?
A: Not yet. Max only ⁶ _____ me about it this morning.

have	stay	go

A: ⁷ _____ you ever _____ to Paris?
B: ⁸ Yes, I _____ there for a week last year.
A: ⁹ _____ you _____ a good time?
B: Yes, it was great.

4 Complete the sentences with *for* or *since*.

1 Have you lived in your flat _____ a long time?
2 We've owned our car _____ over twenty years!
3 She's worked here _____ 2015.
4 We haven't had a holiday _____ two years ago.
5 I haven't missed a day at work _____ over a year.
6 I've studied Spanish _____ two years.
7 He's been a baseball fan _____ he was a child.
8 I've had a cold _____ over a week.

5 Complete the email with these prepositions.

below	between	in	near	on	opposite

I've just moved into my new flat and I love it! It's ¹ _____ a small building with three floors – I'm ² _____ the top floor. The people in the flat ³ _____ my flat are really friendly and I've been down to their flat twice for dinner already. There's a park ⁴ _____ the building, just on the other side of the road. I often go there for lunch. What else? Oh, my building is ⁵ _____ two amazing restaurants – on the right, there's a great Greek restaurant, and on the left there's a really good Mexican place. I'm also really ⁶ _____ the metro station, so I can get to work really quickly.

6 Look at the map and choose the correct preposition to complete the directions.

Everyone in the office is really looking forward to meeting you. Here are the directions you asked for. First, go ¹ *out of / down* the railway station, and then turn right. Go ² *past / across* the bridge and then walk ³ *along / outside* Bridge Street for about three minutes. Go ⁴ *past / through* the bank and the post office, then turn left and walk ⁵ *through / along* the park. The building is opposite the park gates. Walk ⁶ *inside / up* the steps and you've arrived! Call me when you're there and I'll come ⁷ *out of/ outside* to meet you.

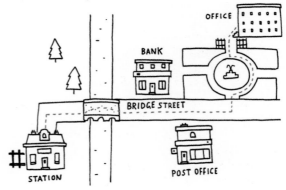

GRAMMAR SUMMARY UNIT 8

Zero and first conditional

Zero conditional

We use the zero conditional to talk about things that are generally true. The form is:

If + present simple + present simple
*If there's important news, everyone on Twitter **talks** about it.*
*If I **get** an email, I **don't** always **read** it straight away.*
*If the weather's bad, **do** you still **cycle** to work?*

We can also use *when* instead of *if*. The meaning is the same.

▶ **Exercise 1**

First conditional

We use the first conditional to talk about a possible future situation. The form is:

If + present simple + will/won't
*If I **hear** something about the job, I'**ll send** you a message.*
*If you **don't read** my blog, you **won't hear** all my news.*

Note: we never use a future form in the *if* clause.
*If it ~~will rain~~ at the weekend, we'**ll stay** at home.*
*If it **rains** at the weekend, we'**ll stay** at home.*

Order in conditional sentences

Conditional sentences have two parts: the *if* clause and the main clause. The main clause describes the result of the situation in the *if* clause.

If it rains, we'll stay at home.
IF CLAUSE   MAIN CLAUSE

We can put the *if* clause first or the main clause first. When the *if* clause comes first, we put a comma before the main clause. When the *if* clause comes second, we don't need a comma.

*We'll stay at home **if** it rains.*

▶ **Exercises 2 and 3**

Defining relative clauses

Defining relative clauses give essential information about a person, thing or place. They say exactly which person, thing or place we are talking about.

*Look at the box **that's on the table**.* (the relative clause tells us exactly which box)
*He's the scientist **who was on the TV news yesterday**.* (the relative clause tells us exactly which scientist)

Form

To make a relative clause, we add a relative pronoun after a noun. The choice of relative pronoun depends on the type of noun:

* for a relative clause about a person, use *who*:
  *That's the woman **who we saw yesterday**.*

* for a relative clause about a thing, use *which*:
  *Did you get the message **which I sent you**?*

* for a relative clause about a place, use *where*:
  *This is the place **where they made the first battery**.*

We can also use *that* instead of *who* or *which* (but not *where*).

*She's the artist **that I told you about**.*
*I'd love to have a machine **that can cook dinner while I'm at work**.*

The relative pronouns *which*, *who* and *that* can be the subject or the object of a relative clause. If it is the subject, we don't need another subject:

This is an invention that ~~it~~ could change the world!

If it is the object, we don't need another object:

Did I tell you about the film that I saw ~~it~~ last week?

▶ **Exercises 4, 5 and 6**

Exercises

1 Match the sentence beginnings (1–7) with the endings (a–g)

1 If I get a message,
2 If she doesn't sleep well at night,
3 It's bad for your skin
4 When he has an exam,
5 If it rains,
6 Babies cry
7 My boss gets angry

a he has to study hard.
b when they are hungry.
c if you sit out in the sun for a long time.
d if I am late for work.
e she feels tired the next day.
f I reply straight away.
g the roads are always busy.

2 Make first conditional sentences with the correct form of the verbs in brackets.

1 If we _____ (finish) the meeting early, we _____ (go out) for a coffee.
2 You _____ (miss) the train if you _____ (not leave) the house now.
3 If the weather _____ (be) bad tomorrow, I _____ drive to work.
4 He _____ (not come) to the party if he _____ (feel) ill.
5 If I _____ (go) to the supermarket, I _____ (buy) you some chocolate.
6 If she _____ (not do) her homework, her teacher _____ (be) angry.
7 I _____ (not answer) my phone if I _____ (be) busy.

3 In each section, match the sentence beginnings (1–4) with the endings (a–d) and complete the sentences with the correct form of the verbs.

A Zero conditional
1 When it _____ (be) cold,
2 If I _____ (not sleep) well at night,
3 Plants _____ (die)
4 She _____ (like) to go for a run

a I _____ (have) a strong coffee in the morning.
b if you _____ (not give) them water.
c when she _____ (wake) up.
d we _____ (prefer) to stay at home.

B First conditional
1 If she _____ (be) free tomorrow evening,
2 If we _____ (not eat) now,
3 They _____ (not get up) early
4 We _____ (travel) by plane

a we _____ (feel) hungry later.
b if we _____ (can) find cheap tickets.
c I _____ (invite) her to the party.
d if they _____ (not have to) work.

4a Complete the sentences with *who*, *which*, or *where*.

1 That's the man _____ lives next door to me.
2 This is the book _____ helped me pass the exam.
3 He visited the town _____ his parents were born.
4 We liked the chocolate _____ you bought us.
5 I got this present from the old lady _____ lives on our street.
6 This is the café _____ I first met my wife.
7 Can you see the cat _____ is lying on top of the car?

4b Tick the sentences in 4a in which *that* can be used as a relative pronoun.

5 Correct the mistakes in these sentences. Two sentences are correct.

1 They have a daughter who is a doctor.
2 This is the house that I want to buy it.
3 She bought the car who she saw last week.
4 Look! That's the friend which I was talking about yesterday.
5 Those are the students who they are looking for a flat.
6 I watched the documentary that was on TV yesterday evening.
7 He didn't see the person who he took his wallet.

6 Complete the text with the phrases below and *who*, *which*, *that* or *where*.

a I didn't want to be friends with again
b lived next door to me
c she gave me for my eighth birthday
d we always played together
e we did together
f you haven't seen for a long time

Facebook is a fantastic way to find old friends ¹_____ . When I was a small girl, I was best friends with Elena, the girl ²_____ . I have a lot of memories of the things ³_____ and I still have the doll ⁴_____ ! When I joined Facebook, I wasn't sure about it at first. There were a lot of people ⁵_____ . But one day I saw that Elena wanted to be friends with me. We started chatting online and after a few months we agreed to meet – in the park ⁶_____ when we were children. It was so nice to see her and to be friends again. And it's all thanks to Facebook!

Past perfect simple

Form

We form the past perfect simple with *had* + past participle. See page 180 for a list of irregular past participles.

	+	–	?
I/you/we/they	*I had arrived.*	*They hadn't arrived.*	*Had you arrived?*
he/she/it	*He had arrived.*	*She hadn't arrived.*	*Had it arrived?*

In spoken English and informal written English, we use *'d* instead of *had*, especially after pronouns.
> *I'd already seen her.*

Use

We use the past perfect simple when we need to make it clear that one past action happened before another past action. For the action that happened first, we use the past perfect. For the action that happened second, we use the past simple.
> *When we arrived at the airport, the plane had left.*

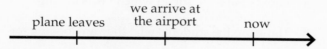

plane leaves   we arrive at the airport   now

We only use the past perfect when we need to make it clear which action happened first. If the order is obvious, we just use the past simple for all the actions.
> *When I got to the station, I bought a ticket and waited for the train.* (all past simple)

We often use linking words and phrases like *but*, *because*, *so* and *as soon as* to link past simple with past perfect sentences.
> *I'd booked the hotel months before, but when I got there they said they were full.*
> *I was tired because I'd been at work all day.*
> *It had rained all night so the roads were very wet.*
> *The children ran outside as soon as the sun had come out.*

▶ Exercises 1, 2 and 3

Subject questions

Other questions

We can use questions to ask about different things, for example time, places, things, or reasons:
> *When did you visit Brazil?* (asking about a time)
> *Where are you staying?* (asking about a place)
> *What are you eating?* (asking about a thing)
> *Why didn't you like the hotel?* (asking about a reason)

To form most questions, we put an auxiliary verb before the subject. To form present simple questions, we need to add the auxiliary verb *do* or *does*. To form past simple questions, we need to add the auxiliary verb *did*.

Subject questions

We can also use questions to ask about the subject of a sentence:

Who lives here? (Answer: <u>Katrin</u> lives here.)
                          SUBJECT

Who likes the food? (Answer: <u>We all</u> like the food.)
                          SUBJECT

The grammar in subject questions is different from other questions. In subject questions:

- the word order is the same as a statement and the question word replaces the subject:

Gheorghe lives here.   Who lives here?

- we do not use the auxiliary verb *do* or *did*
> Who ~~does want~~ a coffee?
> Who wants a coffee?

▶ Exercise 4

We often ask subject questions using *who, which, what,* and *how many.*
> **Who** put this suitcase here?
> **Which** hotel has the best prices?
> **What** caused the delay?
> **How many** people came to the party?

▶ Exercises 5 and 6

Exercises

1 Match the beginnings of the sentences (1–8) with the endings (a–h).

1 As soon as the rain had stopped,
2 When I got home,
3 He checked his phone,
4 She was so happy
5 She realized she'd forgotten to bring any money,
6 They told him to get off the train
7 I arrived late at work
8 Sarah had had an argument with her best friend,

a because he hadn't bought a ticket.
b so she was very upset.
c because she'd passed her exam.
d but the message still hadn't arrived.
e because I'd had a problem with my car.
f I realized I had forgotten my door key.
g so she needed to go home and get some.
h we went for a walk.

2 Complete the text with the past perfect of these verbs.

ask	buy	not check	happen	spend
think	try			

I decided to have a holiday with a difference last summer – I stayed at home for a week! Why? Well, I ¹ _____ just _____ my first home and I didn't have any money. I did lots of different things during my holiday. I went to a museum and learnt about the local history – I didn't know that so many interesting things ² _____ where I live. One evening, some friends came to my new house for a barbecue. I ³ _____ everyone to bring something to eat and it was great! Another day, I went to my local swimming pool for the first time. I ⁴ _____ always _____ it looked a bit old and dirty, but it was really nice inside. Most nights I ate at local restaurants. There were some excellent places – I ⁵ _____ never _____ Ethiopian food before. The only bad day was when I decided to go walking in the local countryside. I ⁶ _____ the weather and it rained all day! At the end of the week, I felt really relaxed. And I ⁷ _____ much less money than I normally do on a holiday. I might even do it again next year!

3 Complete the sentences with these pairs of verbs. Use one past simple form and one past perfect form in each sentence.

call + receive	feel + forget	not go + see
say + help	sleep + feel	study + fail

1 I _____ to the cinema with my friends because I _____ already _____ the film.
2 We _____ hungry because we _____ to bring any lunch.
3 I _____ Martino on his mobile as soon as I _____ his message.
4 Lisa _____ 'thanks' to her brother because he _____ her so much.
5 All of us _____ really well so we _____ great in the morning.
6 Sally _____ hard but she still _____ the exam.

4 Tick the subject questions.

1 Who wrote this message?
2 Where did you buy this?
3 What did she tell you?
4 How many people live here?
5 Who wrote this song?
6 Why didn't you come?
7 Who called you earlier?
8 When did it happen?

5 Put words in order to make subject questions.

1 put / bag / here / who / this
2 which / best / computer / works
3 my / broke / glasses / who
4 speaks / French / who
5 work / how / many / people / here
6 the / won / who / race

6 Write questions about the underlined words in each sentence. Some are subject questions.

1 I went to Spain last year.

2 Kate's behaviour made me really angry.

3 270 people live in this building.

4 I went outside to get some fresh air.

5 Isabella left her coat here.

6 Julia has spoken to Paolo today.

The passive (present simple, past simple)

Active vs. passive

Verbs in English can be active or passive. We normally use the active form when the focus of the sentence is on the 'agent' – the person or thing that does an action.

> Apple **produced** the first Macbook in 2006.
> My father **built** this house in 2004.

When we use the passive, a sentence isn't about the 'agent' any more.

> The first Macbook **was produced** in 2006.
> This house **was built** in 2004.

The focus of the first sentence here is 'the first Macbook', not the company that produced it. The focus of the second sentence is 'this house', not the person who built it.

Form

When we use the passive, the object of the active sentence becomes the subject of the passive sentence.

> People all over the world love <u>Rihanna's music</u>.
> OBJECT

> <u>Rihanna's music</u> **is loved** by people all over the world.
> SUBJECT

We form the passive with the verb *be* and the past participle of the main verb. We can use the passive in affirmative sentences, negative sentences and in questions. The form of *be* shows the tense.

	Present simple	Past simple
+	Rihanna's music **is loved** by people all over the world.	The London Underground **was used** by over 2 billion passengers last year.
–	This film **isn't known** outside of Europe.	Bruce Willis **wasn't born** in the USA.
?	**Is** this product **sold** in Asia?	When **was** the first PC **invented?**

▶ Exercises 1 and 2

Common uses of the passive

We often use the passive voice when it's obvious or not important who does an action.

> Millions of smartphones **are sold** every year.
> (obviously shops sell smartphones)

by

We can use *by* + noun to say who does or did the action in a sentence with a passive verb.

> Facebook **was created by** Mark Zuckerberg.

When we do this, we make this information sound new or important.

▶ Exercises 3 and 4

used to

Use

We use *used to* to talk about habits or situations in the past that are not true now.

> I **used to live** in California but now I live in New York.
> I **used to go** to concerts often, but now I don't have time.

We don't use *used to* to talk about single actions at a specific time in the past. We use past simple instead.

> ~~I used to hear a really good song on the radio yesterday.~~
> I **heard** a really good song on the radio yesterday.

▶ Exercise 5

Form

Used to is always followed by the infinitive. We use the same form for all persons (*I, you, he/she/it* etc.) In negatives and questions, we use the form *use to* not *used to*.

+	I **used to love** rock music.
–	I **didn't use to** like listening to music at work.
?	**Did** you **use to own** a Walkman?

There is no present form of *used to*. To talk about habits in the present, we use the present simple with *usually*.

> ~~I use to go to the gym twice a week.~~
> I **usually go** to the gym twice a week.

▶ Exercises 6 and 7

Exercises

1 Read the sentences. Say if each one is active (A) or passive (P).

1 Most people recognize the Coca Cola logo.
2 The book was written over fifty years ago.
3 The clothes are made in that factory.
4 My question wasn't answered.
5 Apple products are popular all around the world.

2 Complete the sentences with the passive form of the verb. Use the present simple or past simple.

1 The logo _____ (design) fifty years ago.
2 Public transport _____ (use) a lot in my country.
3 About 400 million cups of coffee _____ (drink) every day in the USA.
4 The first Levi jeans _____ (produce) in the 19th century.
5 New articles _____ (write) for the website every month.
6 Professional sports stars _____ (recognized) all over the world.

3 Rewrite the sentences in the passive. Include the 'agent', using *by*.

1 Jeff Bezos created Amazon in 2005.
_____ in 2005.
2 Over one billion viewers watched the final of the World Cup in 2014.
_____ in 2014.
3 Readers in the USA buy more books online than in shops.
_____ than in shops.
4 Up to four million people visit the Taj Mahal in India every year.
_____ every year.
5 Workers in large car factories make one thousand cars every day.
_____ every day.

4 Choose the correct option to complete the text about tablets.

Before 2010, the word 'tablet' [1] *was normally used / normally used* to talk about medicine. But that all changed when the first iPad [2] *released / was released*. Not everyone thought the iPad was a good idea, but 300,000 [3] *are sold / were sold* on the first day. Now, hundreds of different tablets [4] *sold / are sold* by hundreds of different manufacturers and we [5] *spend / are spent* millions of dollars on apps every year. Most tablets [6] *are bought / are buying* for games, photos and the internet, but tablets are also [7] *found / find* in schools, universities and workplaces around the world.

5 Change the past simple verbs in the sentences to a form with *use(d) to* + infinitive when possible. Tick the sentences that cannot be changed.

1 I took guitar lessons every week when I was younger.
2 Did you see Jack at the concert?
3 I took two really good photos this morning.
4 I didn't like going to the cinema when I was young.
5 I played guitar in a band when I was at university.
6 I didn't enjoy the food last night.
7 Did you like football when you were younger?
8 I met a really famous musician last year.

6 Look at the pictures. Write affirmative and negative sentences about Tony when he was a teenager with a form of *use(d) to* and the prompts.

When Tony was a teenager, he …

1 _____ (listen / to music / on CDs)
2 _____ (have / a smartphone)
3 _____ (buy / CDs)
4 _____ (own / a car)
5 _____ (use / a skateboard)
6 _____ (wear / glasses)
7 _____ (be / a student)
8 _____ (wear / a suit)

7 Complete the blog post with the correct form of *use(d) to* and a verb from the box.

be	get up	go out	have	own	play
practise					

Well, it's six months since I started my job. Life is so different now. When I was at university, I [1] _____ early – never before 9.30 a.m. Now I have to be at work at 9 a.m.! I [2] _____ with friends a few times a week, but I'm always too tired after work now. I also [3] _____ the saxophone in a band – we [4] _____ two afternoons a week, but I can't do that any more!

Of course, it's not all bad. I [5] _____ much money when I was a student. I [6] _____ a really cheap mobile phone, but now I've got a smartphone. What about you? How [7] _____ your life _____ different before you started working?

Reported speech

When we want to say what another person said, we can use direct speech. This means we try to use exactly the words the person said.

> *Mike said, 'I'll see you tomorrow.'*

We can also use reported speech.

> *Mike said that he'd see me tomorrow.*

When we use reported speech, we normally change the verb forms.

- present simple becomes past simple:
  *'I **live** in Brighton.'* → *She said she **lived** in Brighton.*

- present continuous becomes past continuous:
  *'I'**m waiting** for the bus.* →
  *Julie said she **was waiting** for the bus.*

- present perfect becomes past perfect:
  *'We'**ve seen** this film before.'* →
  *They said they'**d seen** this film before.*

- past simple becomes past perfect:
  *'I **passed** my exam.'* → *He said he'**d passed** his exam.*

- *will* becomes *would*:
  *'I'**ll** help you.'* → *Mike said he'**d** (= would) help me.*

▶ Exercise 1

We often also need to make changes to other words, like pronouns and possessive forms, in reported speech.

> *'**I** love **you**.'* → *He said **he** loved **me**.*
> *'This is **my** Xbox.'* → *He said this was **his** Xbox.*
> *'**We** live **here**.'* → *They said **they** lived **there**.*
> *'**I**'ll see **you** **tomorrow**.'* →
> *He said **he**'d see me **the next day**.*

▶ Exercises 2, 3 and 4

Reporting verbs (*say* and *tell*)

We use both *say* and *tell* to report another person's words. We normally use *say* and *tell* in the past simple.
With *tell*, we always use an object before the reported speech. The object is often a pronoun.

> *Sam **told me** he wanted to come.*
> *Clara **told Simon** she would be late.*

With *say*, we never use an object before the reported speech.

> *He said ~~me~~ that he was really happy.*

After both *say* and *tell*, we can use *that* but it is not necessary.

> *I said (that) he had won the game.*
> *They told us (that) we needed to leave.*

▶ Exercises 5 and 6

Exercises

1 Choose the correct option to complete the reported speech.

1 'I'll have the pasta.'
   She said she *would have / will had* the pasta.
2 'I'm playing a game.'
   He said he *was playing / had played* a game.
3 'I really don't like this film.'
   She said she really *wasn't liking / didn't like* the film.
4 'I've visited Canada twice.'
   She said she *visited / had visited* Canada twice.
5 'I lost my phone.'
   He said *he lost / he'd lost* his phone.

2 Complete the reported speech with these words and phrases.

his	me	the day before	the next day
their	then	there	they

1 'I want to go there tomorrow.' → She said she wanted to go there _____.
2 'It's my new car'. → He said it was _____ new car.
3 'We love this restaurant.' → They said _____ loved that restaurant.
4 'We live here'. → They said they lived _____.
5 'I'll help you.' → He said he'd help _____.
6 'I'm at home now.' → She said she was at home _____.
7 'We missed our flight.' → They said they'd missed _____ flight.
8 'We went there yesterday.' → They said they'd gone there _____.

3 Complete the direct speech.

1 She said Mike had already left.
   'Mike _____ already _____.'
2 Sally said she'd help me with my work.
   'I _____ help you with your work.'
3 Greta said she didn't speak Portuguese.
   'I _____ Portuguese.'
4 Martin said it had been cold the day before.
   'It _____ cold yesterday.'
5 Fatima said she was arriving at 9 p.m.
   'I _____ at 9 p.m.'

4 Look at these sentences and complete the reported speech.

1 'I lost the match.'
   Jan said _____
2 'I'll see you tomorrow.'
   She said _____.
3 'Your email hasn't arrived.'
   Mehmet said _____.
4 'I don't want to speak to you.'
   He said _____.
5 'I'm trying to watch the TV.'
   Luke said _____.

5 Three of these sentences are incorrect. Correct the sentences by adding or deleting a word.

1 He told that he was really tired.
2 Laura said the food was good.
3 She said me that she needed my help.
4 Stephen told me that he had got the job.
5 He said that he would fix my computer.
6 Anna told she was working today.

6 Read the dialogue. Then complete the sentences (1–5) with reported speech.

John: I've found something interesting.
Jack: You're holding an ancient Greek vase!
John: It's really beautiful.
Jack: It was probably lost in the sea for thousands of years.
John: I'll call the museum right away!

1 John said _____.
2 Jack told _____.
3 John said _____.
4 Jack said _____.
5 John told _____.

Second conditional

We use the second conditional to talk about impossible or unlikely situations in the present or future. The form is:

If + past simple + *would* + verb

> *If I **had** enough money, I **would love** to visit the USA.*
> *What **would** you do **if** you **saw** a tornado?*

In spoken English and informal written English, we use *'d* instead of *would*, especially after pronouns.

Note: we never put *would* in the *if* clause. We always use a past tense.

> ~~*If I would have more time*~~, *I'd go out more.*
> *If I **had** more time, I'd go out more.*

When the main clause comes before the *if* clause, we don't add a comma between the two clauses.

▶ Exercises 1, 2 and 3

anywhere, everyone, nobody, something, etc.

Words like *anywhere, everyone, nobody* and *something* are 'indefinite pronouns'. They can end in *-where, -one, -body,* or *-thing*. We use pronouns ending in:

- *-where* to talk about places.
- *-one* or *-body* to talk about people (there is no difference in meaning).
- *-thing* to talk about objects.

Positive meaning

We use *everywhere, everyone/everybody*, or *everything* to talk about all places, people or objects.

> *I think that **everywhere** in Spain is beautiful.*
> ***Everybody** can do more to help the environment.*
> ***Everything** in the shop was really expensive.*

We use *somewhere, someone/somebody*, or *something* to talk about places, people or objects without being specific.

> *We need to find **somewhere** to eat.* (= It's not important where.)
> ***Somebody** told me about this place.*
> *I think **something**'s moving in the forest.*

Negative meaning

We use *nowhere, no one/nobody* and *nothing* to say there is no place, no people or no things.

> *I found **nowhere** to sit on the train.*
> *We saw **nobody** in the mountains all day.*
> *There's **nothing** interesting to do in my city.*

We also use *anywhere, anybody/anyone* and *anything* with a negative verb (e.g. *isn't, haven't, don't want*) for the same meaning.

> *I **didn't** find **anywhere** to sit on the train.*
> *We **didn't** see **anybody** in the mountains all day.*
> *There **isn't anything** interesting to do in my city.*

Note that *anything, anyone/anybody* and *anywhere* don't have a negative meaning without a negative verb.

> *Who lives in this old house?*
> ~~*Anybody.*~~ *Nobody. It's empty.*

In questions

We use *anywhere, anyone, anybody* or *anything* to ask general questions.

> *Is there **anywhere** to park near here?*
> *Can **anybody** help me?*
> *Did you see **anything** interesting in the park?*

We use *something, someone, somebody* and *somewhere* in questions when we make offers.

> *Would you like **something** to eat?*
> *Do you want me to ask **somebody** to help you?*
> *Would you like to go **somewhere** quieter?*

▶ Exercises 4, 5 and 6

Exercises

1 Complete the first and second conditional sentences with the correct form of the verb.

1 If it rains, all the clothes *will / would* get wet.
2 If there was a snowstorm, we *will / would* be stuck at home.
3 There would be lots of problems if our water supply *becomes / became* polluted.
4 If we didn't have air conditioning, it *will / would* be impossible to work here.
5 If the world gets hotter, farmers *won't / wouldn't* be able to grow some kinds of food.
6 Sailors would have problems if they *don't / didn't* check the weather forecast.

2 Match the beginnings of the second conditional sentences (1–6) with the endings (a–f).

1 If it was hotter here in summer,
2 If he worked harder,
3 You wouldn't need to ask me for money
4 If you didn't drive so fast,
5 If it wasn't so windy,
6 If I could move to a different country,

a he'd have a better job.
b I'd definitely go to South Africa.
c if you didn't spend so much.
d lots of tourists would come to visit.
e we could go out for a walk now.
f you wouldn't always get in trouble with the police.

3 Complete the second conditional sentences with the correct form of the verbs.

1 If I _____ (not be) so tired, I _____ (be able to) work better.
2 If I _____ (have) more money, I _____ (buy) a new car.
3 If Michael _____ (speak) more slowly, everyone _____ (understand) him.
4 I _____ (not tell) you to do this if I _____ (not think) it was important.
5 We _____ (save) lots of water if people _____ (be) more careful.
6 _____ you _____ (come) to visit me if I _____ (pay) for your ticket?

4 Choose the correct option.

1 I know *somewhere / something* really nice to stay in this city.
2 Can I bring you *something / nothing* to eat?
3 A: Where are you going now?
  B: *Nowhere. / Anywhere*. I'm staying here.
4 She didn't speak to *anybody / nobody* at the party.
5 *Everywhere / Everyone* here has been to university.
6 We don't have *anything / nothing* to do today.

5 Complete the text with the words in the box.

anything	everywhere	nobody	nothing
something	somewhere		

Ten years ago, I decided I wanted to live
¹ _____ different. I was living in a big city and I was tired of the traffic and pollution ² _____ . So I moved to a small village near the sea. The first few years were a bit difficult. When I moved, there was almost ³ _____ else living here. I enjoyed the peace and quiet but there was ⁴ _____ to do in the evening or at the weekend. But gradually, more and more people have come and now there's always ⁵ _____ happening. Now I think it's a perfect place to live – I wouldn't change ⁶ _____ !

6 Rewrite the sentences, using an indefinite pronoun to replace the underlined phrases.

1 Giulia lives <u>in a place</u> near here.

_____

2 There was <u>not one person</u> on the beach so it was really quiet.

_____

3 I've been <u>to all the places</u> in this city and the parks are my favourite.

_____

4 A: Where do you want me to leave this box?
  B: <u>Any place</u> in the room will do.

_____

5 Mike didn't have <u>any objects</u> with him – he'd left his bag at home.

_____

6 There's <u>a person</u> waiting for you outside.

_____

INFINITIVE	PAST SIMPLE	PAST PARTICIPLE
be	was/were	been
become	became	become
begin	began	begun
bring	brought	brought
build	built	built
buy	bought	bought
choose	chose	chosen
come	came	come
cost	cost	cost
do	did	done
drink	drank	drunk
eat	ate	eaten
fall	fell	fallen
feel	felt	felt
find	found	found
fly	flew	flown
forget	forgot	forgotten
get	got	got
give	gave	given
go	went	gone
grow	grew	grown
have	had	had
hear	heard	heard
hurt	hurt	hurt
keep	kept	kept
know	knew	known

INFINITIVE	PAST SIMPLE	PAST PARTICIPLE
leave	left	left
learn	learned	learned
let	let	let
make	made	made
meet	met	met
pay	paid	paid
put	put	put
read	read	read
run	ran	run
say	said	said
see	saw	seen
sell	sold	sold
send	sent	sent
sit	sat	sat
sleep	slept	slept
speak	spoke	spoken
spend	spent	spent
swim	swam	swum
take	took	taken
teach	taught	taught
tell	told	told
think	thought	thought
understand	understood	understood
wake	woke	woken
wear	wore	worn
write	wrote	written

Unit 1

▶ 1

Normally, national parks are in the countryside. But Bukhansen National Park in South Korea is part of the city of Seoul. It's about forty-five minutes from the city centre by subway and about ten million people visit the park every year. People in Seoul go walking there at weekends. It's a good way to relax.

▶ 5

P = presenter, D = David McLain
(The words of David McLain are spoken by an actor.)

P: No one knows exactly the reason why some people live longer than others. Why are they so healthy? Is it their diet? Do they go to the gym more than other people? Well, one man is trying to answer these questions and that man is photographer David McLain. He's currently travelling to different places around the world with large numbers of people aged a hundred and over and asking the question: Why are they so healthy? At the moment he's working on the island of Sardinia in Italy and he's speaking to us right now on the phone. David, thank you for joining us today.

D: Hello.

P: So, first of all, tell us why you decided to visit Sardinia.

D: Well, Sardinia is an interesting place because men live to the same age as women. That isn't normal for most countries. Men normally die younger.

P: And does anyone know the reason why people live longer in Sardinia?

D: There are different ideas about this. One explanation is that the family is so important here. Every Sunday the whole family eats a big meal together. Research shows that in countries where people live longer, the family is important.

P: I see. So, do you think people live longer in traditional societies?

D: That's an interesting question. Sardinia is quite a traditional place but, even here, the younger generation are eating more food like chips and burgers. Also, young people are moving to the city, so they are doing less exercise because of their lifestyle. It'll be interesting to see what happens in Sardinia in the next twenty or thirty years.

▶ 8

C = customer, P = pharmacist
1

P: Hello, how can I help you?

C: Hello. I've got a runny nose and a sore throat. I feel terrible.

P: Have you got a temperature as well?

C: No, it's normal.

P: Well, you should take this medicine twice a day. It's good for a sore throat.

C: Thanks.

P: And try drinking hot water with honey and lemon. That helps.

C: OK. I will.

P: Oh, and why don't you buy some cough sweets? They should help. If you still feel ill in a few days, see a doctor.

P = patient, D = doctor
2

D: Good morning. So what's the problem?

P: I've got earache in this ear. It's really painful.

D: Let me have a look. … ah … yes, it's very red in there. What about the other one?

P: It feels fine.

D: Hmm. It's a bit red as well. Do you feel sick at all?

P: No, not really.

D: Let me check your temperature. … Yes, it's higher than normal. OK, I'll give you something for your earache. You need to take one of these pills twice a day for seven days. They might make you sleepy so go to bed if you have to. And if you still feel ill, then come back and see me again.

Unit 2

▶ 9

An Ironman competition has three different races. In the swimming race, the competitors swim for 3.86 kilometres. Then they cycle for 180 kilometres, and finally they run a marathon at the end. The world final of the Ironman Championship is in Hawaii and it's very competitive. Every year, around 1,900 people compete against each other in front of thousands of spectators.

▶ 11

1
Learning to win and lose is important in a child's education because it teaches you about life. So I think competitive sports in schools are good for teaching children. They're also good for their physical health, because when children try to win, they work harder and get more exercise. The other good thing about competitive sports is that you learn to work well in teams when you play in matches. Competitions are a great lesson in teamwork.

2
Some children aren't good at sport, so when school sports are competitive, they always lose. That's really bad for the child. The fact is that not all children are the same and some children don't like doing sport. I think schools in my country should be more like the schools in Finland. They get good results but they aren't competitive and they don't have competitive sports either. So when a child can't do a sport very well, that's ok as long as they do their best and try hard at everything they do.

3
We have a sports day at my school and the children love it. Yes, winning is nice for a child, but the whole day is also a lot of fun. So overall I don't think there's a problem with having competitive sports in school – the problem is with some of the mothers and fathers. Some parents hate losing and they get very competitive. When there's a race or a match some of them shout at their kids. They think it's the Olympic Games or something!

▶ 12

A: What's on TV?
B: Cycling from France. It's the Tour de France. I love watching it.
A: Oh no! I think it's boring!
B: I really enjoy seeing them on the mountains.
A: Sitting in front of the TV all day is not exciting. I'm bored with doing nothing. Are you any good at tennis? We could play this afternoon.
B: But I want to watch this.
A: I see. Are you afraid of losing?

▶ 13

1 thing, 2 win, 3 bank, 4 sing, 5 ran, 6 pink

▶ 15

A: Hey! Have you seen this?
B: What?
A: This advert. You're really good at doing that.
B: Yes, but I have so much work at the moment, I don't have time.
A: So this is a good way to relax.
B: I can take a good picture of friends and family, but I'm not very creative with it.
A: Alright. Well, what about joining something else? Er, this one! Are you interested in acting?
B: You're joking. I hate standing up in front of people. You're more of a performer than me.
A: Yes, but it's a musical. I'm not very good at singing.
B: Let's have a look at that. But it says here enthusiasm is more important than talent. Go on. I think you'd enjoy it.
A: Mm, well maybe, but I think I'd like to join this on Wednesday evenings.
B: What? You? Do exercise?
A: What do you mean? Anyway, it looks like fun. Why don't you come too?
B: But I can't run!
A: No, but that's the point. There's a beginner's group. You should do it with me.

Unit 3

▶ 17

This photo is on a train in Bangladesh. It was the end of Ramadan and lots of people travel home at that time of year. Train tickets sell out quickly, so you often see people riding on top of the trains and the carriages. In this picture the woman is sitting between the carriages because there isn't space on top of the train. It looks a bit dangerous, but she doesn't look very worried.

▶ 19

A: Sorry I'm late. Eight thirty in the morning is the worst time for traffic.
B: I know what you mean. My bicycle is faster than your car in the rush hour!
A: I'm sure it is, but I travel further than you. It'd take me hours by bicycle.
B: There's also the cost of petrol. It's so expensive!
A: Tell me about it. In fact, last week I went to look at an electric car.
B: Good idea. They're better for the environment.
A: They're better, but they're also more expensive. In fact, a new electric car is the most expensive type of car.
B: Really? Anyway, what about public transport? Isn't there a bus stop near your house?
A: Yes, but the fastest bus takes over an hour. It stops everywhere!

▶ 21

When we talk about transport, most people think of buses, cars, bicycles and so on. But in some parts of the world, animal transport is as popular as these modern types of transport, and sometimes more popular. Because at certain times of year, animals are the only way to travel. Take the desert for example, with its 50-degree temperatures. Yes, you can cross it in the right vehicles, but for long distances, modern vehicles are not as good as camels. A camel can travel over 40 kilometres per day and go without water for three to five days. Yes, it's slower, and maybe a camel isn't as comfortable as a car. But a camel's big feet make it more reliable in the sand – unlike a car, it doesn't get stuck. Camels are so important in the desert that there are around 160 different ways of saying the word 'camel' in Arabic.
In winter, northern Alaska can be as cold as the North Pole. Temperatures go down to minus 50 degrees. Your engine can freeze, and even if your car starts, snow and ice on the road can make driving impossible. When the weather is as bad as this, the only way to travel is by sledge with a team of between six and eight huskies. These famous dogs can pull heavy sledges for hundreds of kilometres. There is even a race for huskies in Alaska called the Iditarod, where large teams of huskies pull sledges over 1,600 kilometres.

▶ 24

J = Javier, D = driver
1
J: Hello? Are you the next taxi?
D: Yes, that's right.
J: I'd like to go to the station, please.
D: Bus or train?
J: Oh, sorry. The train station.
D: OK. Get in then.

2
D: There are road works up by the entrance.
J: You can stop here. It's fine. How much is that?
D: Six pounds thirty.
J: Sorry, I only have a twenty-pound note. Do you have change?
D: Sure. So, that's thirteen pounds seventy. Do you want a receipt?
J: No, it's OK, thanks. Bye.

S = Shelley, D = driver
3
S: Hi. Do you stop at the airport?
D: Yeah, I do. Which terminal is it? North or south?
S: Err. I need to get to the … north terminal.
D: OK. A single or return ticket?
S: Single, please.
D: That's two pounds.

J = Javier, T = ticket office clerk
4
J: A return ticket to the airport, please.
T: OK. The next train goes in five minutes.
J: Right. That one, please.
T: First or second class?
J: Second.
T: OK. That's fourteen pounds fifty.
J: Wow! I don't think I have the cash.
T: Credit card is fine.
J: Oh, no … maybe I have enough left.
T: OK. Here you are.
J: Which platform is it?
T: Err, platform six.

A = attendant, S = Shelley, J = Javier
5
A: Hello. Can I see your passport?
S: Here you are.
A: That's OK. How many bags are you checking in?
S: None. I only have this carry on.
A: OK. Window or aisle?
S: Err, I don't mind, but can I have a seat next to my friend?
A: Has he already checked in?
S: No, I'm waiting for him.
A: Well, I can't …
J: Shelley!
S: Where have you been?
J: It's a long story.

Unit 4

▶ 26

My name's Vic and I live in the state of Tennessee. During the week I work in a bank. I like my job, but most of the time I'm sitting at a desk, so I need to get exercise after work and at the weekends. Most people go running or play sports, but I like caving. My colleagues think I'm a bit crazy because they say it's dangerous. It's true that sometimes you have to take a risk when you go caving, but I always go with other cavers and we look after each other. It's important to work as a team when you go down into a new cave because every cave gives you a different challenge. The most difficult cave was called Rumbling Falls Cave. You have to use a rope and climb down a hole that's about twenty metres into the ground. At the bottom, you are on your hands and knees for nearly a kilometre, so you need to be physically fit. Then at the end, you come into the main part of the cave. It's an incredible place, like a huge room. Getting to Rumbling Falls cave was probably my biggest achievement as a caver.

▶ 29

In May 1985, Joe Simpson and Simon Yates climbed the Siula Grande mountain in the Andes. It's a dangerous mountain, but Simpson and Yates were very experienced climbers and positive about the challenge. The sun was shining when they left their tents on the first day and everything went well. Three days later, they reached the top of the mountain, but they didn't stay there long. It was snowing and the weather was getting worse. While they were going down the mountain, Simpson fell and broke his knee. Yates tied a rope between them and slowly lowered Simpson down the mountain with the rope. Sometime later, when they were getting nearer to the bottom of the mountain, Simpson slipped and fell over a cliff. For an hour, Yates held the rope while his friend was hanging in the air. But the rope was getting too heavy and it was pulling Yates off the mountain. Simon Yates had an impossible decision. Either he could hold the rope, but then they might both die, or he could cut the rope and save himself. …

▶ 30

(The first part of the story is repeated from track 29.)
… At the last second, Yates cut the rope. The next day, Yates looked for his friend, but couldn't find him. Sadly, he decided he was dead. But amazingly, Simpson was still alive and he started to crawl towards their camp. Three days later, Yates was sleeping in his tent and planned to go home the next morning. But at midnight he suddenly woke up. Someone was shouting his name. He ran outside and looked everywhere. Finally, he found Simpson on the ground. He wasn't moving, but he was still breathing. Yates carried him to the tent and Simpson survived. Later, their story became famous as a book and a film.

▶ 31

1 I was working on my own when a group of people came in to my office.
2 We met them when they were living above our apartment.
3 They weren't getting on very well, so the team agreed to have a meeting.
4 The weather was cold this morning but it wasn't raining so I cycled to work.

▶ 33

A: Hi Mark. How was your camping trip?
B: It was great in the end, but we had a terrible time at the beginning.
A: Why?
B: First, we left the house late, and then after only half an hour the car broke down.
A: Oh no! What did you do?
B: Fortunately, there was a garage nearby and the mechanic fixed the problem. But when we arrived at the forest, it was getting dark. After we drove around for about an hour, we finally found the campsite, but it was completely dark by then. And it was raining!
A: Really? So what happened?
B: We found a nice, warm hotel down the road!
A: That was lucky!
B: Yes, it was a great hotel and in the end we stayed there for the whole weekend.
A: Sounds great!

Unit 5

▶ 35

Every day we throw away objects such as wood, old household appliances, and glass bottles. But an artist from Uruguay called Jaime built a house made from these types of objects. The house is in Brazil and it has a bedroom, a kitchen, and a bathroom. There are shelves made from trees and old wood and there's lots of light. That's because Jaime used coloured glass from bottles in the walls. When people visit the house, Jaime wants them to think about the environment and about how we recycle and reuse everyday objects.

▶ 37

Nearly thirty percent of the land on Earth is desert. While the ice in the two cold deserts of the Arctic and Antarctica is starting to melt, hot deserts such as the Gobi Desert and the Sahara are getting bigger. Some countries are trying to stop them growing.
Take China, for example. People know about the Great Wall of China, but China has another wall called the Great Green Wall. In 1978, the Chinese started planting a wall of trees to stop the Gobi Desert growing towards the cities of northern China. Now the wall has about 66 billion trees and by 2050 it will be 4,500 kilometres long with about 100 billion trees. There is a similar problem with the Sahara Desert, which is the largest hot desert in the world. Twenty countries in Africa are working together to build a wall of trees all the way from Senegal to Djibouti. The new forest will stop the desert destroying more homes and farms in the region. Eventually, the forest will be about fifteen kilometres wide and 7,775 kilometres long.

▶ 41

V = recorded voice, C = customer care assistant, J = Jane
V: Thank you for calling Teco Art dot com. Your call is important to us. For information about our latest products, press one. For orders, press two. For problems with your order, press three. … All our customer service assistants are busy. We apologize for the delay. Your call is important to us. One of our customer service assistants will be with you as soon as possible.
C: Good morning. Can I help you?
J: Hi, I'm calling about an order for a Computer Circuit Board Clock from your website but I received an email saying I have to wait seven more days.
C: One moment … Do you have the order number?
J: Yes, it's 8-0-5-3-1-A.
C: Is that A as in alpha?
J: That's right.
C: Is that Ms Jane Powell of 90 North Lane?
J: Yes, it is.
C: Hmm. Can I put you on hold for a moment?
J: Sure.
C: Hello?
J: Yes, hello.
C: I'm very sorry but this product isn't in stock at the moment. We'll have it in seven days.
J: I already know that. But it's my husband's birthday tomorrow.
C: Ah, I see. Well, would you like to order a similar clock? We have an Apple iPod one for thirty-five pounds.

J: Hmm. I really liked the one I ordered.
C: Oh, I'm sorry about that. Would you like to cancel the order?
J: Yes, I think so. How does that work?
C: Well, we'll refund the amount of thirty-nine pounds to your credit card.
J: OK. Thanks.
C: And would you like confirmation by email?
J: Yes, please.
C: Let me check. Your email is J powell at S-mail dot com.
J: That's right.
C: Is there anything else I can help you with?
J: No, thanks. That's everything.
C: OK. Goodbye.
J: Bye.

Unit 6

▶ 44

These three people are waiting in a train station in Winterthur in Switzerland. I like the picture because it shows three people at different stages in their life communicating in different ways. The elderly lady and the middle-aged lady are chatting and the young adult woman, maybe she's eighteen or nineteen, is probably texting her friends or using social media.

▶ 46

1 One day I intend to buy my own house.
2 I want to take a year off to travel overseas.
3 I'd be happy to live in another country.
4 In the future I'd like to learn to play a musical instrument.
5 When I get older I hope to spend more time with my family.
6 These days it's difficult not to take work home.

▶ 48

R = reporter, L = Lorette
R: It's about six o'clock in the morning here in New Orleans and the streets are very quiet. But in about six hours the city is going to have the biggest party in the world, with thousands of visitors from all over. However, Mardi Gras is really about the local communities in the city. So, I've come to the traditional Tremé neighbourhood of New Orleans, where there are already some people preparing for the big day. So, I'll try to speak to some of them … Hello? Hello?
L: Hello?
R: Hello. What's your name?
L: Lorette.
R: Hi Lorette. You're wearing a fantastic costume. Are you going to be in the parade this afternoon?
L: That's right. Everyone is meeting at the float at six-fifteen and then we're going to ride through the city.
R: As I say, your dress looks amazing. Did you make it?
L: Yes, we all make our own costumes for Mardi Gras.
R: And do you have a mask?
L: Sure. Here it is. I'll put it on.
R: Wow. That's perfect. So tell me – how important is Mardi Gras for the people in Tremé?
L: It's the most important part of the year. It brings people together.
R: Well, good luck this afternoon. You're going to have a great time, I'm sure!

▶ 49

1 A: Did Geoff email the times of the parade?
  B: I don't know. I'll check my inbox right away.
2 You're going to visit New Orleans! When did you decide that?
3 A: Hey, this costume would look great on you.
  B: Maybe. I'll try it on.
4 One day when I'm older, I'm going to visit Venice.

▶ 51

I = Ian, A = Abdullah

1

I: Hi Abdullah. How's it going?
A: Good. I finished all my courses today so I can relax.
I: Great. Maybe you'll have time for some travelling and sightseeing now.
A: Maybe. But I think I'll take it easy this weekend.
I: Oh! Well, why don't you come to my house? My family is coming over. We're having a barbecue in the back garden. It'll be fun.
A: Thanks, but I have a few things to do at home and it's with your family so you probably don't want other people there …
I: No, really. Don't worry because I'm inviting a few people from our class as well. So you'll know people. I'd really like you to come.
A: OK. Thanks, that would be great. Is it a special occasion?
I: Well, my oldest sister has a new baby girl, so it's a bit of a celebration for that.
A: Oh! So I should bring something.
I: No, please don't. It isn't like that. There's no need …

J = Joanna, S = Sally

2

J: Hello Sally. How are you?
S: Fine, thanks. It's been a busy week.
J: Yes, I imagine. When do you finish?
S: Tomorrow.
J: Oh, really. I didn't realize it was so soon.
S: Well actually, my flight home is on Saturday.
J: But you're staying for another week?
S: No.
J: Oh. Well, what are doing tonight?
S: Nothing at the moment. I'll be at my hotel.
J: Well, would you like to come out for dinner? Let's go somewhere this evening.
S: Really? I'd love to.
J: Of course. I'd like to take you to my favourite restaurant.
S: That would be wonderful. I'd like that very much.
J: Great. Let's go straight after work. I'll meet you downstairs in reception.
S: OK. What time?
J: I finish at six. Is that OK for you?
S: Sure. I'll see you then. Bye.

Unit 7

▶ 53

When I left school at 18, I didn't have a proper job at first. I worked part-time in a restaurant and I also did some manual work for a construction company. In the end, I applied for a job as a steel worker at our local steel mill. Pennsylvania has a large steel industry, though it doesn't employ as many people nowadays. Anyway, I've been here for about five years now. At first it was all low-paid work, but I did a lot of training and learned new skills so now my salary is better.

There are eight people in my team: six men and two women, and we all get on really well. It's hard work and the hours are long. You're inside most of the day and you're working with steel at temperatures which can reach three thousand degrees, so it gets pretty hot round here! Sometimes people are surprised when I tell them where I work. I don't think they expect women to work in a place like this, but there are quite a few other women working in this kind of industry. In fact, my supervisor is also a woman.

▶ 55

I = interviewer, S = scientist

I: How long have you worked for your company?
S: For five years. Since I left college.
I: When did you go to college?
S: I started when I was nineteen and I qualified with my degree about four years later.
I: And have you always lived in Pennsylvania?
S: No, I haven't. I grew up here but then I went to university in Boston and I've lived in one or two other places.
I: So, when did you move back here?
S: In 2015.
I: Have you ever worked overseas?
S: Yes, I have. I worked in Dubai, in the Middle East, two years ago.
I: And how does Pennsylvania compare with other places? Has it been easy living here?
S: Yes, it has, overall.

▶ 56

1

A: Hello? Kristina speaking.
B: Hi Kristina. It's Geoff.
A: Hi Geoff. Where are you calling from?
B: I'm at home but I'm about to leave for a meeting. Can you help me? I've left a list of prices in the office and I need it for the meeting.
A: Sure. Is it on your desk?
B: I think it's next to my computer.
A: I can't see anything.
B: Oh. Well maybe I left it in one of the drawers behind you.
A: OK. Which one?
B: Try the top drawer on the left.
A: Let me look. Yes, there's a folder called 'price lists'?
B: That's the one! Can you email me a copy of the list with prices for next year?
A: Sure, I'll do that now…

2

C: Hello, Richard Roberts speaking.

D: Hi. I'm here to fix your photocopier, but I don't know which office. I'm standing at the entrance to the building.

C: OK. Great. So you need to come into the entrance and go up to the third floor. Go through the door on your right and the photocopying room is there. My office is next to it, so I'll meet you.

D: OK. See you in a minute.

▶ **59**

H = Hania, M = manager

M: Right. Have a seat, Hania

H: Thanks.

M: I've looked at your CV and see that you're from Poland. How long have you been in England?

H: I worked here last year to improve my English and then I came back to study fashion this year.

M: I see. So why do you want this job?

H: I have some spare time in the evenings after college and I'd like to earn some extra money.

M: OK. And last year you worked in another restaurant. What did you like about your last job?

H: Helping the customers and trying to give good service.

M: How did you deal with any difficult situations?

H: At the weekends we were very busy in the evenings so sometimes customers had to wait for their food. But I found that most customers are OK if you are friendly and polite. Also you need to apologize when the food is late.

…

M: Good. Well, I think that's everything. Do you have any questions for me?

H: Yes, it says in the advert you provide training. Can you give me more information about that?

M: Well you have lots of experience, so you probably won't need very much. But on your first day, you work with another waiter and learn about the menu and the different kinds of pizza …

Unit 8

▶ **60**

It's difficult to remember what life was like before the types of modern technology we have today. Technology solves mathematical problems for us. It sends messages to friends in a second. It even cooks dinner for us. When technology makes a mistake, it's only because a human has given the wrong instructions. So, what's the next big step in technology? Robots are common in industries such as car manufacturing, and recently NASA sent the first humanoid robot into space, where it works on the International Space Station. It's called Robonaut 2 or R2 and it does all the simple or repetitive jobs so the astronauts can spend more time doing experiments. Perhaps in a few years' time every home will have their own robot to do all the boring work around the house.

▶ **62**

1 If I go on holiday, I take lots of sun cream.
2 We'll need a torch if we go out late tonight.
3 We always get lost if my brother drives.
4 If we see a supermarket, I'll stop and buy some sandwiches for the journey.
5 If that old phone stops working, I'll buy a new one.
6 I can't buy food if the supermarket isn't open.
7 You ring this number if you have any questions.
8 If you don't try harder, you won't pass your exam.

▶ **63**

More than one billion people in the world need glasses but cannot get them, because they live in places where there aren't any opticians. But now there's a scientist who has solved the problem. Joshua Silver has invented glasses which don't need an optician.

They look like a pair of normal glasses, but there is a pump on each side which uses silicone oil. First, you turn a wheel which controls the pump. The pump pushes the silicone oil through the pipe and it moves into the lenses. As the lens fills with oil, the shape of the lens changes and you turn the wheel until you can see correctly.

Silver had the idea a few years ago and he did many experiments before he got it right. A man in Ghana was the first person who used the new glasses. The man made clothes, but he had bad eyesight and found it difficult to work. When the man put on the glasses, he could start working again. Silver says, 'I will not forget that moment.' As a result of this successful test, Silver started an organization which is called the 'Centre for Vision in the Developing World'. The glasses are cheap to produce and over one hundred thousand people now wear them. In particular, the centre works with schools in countries where people can't get glasses easily. Being able to see well can have a big effect on their education.

▶ **68**

A: What's the problem?

B: A friend gave me this drone as a present, but I don't understand the instructions.

A: Oh yes. I have one like this.

B: Can you show me how this works?

A: Sure. It looks complicated, but it's really easy to use. First of all, have you charged the battery?

B: Yes, I've done that.

A: So now, turn on the remote control.

B: How did you do that?

A: I turned it on here. It's the button on the side.

B: Oh, ok.

A: So, you have two levers. The left and the right. Let's start with the left. If you push it forwards, the propellers go faster and the drone starts to go up. If you pull it back, the propellers slow down and it comes back down.

B: And what is this other one for?

A: When your drone is in the air, you can move this right lever forwards, backwards, right or left and the drone flies in that direction.

B: OK. And what happens if I press this button?

A: It takes photos. Or if you hold it for longer, it makes a video.

B: Cool. Let's try it.

Unit 9

▶ 69

(The words of Zoltan Takacs are spoken by an actor.)

1

My name's Zoltan and I spend a lot of time travelling and studying snakes around the world, from the rain forests to the oceans. For me, my work and my holiday is the same thing. When I travel with my family and friends, I often go diving and looking for sea snakes. I've even kept sea snakes in the hotel bath. That's what I call a holiday.

2

My name's Greg and I have a camping and caravan site in the south of England. Our busiest time is the summer, so I always have my holiday later in the autumn. Because England can be cold later in the year, I put my tent in the car, drive to southern Europe and go camping and hiking in the mountains. My friends think I'm a bit crazy. They think I should do something different for my holidays, but I love camping.

3

I'm Moira and I'm a pilot for an international airline. People think my job is a good way to see the world. Sometimes I have a few hours in a city to go sightseeing, but usually I only see the airport and a hotel room. However, the good thing about my job is that I get a discount on flights, so when I have a holiday, I like flying back to some of the interesting cities I've been to and spending more time there. I also prefer to stay in bed and breakfast accommodation instead of hotels because I think you meet more of the local people that way.

▶ 71

A: How was your holiday?

B: To be honest, I'm really happy to be home!

A: Why? What happened?

B: Well, on the first day at the hotel, someone stole my bag at the reception desk.

A: Did you catch the person?

B: No. He'd run out of the hotel entrance so it was too late. The hotel reported it to the police, but I never got it back. Fortunately, I'd packed my passport and money in a different bag, so as soon as I'd bought some new clothes I went sightseeing.

A: Great.

B: The rest of the holiday went well until the last evening. Suddenly there was no electricity in the hotel. I went to find the manager, but she 'd left for the night. But luckily the assistant manager had some torches and candles and all the hotel guests sat in the reception area and sang traditional songs from their different countries. That was fun. In fact, that was probably the best night of the holiday!

▶ 72

We'd had a wonderful meal, so we gave the waiter a big tip. I'd left my passport at home by mistake, so I had to go back.

▶ 73

I = interviewer, M = Madelaine

I: So, Madelaine. I know that you're very excited about your new job. What is it exactly?

M: I'm going to be a tour guide for a travel company.

I: OK. Why do you want to be a tour guide?

M: Well, I've always been interested in different countries and I've done a lot of independent travel – last year I spent six months travelling on my own in South America. So I know all about visiting new places.

I: But going travelling on your own isn't the same as taking groups of tourists round famous cities or taking them from one hotel to another. Aren't you worried that it might be a bit boring for someone like you?

M: Actually, it'll be fascinating because the tour company specializes in adventure holidays. My first tour is very exciting. I'm leading a group to the Galápagos Archipelago, which is a place I've always wanted to visit.

I: That sounds amazing! So, who books these types of holidays?

M: They're usually people who are bored of traditional sightseeing and want something a bit different.

I: So what can you do on the tours?

M: Well, for example, on day one we go walking along the coast and photographing plants and animals. Day two is kayaking. So I have to organize and plan different group activities for every day.

I: I see. How many people go on the tour?

M: Usually eight. People often come on their own and make new friends. And if someone wants a day on their own, that's fine. I think the main thing is that they are never bored!

I: No, it doesn't sound like they will be! One last question. How much does it cost?

M: Err, actually I don't know the answer to that.

▶ 74

1   amazed, amazing
2   bored, boring
3   fascinated, fascinating
4   interested, interesting
5   frightened, frightening
6   worried, worrying
7   annoyed, annoying
8   tired, tiring

▶ 75

Ryan: OK, so first of all, how much money do we want to spend this year?

Margaret: Not much! It needs to be cheap. How about going camping?

Ryan: Good idea. Who wants to go camping?

Adriana: Only if we can go somewhere hot!

Margaret: But we'll have to fly to go somewhere hot, and flying is expensive.

Peter: Who has a car? We could drive somewhere with the tents. That's cheaper than flying.

Ryan: I can probably borrow my brother's car. I drove to Spain last summer. It was really hot.

Adriana: Which cities did you visit?

Ryan: Barcelona and Madrid. I don't mind going again.

Margaret: Great. How many people agree with going to Spain?

▶ 77

TI = tourist information, T = tourist
TI: Hello? Can I help you?
T: I'm interested in visiting the Tarxien Temples. Do you know the opening times?
TI: Sure. Let me check. Tomorrow is Monday so it might be closed. A lot of places are closed on Mondays in Malta. Oh, wait! The site is open every day.
T: Great! What time does it open?
TI: At ten and it closes at five.
T: Oh right. Could you tell me the price?
TI: It's six euros and you can book a ticket here, if you want. But are you a student?
T: Yes, I am.
TI: Then it's four euros fifty. Also, how about booking a guided tour?
T: Um, I'm not sure. How much is that?
TI: The guided tour is an extra twenty euros. It's a good tour, it lasts two hours.
T: Oh. I think I'll just buy the ticket. One other thing – is there any public transport?
TI: There's a bus every hour from outside this tourist information office. Or another option is to take a taxi. It isn't too expensive.

Unit 10

▶ 79

This man and his family make these baskets in his home in Hung Yen in Vietnam. Local fishermen buy them for catching fish, but some people also use them in the home for storing food. Every morning the man puts as many baskets as he can on his bicycle and slowly cycles around the area. As he goes, people stop him to look at the baskets and discuss a price. At the end of the day he hopes to arrive back home with none left.

▶ 82

On your way to school or work this morning, you probably listened to music on your headphones. Maybe you downloaded your favourite music onto a device which holds thousands of songs, or played your favourite songs through your phone. These days, listening to music is a personal activity that we all do on our own, but it didn't use to be so easy to get music or to listen when you were on the move. In the seventies, people used to buy music on vinyl records and play them on record players at home.
But in 1979, the Sony Walkman changed the way people listened to music. In the eighties and nineties, you used to see people everywhere with their Sony Walkman, a few cassettes and a set of headphones on. In the end, Sony's product was so successful that other companies copied the idea, but Sony's original Walkman was always the most popular. By 1986 the name Walkman was included as a word in the English dictionary.
Looking back, the idea of the Walkman seems so simple, but simplicity was the reason for its success. At the time, some people thought it was a crazy idea; after all, who wanted a music player with no radio, no speakers, no way to record, and small headphones? They were wrong, of course. The Walkman did everything people wanted: it was small enough to carry, it played music, and it was personal.

▶ 85

Sergio: So how's it going? Did you find out about the website name?
Rachel: Yes, I've checked it and no one else has the website name RetakeRecords.com.
Sergio: Great. I think we should buy it today. Oh, and I also started to design the home page. Let me show you. What do you think?
Rachel: Err, it's OK. But there's a lot of text.
Sergio: Sure. But I think people will want to know about us.
Rachel: I see what you mean, but we can have a photo of the shop at the top, and then maybe a contact page with more information. In my opinion it's more important that people see the records for sale as soon as they arrive on the home page. Also, it needs a search box so they can find the record they want.
Sergio: Yes, you're right.
Rachel: Lots of other websites have an 'about us' page. Maybe you could put the text there?
Sergio: Good idea. Also, I think we could have a video of the shop on the page with both of us talking about who we are and what we do.
Rachel: Yes, I agree. A video would be nice there. Customers will like it because it's personal. Maybe they can also contact us on that page.
Sergio: I'm not sure about that. Regular customers will want to call or email us directly, so I think we need a simple contact page and put information on the 'About us' page.

Unit 11

▶ 86

Just over one hundred years ago, the British explorer Captain Robert Falcon Scott died with his team of men in the snow and ice of Antarctica. He had reached the South Pole, but never returned to this hut, which was the starting point for his expedition. Now the hut is falling down under the snow, and we would like to save it – not just because of its connection to Scott, though this of course is important. Actually, we are more interested in what you find inside the hut. Because of the freezing temperatures in this part of the world, the hut has become a time capsule. There are items of food, such as butter, biscuits and tins of meat, which are one hundred years old. The ice has preserved them all. There are even some of Scott's old possessions and equipment, and things like soap and medicine bottles. When you go inside the hut, it's almost as if he has only just left it. I think we need to look after it because it tells us so much about Scott, but also about our own past.

▶ 88

Jack: I need the TV for my game.
Sonia: I'm watching a really interesting programme.
Jack: But I want to get to the next level!
Sonia: You're always using the TV. I haven't watched it for ages.
Jack: I'll play it later.

▶ 89

Last week the captain of a Scottish fishing boat pulled an old bottle out of the sea in one of his fishing nets. He told news reporters that he had been very curious when he'd seen the message inside. However, the message was a bit disappointing. It wasn't a love letter or a message from someone lost at sea. Instead, the writer said the message needed to be returned to an address.

In fact, the bottle was part of a scientific experiment which had begun 98 years before, when scientists threw 1,900 bottles into the sea in order to find out more about the movement of the oceans. It took nearly one hundred years for someone to find this bottle. So it's the oldest message in a bottle ever found – it's a world record.

Of course, the history of messages in bottles goes back many hundreds of years. Over two thousand years ago, the ancient Greeks put bottles in the sea to find out if the Mediterranean Sea and the Atlantic Ocean were connected. And sailors in World War I sent messages home by bottles. For example, one sailor in 1915 wrote a love letter to his wife. The message said that his boat was sinking and that he loved her.

▶ 91

Good morning and thank you all for coming. Today I'd like to talk about my holiday in Peru, and in particular, about my journey to Machu Picchu. It's also called 'The Lost City of the Incas'. Let me begin by telling you about the history of Machu Picchu. It was discovered by the explorer Hiram Bingham in 1911 …

So, that's everything I wanted to say about Hiram Bingham. Now, let's look at the history of the Incas and why they built Machu Picchu. The first Incas lived in the region of Peru around the thirteenth century …

OK. Now, the next part of my presentation is about my own journey through Peru and up to Machu Picchu. For this, I'd like to show you some of my photos. So, this first one is a picture of me in the town of Aguas Calientes. You have to catch the bus from here to Machu Picchu …

OK. So, to sum up, Peru, and especially Machu Picchu is a magical place and anyone who's interested in history should go there. Are there any questions?

Unit 12

▶ 93

When a tornado is coming, most people drive in the opposite direction. But storm chasers look for tornadoes and drive towards them. Some storm chasers are scientists and they try to learn more about how tornadoes are formed. Other storm chasers are just everyday people who are interested and want to get good photos. The most common time of day to see a tornado is between 4 p.m. and 9 p.m., but they can be very unpredictable. They can change direction at any moment and so they are difficult to follow. That also makes them extremely dangerous. They can destroy trees and houses in seconds and some storm chasers have died while they were following tornadoes.

▶ 95

A: Would you move to another country if the weather became much hotter in your country?
B: No, I'd love it if the weather became hotter.
A: I'd go and live somewhere else.
B: Would you?
A: Yes, I wouldn't want to stay. I'd find a country with a colder climate.
B: Oh, I wouldn't. I'd spend every day outside by the pool.

▶ 96

If you live in the middle of the city, maybe you think that there's nowhere to look at nature. Or if you have a local park, perhaps you don't see anything except people walking their dogs. However, David Liittschwager, the photographer, wants to show us that everyone can find nature. Different species of plants and animals are always somewhere nearby.

David spent five years recording living things in different places around the world. He used a green metal frame which measured one cubic foot and took it to different locations. Then he spent three weeks in that place and photographed everything living inside the green metal cube. That included leaves, animals, plants, fish, even living things which were smaller than one millimetre in size. Some of his photos were taken in places far away from any towns, such as the middle of a forest, the side of a mountain, the ocean or a river, but some of them were taken in parks in the middle of cities.

▶ 98

Z = zoo manager, C = city council leader
Z: I'm very worried about the situation. The problem is that the zoo will close without the council's help. How about giving us more money?
C: I'm sorry, but the council doesn't have any more money for the zoo.
Z: But if we don't find a solution soon, then we'll have to close it. And the zoo is part of the city. It's a tourist attraction.
C: Yes, but that's the point. It just isn't attracting enough tourists. You're going to have to find the money from somewhere else.
Z: It's also an important place for animal conservation. If we didn't have zoos, some of these animals wouldn't survive.
C: I understand that, but we need to find a different solution. What if you advertised the zoo more? In the newspaper, on the radio or online, for example.
Z: But if we don't have any money, we can't advertise.
C: Well, why don't you try sponsorship? You know, ask a company to support the zoo.
Z: Actually, that isn't a bad idea. You might be right!
C: I have the names of some company bosses you could contact …

NATIONAL GEOGRAPHIC
L E A R N I N G

Life Pre-intermediate Student's Book, **2nd Edition**
John Hughes, Helen Stephenson, Paul Dummett

Vice President, Editorial Director: John McHugh

Executive Editor: Sian Mavor

Publishing Consultant: Karen Spiller

Project Manager: Sarah Ratcliff

Development Editor: Clare Shaw

Editorial Manager: Claire Merchant

Head of Strategic Marketing ELT: Charlotte Ellis

Senior Content Project Manager: Nick Ventullo

Manufacturing Manager: Eyvett Davis

Senior IP Analyst: Ashley Maynard

Senior IP Project Manager: Michelle McKenna

Cover: Lisa Trager

Text design: emc design ltd.

Compositor: emc design ltd.

Audio: Prolingua Productions and Tom Dick and Debbie Productions Ltd

Contributing writers: Graham Burton (grammar reference), Mike Downie, David Gray (some video activities)

For product information and technology assistance, contact us at
Cengage Learning Customer & Sales Support, cengage.com/contact
For permission to use material from this text or product, submit all requests online at **cengage.com/permissions**
Further permissions questions can be emailed to
permissionrequest@cengage.com

ISBN: 978-1-337-28570-4

National Geographic Learning
Cheriton House, North Way,
Andover, Hampshire, SP10 5BE
United Kingdom

National Geographic Learning, a Cengage Learning Company, has a mission to bring the world to the classroom and the classroom to life. With our English language programs, students learn about their world by experiencing it. Through our partnerships with National Geographic and TED Talks, they develop the language and skills they need to be successful global citizens and leaders.

Locate your local office at **international.cengage.com/region**

Visit National Geographic Learning online at **NGL.Cengage.com/ELT**
Visit our corporate website at **www.cengage.com**

CREDITS
Although every effort has been made to contact copyright holders before publication, this has not always been possible. If notified, the publisher will undertake to rectify any errors or omissions at the earliest opportunity.
Text: Text: p10 Adapted from: (from question 2 onwards) http://ngm.nationalgeographic.com/2010/05/sleep/quiz/sleep#/sleep; p11 Adapted from: http://ngm.nationalgeographic.com/2010/05/sleep/max-text; p12 Adapted from: http://ngm.nationalgeographic.com/ngm/0511/feature1/index.html; p13/181 Adapted from: http://ngm.nationalgeographic.com/ngm/0511/sights_n_sounds/index.html; p15 Adapted from:http://www.natgeotraveller.in/web-exclusive/web-exclusive-month/this-is-your-brain-on-nature/; p22 Adapted from: http://americanfestivalsproject.net; p23 Adapted from: http://americanfestivalsproject.net; p24 Quotations, www.brainyquote.com; p27 Adapted from: http://ngm.nationalgeographic.com/2008/09/wrestlers/guillermoprieto-text called 'Bolivian wrestlers'; p34 Adapted from: http://news.nationalgeographic.com/news/energy/2011/11/pictures/111123-amazing-transportation-ideas/; p37 Adapted from: http://news.nationalgeographic.com/news/special-features/2014/08/140808-london-cabbies-knowledge-cabs-hansom-uber-hippocampus-livery/; p39 Adapted from: http://ngm.nationalgeographic.com/2008/04/kolkata-rickshaws/calvin-trillin-text; p44 Adapted from: https://www.itdp.org/2017-sustainable-transport-award-winner/; p46 Adapted from: http://adventure.nationalgeographic.com/adventure/adventurers-of-the-year/2016/vote/pasang-lhamu/; p47 Adapted from: http://www.nationalgeographic.com/field/explorers/reza/; p48/183 Source: Daily Telegraph 22.10.07. http://www.telegraph.co.uk/news/features/3634463/Joe-Simpson-My-journey-back-into-the-void.html; p51 Adapted from:http://solution-dailybrainteaser.blogspot.co.uk/2015/09/classic-matchstick-puzzle.html; p56 Adapted from: http://www.nationalgeographic.com/adventure/adventurers-of-the-year/2015/aleksander-doba/; p58 Adapted from: http://ngm.nationalgeographic.com/2008/01/high-tech-trash/carroll-text/1; p60 Adapted from: http://www.theguardian.com/environment/2016/may/18/portugal-runs-for-four-days-straight-on-renewable-energy-alone; p60/184 Adapted from: http://www.economist.com/news/international/21613334-vast-tree-planting-arid-regions-failing-halt-deserts-march-great-green-wall; p61 Source: BBC Focus April 2016, page 64; p61 Source: http://www.dailymail.co.uk/news/article-2301226/Fog-catchers-attempt-harvest-moisture-huge-nets-Chilean-desert.html; p63 Source: http://ngadventure.typepad.com/blog/pastiki/; p64 Source: http://www.tecoart.com/; p71 Adapted from: http://www.nationalgeographic.com/adventure/photography/adventure-dreams/road-trip/lessons-learned.html; p72 Adapted from: Nat Geo Magazine, February 2007 'Culture: World Party; p75 Adapted from: http://www.bbc.co.uk/nature/humanplanetexplorer/life_events/coming_of_age; p77

Printed in Greece by Bakis SA
Print Number: 01 Print Year: 2017

Adapted from: http://glimpse.org/a-wedding-story/; p82 'Faces of the Gas Rush', National Geographic Partners, LLC, October 22, 2010. Reprinted by Permission. p82 Marianne Lavelle, 'Natural Gas Stirs Hope and Fear in Pennsylvania', National Geographic Partners, LLC, October 30, 2010. Reprinted by Permission. p82 Source: http://www.telegraph.co.uk/finance/jobs/11602670/Here-are-the-workers-most-in-demand-in-the-UK.html; p87 Source: http://ngm.nationalgeographic.com/2007/12/vaquero/draper-text; p94 Jay Gifford, National Geographic Partners, LLC, July 15, 2010. Reprinted by Permission. p96 Adapted from: 'The Eyes Have It' from NG archive, July 2009, page 25. p99 Adapted from: Article on Biomimetics 2008 April (pg68-90). http://archive.nationalgeographic.com/?iid=52096#folio=70; p105 Zoltan Takacs; p106 Adapted from: The Tap dance of tipping from NG Traveller Now-Dec 2010 page 16 and also at http://travel.nationalgeographic.co.uk/travel/traveler-magazine/real-travel/tipping/; p108 Source at first edition: sources: http://www.nationalgeographicexpeditions.com/natgeoadventures?utm_source=NGdotcom-Adventure&utm_medium=Link&utm_content=TopNav&utm_campaign=Ngdotcom; p110 http://ngm.nationalgeographic.com/2011/02/paris-underground/shea-text; p118 Christina Bonnington, 'Former Apple Employee Explains Origins Of Upside-Down Logo', Wired, May 21, 2012. http://www.wired.com/2012/05/upside-down-apple-logo/; p123 Information on why boredom is good for you comes from April 2016 of BBC Focus magazine page 106; p129 Source: http://news.nationalgeographic.com/news/2010/01/photogalleries/100111-100-year-antarctic-hut-scott-pictures#/antarctic-terra-nova-hut-robert-falcon-scott_11856_600x450.jpg; p130 Adapted from: http://tvblogs.nationalgeographic.com/2013/04/16/from-pac-man-to-wow-the-evolution-of-video-games/;

p132 Adapted from: http://news.nationalgeographic.com/news/2012/09/120918-oldest-message-in-a-bottle-science-history-messages/; p135 Tom Mueller, 'How Tomb Raiders Are Stealing Our History', National Geographic Partners, LLC, June 2016. p137 Adapted from: http://ngm.nationalgeographic.com/2006/11/reinhold-messner/alexander-text; p142 'What if ...?', xkcd. https://what-if.xkcd.com/16/; p144 Adapted from: 'Nature In One Cubic Foot', http://ngm.nationalgeographic.com/2010/02/cubic-foot/liittschwager-photography#/explore/; p147 Adapted from: http://ngm.nationalgeographic.com/2010/10/jane-goodall/quammen-text;

Javier Jaen/National Geographic Creative; 136 © Alexey Stiop/Shutterstock.com; 137 imageBROKER/Alamy Stock Photo; 138 © Vincent DiFate/National Geographic Creative; 139 © NASA/JPL; 140 (t) Llama, alpaca and woman, from Lake Titicaca, Bolivia, c.1475–1532 (silver), Incan/American Museum of Natural History, New York, USA/The Bridgeman Art Library; 140 (m) © Marine Scotland; 140 (b) © rvlsoft/Shutterstock.com; 141 © Jim Reed/National Geographic Creative; 142 (t) imageBROKER/Alamy Stock Photo; 142 (ml) © TongFotoman/Shutterstock.com; 142 (mr) Rob Matheson/Alamy Stock Photo; 142 (b) © Salienko Evgenii/Shutterstock.com; 144 (all) © David Liittschwager/National Geographic Creative; 145 © David Liittschwager/National Geographic Creative; 147 © Michael Nichols/National Geographic Creative; 148 © David Cheskin/Press Association Images/AP Images; 149 Marc Hill/Alamy Stock Photo; 150 © Nadia Isakova/Alamy Stock Photo; 150 (inset) © National Geographic Creative/Alamy Stock Photo; 152 (tl) imageBROKER/Alamy Stock Photo; 152 (tm) © TongFotoman/Shutterstock.com; 152 (tr) Rob Matheson/Alamy Stock Photo; 152 (b) © David Liittschwager/National Geographic Creative; 153 (l) John Kellerman/Alamy Stock Photo; 153 (ml) © Design Pics Inc/National Geographic Creative; 153 (m) © Richard Nowitz/National Geographic Creative; 153 (mr) © Design Pics Inc/National Geographic Creative; 153 (r) © rvlsoft/Shutterstock.com; 154 (tl) © Happy Together/Shutterstotck.com; 154 (tml) © Gordon Wiltsie/National Geographic Creative; 154 (tm) © Sam Abell/National Geographic Creative; 154 (tmr) © Rose Carson/Shutterstock.com; 154 (tr) © Jonathan Irish/National Geographic Creative; 154 (bl) © RIEGER Bertrand/Getty Images; 154 (br) © Todd Keith/iStockphoto; 155 (l) © RIEGER Bertrand/Getty Images; 155 (r) © Todd Keith/iStockphoto.
Illustrations: 16, 20 Eric Olsen/Sylvie Poggio Agency; 41, 50, 130, 155 emc design; 48, 175 John Batten/Beehive Illustration; 53, 72, 143 David Russell; 56 Kevin Hopgood; 73 Mark Turner/Beehive Illustration; 100, 142 Laszlo Veres/Beehive Illustration; 168, 169 Matthew Hams.

ACKNOWLEDGEMENTS

The *Life* publishing team would like to thank the following teachers and students who provided invaluable and detailed feedback on the first edition:

Armik Adamians, Colombo Americano, Cali, Colombia; Carlos Alberto Aguirre, Universidad Madero, Puebla, Mexico; Anabel Aikin, La Escuela Oficial de Idiomas de Coslada, Madrid, Spain; Pamela Alvarez, Colegio Eccleston, Lanús, Argentina; Manuel Antonio, CEL – Unicamp, São Paolo, Brazil; Bob Ashcroft, Shonan Koka University, Japan; Linda Azzopardi, Clubclass, Malta; Éricka Bauchwitz, Universidad Madero, Puebla, Mexico; Paola Biancolini, Università Cattolica del Sacro Cuore, Milan, Italy; Laura Bottiglieri, Universidad Nacional de Salta, Argentina; Richard Brookes, Brookes Talen, Aalsmeer, Netherlands; Maria Cante, Universidad Madero, Puebla, Mexico; Carmín Castillo, Universidad Madero, Puebla, Mexico; Ana Laura Chacón, Universidad Madero, Puebla, Mexico; Somchao Chatnaridom, Suratthani Rajabhat University, Surat Thani, Thailand; Adrian Cini, British Study Centres, London, UK; Andrew Clarke, Centre of English Studies, Dublin, Ireland; Mariano Cordoni, Centro Universitario de Idiomas, Buenos Aries, Argentina; Monica Cuellar, Universidad La Gran Colombia, Colombia; Jacqui Davis-Bowen, St Giles International, UK; Nuria Mendoza Dominguez, Universidad Nebrija, Madrid, Spain; Robin Duncan, ITC London, UK; Christine Eade, Libera Università Internazionale degli Studi Sociali Guido Carli, Rome, Italy; Leopoldo Pinzon Escobar, Universidad Catolica, Colombia; Joanne Evans, Linguarama, Berlin, Germany; Juan David Figueroa, Colombo Americano, Cali, Colombia; Emmanuel Flores, Universidad del Valle de Puebla, Mexico; Sally Fryer, University of Sheffield, Sheffield, UK; Antonio David Berbel García, Escuela Oficial de Idiomas de Almería, Spain; Lia Gargioni, Feltrinelli Secondary School, Milan, Italy; Roberta Giugni, Galileo Galilei Secondary School, Legnano, Italy; Monica Gomez, Universidad Pontificia Bolivariana, Colombia; Doctor Erwin Gonzales, Centro de Idiomas Universidad Nacional San Agustin, Peru; Ivonne Gonzalez, Universidad de La Sabana, Colombia; J Gouman, Pieter Zandt Scholengemeenschap, Kampen, Netherlands; Cherryll Harrison, UNINT, Rome, Italy; Lottie Harrison, International House Recoleta, Argentina; Marjo Heij, CSG Prins Maurits, Middelharnis, Netherlands; María del Pilar Hernández, Universidad Madero, Puebla, Mexico; Luz Stella Hernandez, Universidad de La Sabana, Colombia; Rogelio Herrera, Colombo Americano, Cali, Colombia; Amy Huang, Language Canada, Taipei, Taiwan; Huang Huei-Jiun, Pu Tai Senior High School, Taiwan; Nelson Jaramillo, Colombo Americano, Cali, Colombia; Jacek Kaczmarek, Xiehe YouDe High School, Taipei, Taiwan; Thurgadevi Kalay, Kaplan, Singapore; Noreen Kane, Centre of English Studies, Dublin, Ireland; Billy Kao, Jinwen University of Science and Technology, Taiwan; Shih-Fan Kao, Jinwen University of Science and Technology, Taipei, Taiwan; Youmay Kao, Mackay Junior College of Medicine, Nursing, and Management, Taipei, Taiwan; Fleur Kelder, Vechtstede College, Weesp, Netherlands; Dr Sarinya Khattiya, Chiang Mai University, Thailand; Lucy Khoo, Kaplan, Singapore; Karen Koh, Kaplan, Singapore; Susan Langerfeld, Liceo Scientifico Statale Augusto Righi, Rome, Italy; Hilary Lawler, Centre of English Studies, Dublin, Ireland; Eva Lendi, Kantonsschule Zürich Nord, Zürich, Switzerland; Evon Lo, Jinwen University of Science and Technology, Taiwan; Peter Loftus, Centre of English Studies, Dublin, Ireland; José Luiz, Inglês com Tecnologia, Cruzeiro, Brazil; Christopher MacGuire, UC Language Center, Chile; Eric Maher, Centre of English Studies, Dublin, Ireland; Nick Malewski, ITC London, UK; Claudia Maribell Loo, Universidad Madero, Puebla, Mexico; Malcolm Marr, ITC London, UK; Graciela Martin, ICANA (Belgrano), Argentina; Erik Meek, CS Vincent van Gogh, Assen, Netherlands; Marlene Merkt, Kantonsschule Zürich Nord, Zürich, Switzerland; David Moran, Qatar University, Doha, Qatar; Rosella Morini, Feltrinelli Secondary School, Milan, Italy; Judith Mundell, Quarenghi Adult Learning Centre, Milan, Italy; Cinthya Nestor, Universidad Madero, Puebla, Mexico; Peter O'Connor, Musashino University, Tokyo, Japan; Cliona O'Neill, Trinity School, Rome, Italy; María José Colón Orellana, Escola Oficial d'Idiomes de Terrassa, Barcelona, Spain; Viviana Ortega, Universidad Mayor, Santiago, Chile; Luc Peeters, Kyoto Sangyo University, Kyoto, Japan; Sanja Brekalo Pelin, La Escuela Oficial de Idiomas de Coslada, Madrid, Spain; Itzel Carolina Pérez, Universidad Madero, Puebla, Mexico; Sutthima Peung, Rajamangala University of Technology Rattanakosin, Thailand; Marina Pezzuoli, Liceo Scientifico Amedeo Avogadro, Rome, Italy; Andrew Pharis, Aichi Gakuin University, Nagoya, Japan; Hugh Podmore, St Giles International, UK; Carolina Porras, Universidad de La Sabana, Colombia; Brigit Portilla, Colombo Americano, Cali, Colombia; Soudaben Pradeep, Kaplan, Singapore; Judith Puertas, Colombo Americano, Cali, Colombia; Takako Ramsden, Kyoto Sangyo University, Kyoto, Japan; Sophie Rebel-Dijkstra, Aeres Hogeschool, Netherlands; Zita Reszler, Nottingham Language Academy, Nottingham, UK; Sophia Rizzo, St Giles International, UK; Gloria Stella Quintero Riveros, Universidad Catolica, Colombia; Cecilia Rosas, Euroidiomas, Peru; Eleonora Salas, IICANA Centro, Córdoba, Argentina; Victoria Samaniego, La Escuela Oficial de Idiomas de Pozuelo de Alarcón, Madrid, Spain; Jeanette Sandre, Universidad Madero, Puebla, Mexico; Bruno Scafati, ARICANA, Argentina; Anya Shaw, International House Belgrano, Argentina; Anne Smith, UNINT, Rome & University of Rome Tor Vergata, Italy; Suzannah Spencer-George, British Study Centres, Bournemouth, UK; Students of Cultura Inglesa, São Paolo, Brazil; Makiko Takeda, Aichi Gakuin University, Nagoya, Japan; Jilly Taylor, British Study Centres, London, UK; Juliana Trisno, Kaplan, Singapore; Ruey Miin Tsao, National Cheng Kung University, Tainan City, Taiwan; Michelle Uitterhoeve, Vechtstede College, Weesp, Netherlands; Anna Maria Usai, Liceo Spallanzani, Rome, Italy; Carolina Valdiri, Colombo Americano, Cali, Colombia; Gina Vasquez, Colombo Americano, Cali, Colombia; Andreas Vikran, NET School of English, Milan, Italy; Helen Ward, Oxford, UK; Mimi Watts, Università Cattolica del Sacro Cuore, Milan, Italy; Yvonne Wee, Kaplan Higher Education Academy, Singapore; Christopher Wood, Meijo University, Japan; Yanina Zagarrio, ARICANA, Argentina.